INSPIRATIONS FROM LIFE

The Complete
"A Word From Father Roy"
Collection

REVEREND ROY SHEPHERD

 FriesenPress

Suite 300 - 990 Fort St
Victoria, BC, V8V 3K2
Canada

www.friesenpress.com

ISBN
978-1-5255-3410-2 (Hardcover)
978-1-5255-3411-9 (Paperback)
978-1-5255-3412-6 (eBook)

1. RELIGION

Distributed to the trade by The Ingram Book Company

7/4/19
For JoAnn -
so many searching
questions and comments
on Thursday morning

God's richest blessings

Roy S✝

Appreciation

Sincere thanks to Archbishop Terence Finlay, Archbishop Colin Johnson, Bishop Arthur Brown, and especially Bishop Michael Bedford-Jones, Bishop Douglas Blackwell, Bishop Linda Nicholls and Bishop Patrick Yu for their support of my intentional interim ministries in the Diocese of Toronto, and to the parish secretaries and administrators who have had to struggle with my handwriting.

Finally, my thanks to my Number One supporter/editor, Audrey, my mate since 1947, without whose commitment and encouragement none of this would have happened.

If you would like to give thanks in a tangible way, please send your tax-deductible donations to:

> Anglican Worship Resources Society
>
> c/o Rev. Canon Jim Woolley, Chair AWRS
>
> 2473 Windjammer Rd
>
> Mississauga, ON, Canada
>
> L5L 1H7

The mission of the Anglican Worship Resources Society is to assist lower-income parishes across Canada to purchase Bibles, Hymn Books, tapes and other resources, using donations, bequests and gifts from parishes and individuals who, like me, are trying to tell the world about Jesus' saving love.

Proceeds from the sale of this book will be given to the Anglican Worship Resources Society.

Foreword

The first 'Word from Father Roy' appeared in the Ship's Log newsletter of St. Wilfred's Episcopal Church in Sarasota, Florida, where I have served as a Winter Assistant since 1992. Then, early in my interim ministry, a parishioner suggested that a short inspirational message would be helpful when taking the Sunday bulletin to shut-in people. That was the beginning of 'A Word from Father Roy', which I have placed in every Sunday bulletin wherever my ministry has taken me.

Most of these reflections come from my own experiences, but some were developed from anecdotes I have heard or read over the years.

Many of the 'Words' have appeared in a number of the bulletins of different parishes. The guiding hand of the Holy Spirit has hopefully given them appropriate placement, according as they were needed. Since an interim ministry is primarily the sharing of a spiritual journey between people and priest, much of the inspiration for these writings comes from my interaction with the members of:

St. Columba and All Hallows	St. John Norway
St. Nicholas Birchcliff	Holy Trinity Guildwood
St. Timothy Agincourt	St. Paul Minden
St. Peter Maple Lake	St. James Kinmount
St. John Irondale	Ascension Port Perry
St. John Blackstock	St. Thomas Brooklin
St. George Grafton	Trinity Colborne
Christ Church Oshawa	St. John Bowmanville
St. Martin Courtice	Nativity Malvern
St. Paul L'Amoreaux	St. Saviour Toronto
St. Bede Scarborough	Epiphany Scarborough
St. George Ajax	St. Theodore of Canterbury
St. Peter Scarborough	Christ Church Scarborough

Shalom! May God's richest blessings be yours.

TABLE OF CONTENTS

By paths they have not known I will guide them. I will turn the darkness before them into light, the rough places into level ground.

Isaiah 42: 16

The tradition at the Stratford Festival Theatre is that, when the trumpets gloriously sound, the audience proceed to their seats. And when the appointed hour arrives, the house lights are dimmed, the ushers close all the doors and there are a few seconds of black darkness before the first stage spots come on.

No one enters the theatre once the doors are closed.

One evening, tradition was broken. A door in the balcony opened for a moment and there was a small circle of light from an usher's flashlight. It shone down on the steep steps, as two latecomers slowly made their way to vacant seats on the aisle.

One of the couple was an older man with a cane. He went down each step, as the light revealed it, until he reached his seat. His companion, equally hesitant, followed. The actors on stage had not begun their play, and you could hear a collective sigh of relief around the theatre as the new members of the audience sat down. The first lines were spoken.

This slow journey down the steps is somewhat like our spiritual journey. It highlights God's patience with us, as he waits for us to take our next step. And if, for any reason, we seem hesitant or even unable to move, he guides us in the right way. He gives us enough light in our lives to show us the next step we should take.

Then, when we have made that step, he gives us more light for the next step, and then for the next … and the next. He does this for each of us on our spiritual journey, and for all of us collectively in our local parish, as we strive to 'Go in peace to love and serve the Lord.'

Take delight in the Lord, and he will give you the desires of your heart.

Psalm 37: 4

Ask and it shall be given to you.

Matthew 7: 7

We read these passages, and we often say, "How come it hasn't happened that way for me?" Today, try something different.

If God gave you three wishes ...

Just three. No more.

What would they be?

Furthermore, if God said to you, "I will give you anything you want in your three wishes".

What would you want?

Think of all the possibilities you could put together in your three wishes.

What would you request?

What are your deepest aspirations, longings?

Your greatest desires?

What do you really want in life?

Before you make a choice, make a decision.

Remember that desires are deeper than decisions.

Desires can change ... decisions are final ...

And needs are greater than wishes.

When you have decided on your three wishes ...

Ask yourself two final questions.

Was God part of your choosing process?

Does God have a place in your three wishes?

"Believe in God. Believe also in me."

John 14: 1

I was working on my computer, using my notes and reflections to put together a hopefully God-guided message for Sunday morning. Suddenly, everything stopped. For ten minutes I vainly tried to make this technological marvel do something except stare at me. Nothing worked, because nothing happened.

It was frozen. Even talking to it didn't help, perhaps because my language wasn't very complimentary. I was completely frustrated and exasperated.

Finally I called to Audrey to help me. I don't know what she did, but a few minutes later the computer and I were friends again. And I'm prepared to admit that the whole thing happened because I did something wrong, even though I don't know what.

There are times when I'm completely frustrated and exasperated in my relationship with God. I spend the day doing what I believe he wants me to do, but the results seem to be non-productive or even counter-productive. And I tell him so.

He listens. He doesn't scold me, but lovingly helps me to understand that things don't always happen as quickly as the wink of an eye. That I should trust him and continue to love and serve him.

I'm thankful that I have an understanding wife, who is able to extract me from my computer dilemmas. I'm thankful to God for guiding me carefully through my life mistakes. Praise the Lord that in neither case are my errors fatal.

"Take courage. It is I. Do not be afraid."

Matthew 14: 27

"COURAGE TO DARE AND FREEDOM TO FAIL" Because we read these words in a church bulletin, we assume they come from the Bible. But they don't. They were spoken by John F. Kennedy in his first inaugural address as President of the United States of America. When we talk about having fire in your heart for God, these words could very well be our call to action.

COURAGE TO DARE to speak out forcefully when someone denies the existence of God.

COURAGE TO DARE to share with others your personal encounters with God.

COURAGE TO DARE to tell others that you love Jesus and that he is the motivating force in your life.

COURAGE TO DARE to stand up for your faith and its value of all human life against the principalities and powers of the world.

COURAGE TO DARE in your relationships with others to give of yourself instead of taking for yourself.

FREEDOM TO FAIL because you know that God forgives you when you turn away from him.

FREEDOM TO FAIL because you know that the joy of being alive comes from doing God's will.

FREEDOM TO FAIL because you know that, in the midst of failure and despair, God has already given you hope through the life, death and resurrection of Jesus.

FREEDOM TO FAIL because you can experience 'God's peace, which passes all understanding' and overcome the stresses and strains of modern life.

FREEDOM TO FAIL because you know that, as the sun shines on the good and the bad, so God loves you and holds you in the palm of his hand, no matter what happens.

COURAGE TO DARE and **FREEDOM TO FAIL** … that's how we can be God's people in the world.

"I give you a new commandment, that you love one another. Just as I have loved you, you also should love one another."

John 13: 34

The salesman had just finished a rather disappointing day. He decided to stop for a cup of coffee on the highway outside of town, before heading to the next stop on his itinerary.

When the waitress brought him a steaming cup of good coffee, he said to her, "What kind of people live in the next town?" As she passed him the cream and sugar, she replied warmly, "What kind of people lived in the town you just left?" Without even a word of thanks for the service, he exclaimed, "They were horrible! People were rude, selfish and inconsiderate." "Well," said the waitress, "I'm sorry to say that's probably what you'll find in the next town." With a scowl, the salesman finished his coffee and went on his way.

A short time later, another salesman stopped for a cup of coffee. After complimenting the waitress on her excellent coffee, he said to her, "What are the folks like in the next town?" With a smile, she said, "What kind of people did you meet in the town you just left?" "Oh, they were friendly, thoughtful and kind," came the answer. As she refilled his cup, she declared with an even broader smile, "I'm delighted to tell you that's the kind of folk you'll find in the next town."

This story is an adaptation of an old American folktale. Speaks of our attitude toward life, and particularly our relationships with each other. Jesus said it even more succinctly, when he told his disciples, "Love one another as I have loved you."

When we accept his love, we are automatically committing ourselves to passing it on to others in the same way and with the same motivation as he did. We are to share his incredible love with everyone we meet. No matter what God calls us to do in our lives, love must be at the centre of our thoughts, words and actions.

A time to seek, and a time to lose; a time to keep, and a time to throw away.

Ecclesiastes 3: 6

We were having refreshments and fellowship after church. I noticed Sally, one of my servers, sitting in a corner with a long, obviously downhearted face. I sat down beside her and gently asked what was bothering her.

Almost in tears, she blurted out her story. At a concert in her school auditorium on Thursday, she had lost her bracelet. After school, she searched everywhere, even getting her friends to help. No luck.

The next day she went through the Lost and Found, and put up a sign. Still no luck. It wasn't that it was so immensely valuable, nor especially beautiful. It was her very favourite bracelet. She was very upset, and couldn't stop thinking about her loss. Twice she said, "My favourite bracelet is lost, gone forever. I think somebody took it."

For a moment, I was unsure what to say to Sally. Then the Holy Spirit came to my rescue, giving me these words, "Nothing is ever lost. You don't have the bracelet anymore, but someone does. So bless that person. Forgive him or her for not returning it, and then LET THE BRACELET GO!"

Sally told me later that, in her prayers that night, she told God she really wanted to forgive the person who took her bracelet, and asked him to help her do that. And when she woke up the next morning it was as if a great weight had been lifted from her mind.

From that experience Sally learned that letting a worry or upset dominate your mind makes you into a different person. Handing it to God with true forgiveness in your heart puts love, joy and peace back into your life. And I learned to listen to and trust the Holy Spirit.

Now there are varieties of gifts, but the same spirit;
and there are varieties of service, but the same Lord;

1 Corinthians 12: 4,5

One of the most popular and best scripted TV programs of all times was 'The Golden Girls'. It was the story of four older women who shared a home and companionship. Their distinctive personalities generated times of laughter and frivolity, and also sorrow and tears. But underneath the ups and downs of their often mercurial relationships there was a solid foundation of mutual respect and loyal support. A 'group hug' ended many episodes.

As I was watching a rerun of the program the other day, I couldn't help thinking of the dozens of golden girls I had met during my years as an Interim Pastor. Every congregation, without exception, had a number of women of every age whose commitment to our Lord and his church was outstanding. Without downgrading the efforts of the men, whenever there was a need in the church or community, you would find church women involved. Some of them were Marys and others were Marthas.

Part of their service for the Lord included the expected - church school - nursery - choir - readers - chalice bearers - greeters - servers - cooks - crafts - Advisory Board - wardens - meals-on-wheels - hospital auxiliary - community fundraising. But they also spoke out against injustice, marched to eradicate poverty, led worshippers in prayer, made pastoral calls to the sick and the shut-in, participated in Bible study and spiritual retreats, ministered to those in need through healing prayers and anointing, put together the church bulletin every week. The depth of their loyalty and involvement because of their faith was beyond measurement.

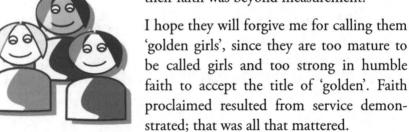

I hope they will forgive me for calling them 'golden girls', since they are too mature to be called girls and too strong in humble faith to accept the title of 'golden'. Faith proclaimed resulted from service demonstrated; that was all that mattered.

"So do not worry about tomorrow, for tomorrow will bring worries of its own. Today's trouble is enough for today."

Matthew 6: 34

I n the famous comic strip, Charlie Brown is at bat. Strike one! Strike two! Strike three! He has struck out again! Dejectedly, he slumps down on the players' bench. "Rats! I'll never be a good baseball player! I just don't have it. All my life I've dreamed of playing in the big leagues, but now I know I'll never make it."

Lucy turns to console him. "Charlie Brown," she says, "you're planning too far ahead. What you need to do is set some short-term goals for yourself." Charlie looks at her in confusion, and says, "What do you mean, short-term goals?" Lucy responds, "Something immediate. Start with the next inning, when you go out to pitch. See if you can walk to the mound without falling down!"

Both Jesus and Charlie Brown remind us that the first step into any future is the step you take today. This is most particularly true of our spiritual life, which is a journey, not a destination. We are all on this journey, both as individuals and as members of our parish family. Each day we try to be more open to God, and to a more loving relationship with him. And we grow 'as living members of the mystical body, which is the blessed company of all faithful people.' *(Book of Common Prayer, page 85)*

When we become members of the worldwide Christian church through the sacrament of Baptism, God's special gift of the Holy Spirit is given to us. At any time, as he did with the Apostle Paul, God can force his Spirit into the forefront of our lives.

But for the most part, God elects to work through the people closest to his children … the parents and god-parents. We always pray that they will ensure that God is an important part of each newly baptized person's life.

We church members also have a responsibility ... to encourage them, to support them, and, whenever we can, to walk with them on their journey, a step at a time. Short-term goals can become long-term gains ... abundant lives, full of God's love.

*As soon as the people heard the sound of the trumpets,
they raised a great shout, and the wall fell down flat;
so the people charged straight ahead into the city and
captured it.*

Joshua 6: 20

I have this picture of Joshua assembling all his senior officers and outlining to them his battle plan for taking the well-guarded and high-walled city of Jericho.

"Well, we're going to march around the city."

"Then what?"

"We're going to do it once a day for six days."

"Uh-huh! Then what?"

"We're going to do it once more on the seventh day."

"Oh! Six days wasn't enough?"

"Then seven priests are going to sound a long note on their trumpets, and we'll give a loud shout."

"Really?"

"Then the walls of the city will fall down."

There was no sense in Joshua's plan. His officers could be forgiven for thinking he was suffering from burn-out. But they followed his instructions and the walls fell down. Joshua trusted God, and the Lord would not let him down. Mission impossible accomplished! As someone once remarked, "With God, the difficult can be done immediately; the impossible takes a little longer."

Living the Christian life is not difficult, it's impossible if we try to do it on our own. Whether as individuals or members of a faith community, our gifts, skills and talents cannot begin to compare to the power of a God who created the universe and raised the

dead. Jesus said, "Without me, you can do nothing." He asks us to trust him. Like Joshua. And when we do, the impossible becomes possible.

"But I have prayed for you that your own faith may not fail;"

Luke 22: 32a

Early in my career I was interviewed for a sales trainee position with a large multi-national insurance company. Having previously learned that my chances would be improved in direct ratio to the amount of talking the Vice-President (and not I) did, I asked,

"What made you a success in this company?"

"Two words," came the reply, "good decisions."

"How did you learn to make good decisions?" I rejoined.

"One word," replied the Vice-President, "experience."

"How did you get the experience?" I persisted.

"Two words" he answered. "Bad decisions."

When I look at scripture, I see men of great stature making bad decisions, failing at something.

Paul failed … Peter failed … all of the apostles failed at one time or another. Adam and Eve failed … faithful Abraham failed. Moses made some bad decisions … so did the great Hebrew king, David … also Isaiah, Ezekiel, Jeremiah, Samson, Judas, and many others. It would be hard to find anyone who didn't.

Some would point to a short, three-year ministry, finishing with death on a cross, and say that Jesus himself failed. True, he didn't convert all the people in his world, especially the religious establishment.

But it isn't making a bad decision that's the problem, it's what you do after you've failed. And what Jesus did was to be the perfect obedient servant to his Creator. He allowed himself to be crucified.

As he lay down his life, he became an incredible success. His act of human perfection gave each one of us the freedom to fail, because we know that God's love and care for us is never limited and never ending.

As our love for each other should always be.

And we sent Timothy, our brother and co-worker in proclaiming the Gospel of Christ, to strengthen and encourage you for the sake of your faith,

1 Thessalonians 3: 2

One evening in the summer, I was toasting marshmallows on the beach with two of my grandchildren … over red hot coals, of course, not a flame. As our stomachs got filled and our hands got sticky, I absentmindedly started poking in the coals with a stick.

Flicking one good-sized piece onto the sand beside the fire, I watched with the children as the red glow gradually turned into a black lump speckled with grey. It seemed quite lifeless. Then I used the same stick to push it back into the fire, and the children blew on it. A short while later, it had returned to its former heat and glow.

The Christian journey of faith is like that piece of charcoal. Like the coal separated from the fire, an individual Christian cannot make the journey alone. Sooner or later the glow is lost and faith appears to be lifeless.

To be rekindled, it is necessary to rejoin the fire, become an active part of a Christian community. Then the glow from fellow believers will help to put the glow back to the returned Christian's faith.

The incredible wonder is that the fire of faith will never go completely out, because it comes from God. But it can be dormant until it is fanned back into life again by the flame of the loving people of God.

Every day the glow of faith grows dim from someone in a parish fellowship. It's the responsibility of the other members of the parish to rekindle that faith. We uncover the need by being sensitive to one another, and we bring back the glow through our prayer and our warm and caring love.

And what does the Lord require of you but to do
justice, to love kindness and to walk humbly with
your God.

Micah 6: 8b

A few years ago, I was asked by a local service club to judge a spelling bee. It was a rewarding experience. But I particularly remember the finals for the eight- and nine-year olds; one girl had to spell 'conscious', which she did correctly. Her young male opponent then spelled 'conscience' correctly.

At the refreshment period afterward, I asked each one what their word meant. "Conscious," said the girl, "is when you're sure of something." "Conscience," piped the young man, "is when you wish you weren't."

The profound inter-relationship of these two 'Cs' for us as Christians didn't strike me until much later. In Isaiah's prophecy, chapter 61, verse 8, we read, ***The Lord says, "I love justice and hate oppression and crime."*** Micah's prophecy, chapter 6, verse 8, says, ***"… what does the Lord require of you but to do justice, to love kindness and to walk humbly with your God."***

Injustice, oppression, greed, hate and bigotry are all around us. The 'Conscious' imperative of our faith is to see them and be aware of them and to name them for what they are. The 'Conscience' imperative of our faith is not to turn our backs on them, but to accept the Lord's command-ment and do something about them.

The prophets spoke God's words to the people - individually and col-lectively. We all have an urge to say, "the problems of the world are too big for me to solve." We forget that one voice, when added to another voice, plus more and more voices, all speaking out against a specific

injustice, has in the course of history, time and time again, created great changes. We forget that the actions of one person, when joined by the actions of many others, con-stantly make a difference in human affairs.

There are challenges for Christians everywhere. Our response in faith is to become aware and knowledgeable about a particular need or injustice, and then to join with other Jesus-believers to be God's conscience for the world.

*"For I was hungry and you gave me food, I was thirsty
and you gave me something to drink, I was a stranger
and you welcomed me,"*

Matthew 25: 35

Her name is Betty. She's seventy-five, short, and what she calls dumpy. She's been a widow for fifteen years, retired for ten, and has no children. Social security, a small pension and a house without a mortgage - comfortable, able to make ends meet, but not wealthy.

She says she's a practical community volunteer. One morning she works in the laundry of a shelter for the homeless, one morning you'll find her in the back room of a secondhand store run by a non-profit agency.

She reads stories to a group of handicapped children, drives for Meals on Wheels one week every month, is an active helper and worshipper in her church. She gives all kinds of practical help to people in need in the community.

I've rarely seen Betty without a smile on her face and friendly warmth in her conversation. A friend told me, "Betty believes God gave her a special gift of making people feel good about themselves, if even just for a little while. She doesn't use that talent to put her own name in lights, but to bring light into the lives of others."

You wouldn't notice it, but she has constant chronic back pain, which is sometimes severe. Betty says, "God tells me he needs me. I listen to him and do what practical things he tells me to do. He is my strength."

She calls herself a practical volunteer. I call her a SILENT EVANGELIST.

Give me understanding, that I may keep your law and observe it with my whole heart.

Psalm 119: 34

I t was the most luscious and beautiful garden you could imagine. In the middle of it was a glorious tree with shiny, ripe fruit.

The man said to the woman, "What a fabulous tree! There are so many juicy fruits it's almost touching the ground with their weight." "I'd love to sink my teeth into one of them," she answered. "What was it God said to you about this tree?"

"He said we could eat from any one of the trees, except this special one", came the reply. "Why? What's so special about it?" she said. "Is it poisonous or something?"

"No, I don't think so." he rejoined, "He said it was the tree that gives knowledge of what's good and what's bad." "What's that mean?" she retorted. "I'm not sure," he replied, "but he warned me that if we ate the fruit from his special tree, we would die." "You're kidding me." she said.

The snake had been listening to this exchange, and now he piped up. "Did God really tell you that you would die if you ate the fruit of the tree of good and evil?" In unison came the answer. "That's right. And we'll die, if we do."

"Not true," said the snake. "God's protecting himself. He knows that, if you eat it, you'll be like God." So the man and the woman ate the fruit of the forbidden tree, and the beautiful garden has never been the same.

Satan was smart. Through the snake, he could have said, "Listen to me, not God. Eat the fruit, and you will end up in Hell." Instead, he said the opposite. "Believe me, and you will be like God." The temptation was not to evil, but to virtue. He made disbelieving

and disobeying God seem desirable and worthwhile. And they fell for his trap.

We know this is a symbolic story. But we also know that it's a true one! It reminds us that God gives us freedom of choice - to follow him or follow our own desires. And every time we choose for ourselves, we take another step away from the beautiful garden into the desert of destruction and despair. But praise be! If we admit our mistake and ask for his forgiveness, the gate of the garden opens wide.

"You are the salt of the earth; you are the light of the world."

Matthew 5: 13,14

God's purpose in the church is to take a group of people, a congregation, and build and mould them into a fellowship whose way of life together will be a sign and a witness of God's presence, activity and purpose in the world.

Whereas life in the world is often characterized by suspicion, isolation, fractiousness, polarization, hostility and confrontation, God's vision is surely that, in the fullness of time, there will be harmony, unity and love.

Every Christian church is supposed to be a working model of the world as God wants it to be. The local congregation is therefore, in a sense, a preview of God's ultimate Kingdom. It is created as a community of people living together. In a world so alienated from the Lord, we are called to be "the salt of the earth and the light of the world."

In any parish there will be many viewpoints on a variety of subjects. Opinions may differ, but we should be united in our hearts and minds, striving for what God wants. He is not asking for uniformity, but unity in diversity.

If we are truly open to the wisdom and power of the Holy Spirit, he will lead us from being a congregation to being a true community of the faithful.

The world around us needs our community, because it is hurting. God will work through us to heal it.

Surely God is my salvation; I will trust, and not be afraid, for the Lord God is my strength and my might;

Isaiah 12: 2

I n my study at home I have a picture taken many years ago at a lake up in cottage country. I'm treading water at the end of the dock. The water is about ten feet deep, and it's cold. My arms are raised out in front of me.

In the air coming towards me is my granddaughter, Jaclyn. She has just jumped off the dock into the water and my waiting arms. She's four years old, and she can't swim very well. She has blown up plastic rings on both arms. And a beautiful smile on her face. Absolutely no fear, because she trusts me.

What an incredible human experience it is to trust someone completely - without fear - without any holding back - not even the slightest kind of uncertainty in the back of your mind! You are wonderfully free. Free to be you, without any pretense. No need to put on a false face or cover up your insecurities. There are no uncertainties or insecurities, because there is absolutely no risk.

If we want it, our relationship with God can be like that. No fear! No uncertainty! No risk! Complete freedom to be the persons God created us to be. Complete trust that God never stops loving us, never stops caring for us. Even when we break that trust, we know that he will forgive us, if we ask.

Having such an intimate and trusting relationship with God, a human experience, gives us the strength and the freedom to carry that trust into the relationships we have with others around us.

And early in the morning Jesus came walking toward them on the sea.

Matthew 14: 25

The Nith River flows through the town of New Hamburg, which is twenty kilometres west of Kitchener, Ontario. In the late 1980s, determined to make the town a better tourist stop-over, the town authorities undertook a major landscaping project on the Nith, right in the centre of town. There were new trees and gardens, lights, pathways, benches and a huge waterwheel. Below the dam and before the bridge, they put a series of stepping-stones across the shallow river.

When my grandchildren came to visit at the rectory, they inevitably wanted to go down to the river and walk across the stepping-stones. We called it 'walking on water'. None of them ever fell in, although when the river was high, they would come home with wet shoes and socks from the spray. Needless to say, there was always adult supervision, usually by grandfather.

Peter was astonished when he saw Jesus walking on water towards him. Told to "Come" by the Lord, he stepped out of the boat and walked on the water to meet Jesus. But then fear entered his mind, and he started to sink.

There are times when we wish we could 'walk on water' and experience a miracle within the turmoil of a difficult life situation. Occasionally we do, but, more often than not, fear prevents us from giving our complete trust to the Lord.

Thankfully, God doesn't let us sink, as Jesus didn't let Peter sink. He provides us with stepping-stones that, if we are paying attention, will take us gradually through our problem.

Like the children crossing the Nith River, we may be somewhat soaked with the stress of the situation, but he brings us to safety and peace on the other side. Thank God for stepping-stones.

And after he dismissed the crowds, he went up the mountain by himself to pray.

Matthew 14: 23

Audrey and I live in an apartment building in Scarborough in which, from time to time, there is a power failure. From a few minutes to over an hour, nothing works. Immediately, the whole atmosphere is different, because it inevitably happens at night, when it is dark.

Even after we light our ever-ready candles, everything seems quieter, calmer, less pressured. The bright lights that fill the corners of every room are replaced by the soft, glowing flicker of candlelight.

But the most striking difference is the silence. All the background noises of our ordinary household are gone - the hum of the computer, the purr of the refrigerator, the whirr of the fans, the continual blare of the television - they are replaced by a different sound - the sound of our two voices, speaking more softly, but being heard more easily.

In this environment I somehow feel more in touch with my own being, and with other people around me. I am more conscious of doing things as I do them. And the longer the blackout lasts, the more disconnected I become from all the things around me, and more aware of the true essence of life.

Then suddenly the power comes back on. We are back in a brightly lit, noisy, distracting world.

After one such power outage, as I was reading my Bible, I understood why Jesus regularly disconnected himself from the busyness around him, so that he could be better connected to God.

Blessed are those who trust in the Lord, whose trust is the Lord.

Jeremiah 17: 7

It was a warm, sunny day. Audrey and I were walking around an Arts and Crafts show near the beach in Sarasota. It was also just before Valentine's Day, and for a week I had been trying to find a gift for her.

Then she saw a beautiful paperweight at one of the booths. The colours were wonderful, but what made it special was its shape. Neither of us had ever seen anything like it before - eye-catching and special. I decided to buy it as her Valentine gift.

Unfortunately, I was in shorts and a tank top, and I discovered that I didn't have the purchase price in cash and the lady crafter didn't take Visa. What's more, the show ended in half an hour.

Seeing my dismay, the crafter smiled and said, "Your wife likes it so much, I'll just wrap it up and you can send me a cheque." She had never seen us before and would probably never see us again, since she lived three hundred miles away. But she trusted us. We exchanged names and addresses, she wrapped up the gift and handed it to me, and I mailed her a cheque as soon as we got home.

Mary, the mother of Jesus, was also trusting. A teenager, engaged to be married, she was told by the angel Gabriel that she was going to have a son by the Holy Spirit. She was afraid, and rightly so. Not only would Joseph, her husband-to-be, discard her, but as an unwed pregnant woman, she would be outlawed by the whole community. Her love of God and Gabriel's assurance not to be afraid gave her the courage to accept a most difficult situation and to trust God to be with her.

Courage and trust. The lady crafter had it. So did Mary. And so did Jesus. With the Holy Spirit to guide and strengthen us, we can have it, too. We need that kind of courage and trust to have a loving relationship with God.

Your word is a lamp to my feet and a light to my path.

Psalm 119: 105

Jerry ran a riding stable. One night, when it was very dark, he decided that his son, Jim, was old enough to go out to the barn and feed the horses. Jim said to his dad, "But I'm only six, and I'm afraid of the dark".

Jerry went out on the porch with his son, handed him a flashlight, and asked him how far he could see with it. "I can see halfway down the path", said Jim. "Walk halfway down the path", said Jerry. Jim did, and when he had reached that point, his dad called out, "How far can you see now?"

"To the gate at the end of the path", replied Jim. "Then walk to the gate", called Jerry. When his son had reached the gate, Jerry yelled, "How far can you see now?" "I can see the barn door", the boy replied.

"With the light in front of you, go to the barn", said Jerry. Courageously, Jim forged ahead, and when he reached the barn, his dad called, "Open the door."

A moment later, Jim shouted, "I can see the horses!" As he stepped back into the house, Jerry called out, "Now feed the horses."

Jim had overcome his fear of the darkness with the help of a flashlight and a wise and encouraging father.

Our spiritual life is like that. Satan puts all kinds of temptations before us. He also provokes our fears by seducing us away from our trust in God.

In reality there is no need to be afraid. God is always our wise and supportive father, and Jesus is the light that shows us the way. God never stops loving and encouraging us, and the light of Jesus' love is powered increasingly by the Holy Spirit.

> ***For he will command his angels concerning you to guard you in all your ways.***
>
> *Psalm 91: 11*

We were in Sarasota for the winter. Just after Easter, Vince, a friend from our Episcopal faith community, offered to fly us to Key West for a day. The trip in the air would take about an hour and a half, in his four-seat, single engine Beechcraft monoplane. Our pilot-host had over a thousand hours of solo experience and an impeccable safety record.

The day arrived. Vince checked the weather and flight conditions. Sunny with cloudy periods, with the threat of a storm coming in from the Gulf of Mexico. He filed a carefully plotted flight plan. Then we helped him go through a two-page checklist of every function and part of the aircraft, which took over half an hour to complete. Finally, we climbed aboard, fastened our seatbelts, put on our earphones and prepared to take off.

The next hour and a half was breathtakingly wonderful. At 5,000 feet, we were in sunshine most of the time, able to see the beaches, the Gulf, rivers, towns, and cities of Southwest Florida. And there were times when we were completely engulfed in billowing white clouds. The flight was a little bumpy for only a few minutes. Vince's skill had something to do with that.

Perhaps the most exciting part was hearing our journey over the earphones, as it was guided by a series of air traffic controllers. Starting with Sarasota, who got us off the ground and into our flight path, then handed us over to Tampa, who asked us to veer a few degrees because of a commercial aircraft in the vicinity; next to Fort Myers, who directed us to change course slightly because of the storm front; picked up by Miami, who took us through until Key West assumed responsibility, reminding us to stay clear of a restricted Navy no-fly

zone, and brought us in. I had an image of one angel after another guiding us safely to our destination.

Lunch in Key West, interesting sight-seeing and warm and stimulating conversations. The return trip was just like the first, in reverse. A never-to-be-forgotten day.

I thank God for the wonder of his creation. I thank God for Vince's friendship and skill. And I thank God for his air traffic 'angels'.

Be still, and know that I am God.

Psalm 46: 10a

The story is told of a young Canadian soldier fighting in Italy during the Second World War. His company was pinned down at the bottom of a small hill, and bullets were flying all around him. He managed to jump into a shallow foxhole just ahead of a deadly hail of fire. He immediately started to make the hole deeper for greater protection. As he was frantically scraping at the dirt with his hands and a sharp rock, he unearthed a silver crucifix, obviously left by a previous occupant of the hole.

A few minutes later, another figure leapt in beside him, as shells screamed and bullets whistled overhead. The soldier recognized his new companion as the regimental chaplain. Holding up the crucifix, he cried out, "Padre! Am I glad to see you! How do you work this thing, anyway?"

So often, when we face a crisis or a major problem, our thoughts instinctively turn to God. Psychologists tells us that this even happens with people who pay no attention to God in their everyday lives. Thankfully, God is always there when we need him.

But our side of the relationship can easily be blocked by our inability to be open to God's love and guidance. We need his help. We want his help. But we don't know how to be still and let his power and wisdom come through. We mirror the soldier, saying, "How do you work this thing, anyway?"

Regular daily prayer. Regular Bible reading. Regular attendance at corporate worship. Regular active participation in the activities of the Christian fellowship. All these are essential to developing our side of the God/me relationship.

God can always break through our barriers of confusion, doubt or indifference. But the more we do on our side to develop the relationship, the more we'll understand him when he reaches out to help us.

"You did not choose me, but I chose you. And I appointed you to go and bear fruit, fruit that will last,"

John 15: 16a

Matthew was a tax-collector, an occupation which helped the Roman authorities tighten their hold over the people of Israel. He was either scorned or hated by his fellow Jews. Even so … Jesus loved him and chose him as one of his apostles.

Mary Magdalene was possessed by demons. Even so … Jesus loved her, freed her from their terrible grasp and encouraged her to become one of his followers.

Peter was impetuous and quick-tempered, easily moved to make emotional responses to situations; he even denied Jesus three times during the Lord's most critical hours of earthly life. Even so … Jesus loved him and selected him as the leader of the early church.

Saul, a highly educated and devout Jew, led raids on the homes of Christians in Jerusalem and had many of them put in prison. He stood silently by, as Stephen was stoned to death. He aggressively sought authority to carry out the persecution of the Jesus followers in other cities. Even so … Jesus loved him, called him to repentance, and chose him to proclaim the Good News to the Gentiles.

Not one of these four was perfect. None of them were logical choices to be leaders in a movement founded on self-giving love. Yet Jesus chose them. He loved them, and he chose them in spite of their imperfections. And each one loved him in return.

Too often, we try to be 'perfect' for the Lord. We feel guilty when we're not, and that makes it difficult for us to love him. He doesn't ask for perfection, just for love. No matter what our flaws, Jesus loves us, even to the extreme act of dying on our behalf on the cross. He asks us to love him, and love each other, in the same way.

The Lord is my rock, my fortress and my deliverer, my God in whom I take refuge, my shield, and the horn of my salvation, my stronghold.

Psalm 18: 2

In the Fall of 1944, having just risen from the lower ranks and been commissioned as a Probationary Sub-Lieutenant in the Royal Canadian Navy, I was posted for some additional training on board H.M.C.S. Acadia, sailing out of St. John, New Brunswick. The day before my nineteenth birthday, the Captain and the other senior officers went ashore, leaving me, full of ego and pride but very wet behind the ears, as a determined but bewildered Officer of the Day.

An hour later an urgent signal arrived, directing the ship to be moved as soon as possible from the eastern jetty to the western jetty. The Petty Officer of the watch recommended that I try to locate the Captain, but I decided to carry out the signal, even though I had never conned a ship before. I got out my Seamanship Manual, alerted the duty crew on board, and proceeded to follow the instructions 'by the book'.

We got away from the eastern jetty with only a few bumps and jars, but after that, disaster was all around me. The Acadia was a single-screw ship, and the tide was coming in. I kept giving commands to the helmsman and the engine room, but I was in way over my head. After I had severely damaged a couple of pilings on the western jetty, the Petty Officer and the rest of the crew disregarded my commands and finally brought us in safely.

When I look back on that humbling experience, three messages emerge.

First, I wasn't prepared to con a ship. I not only didn't know the Manual, I hadn't any real experience in doing what it told me to do. The Bible is God's Manual for life, our set of instructions about how to handle our ship of life. We need to know what is in it, and experience its help and guidance every day.

Second, we don't journey alone. Others share the passage, and we must accept their guidance and support.

Third, we must never be so bound to the book or to other people that we forget that God is at the centre of our voyage. Only a continuing relationship with him will bring us safely home.

For I am convinced that neither death, nor life, nor angels, nor rulers, nor things present, not things to come, nor height, nor depth, nor anything in all creation will be able to separate us from the love of God in Christ Jesus our Lord.

Romans 8: 38,39

There's a path that follows the shoreline of the Avon River in Stratford, Ontario. Swans and ducks paddle close to the shore, always looking for a handout from the many people walking on the grass along the bank. At one point, with the Festival Theatre just up the hill, you come to a bridge, a small bridge, taking you across to a small island. There are trees and flowers, and some comfortable benches to sit on.

We rarely go to Stratford without spending time on this island. It's an oasis of peace and beauty, just a minute away from the hustle and bustle of the footpath. And you need the bridge to get there.

Life is much like the island and the footpath. We need bridges to get from one to the other. Most of our bridges come from the people we meet every day - family, friends, neighbours, work associates, fellow recreationers, even strangers. Sometimes it can be a word of encouragement; sometimes a helping hand; sometimes just a warm smile. But it's always a bridge between busyness and stress and peace and joy, a bridge we tend to take for granted, but without which life would be unbearable.

During his three-year ministry, Jesus continually built bridges. Bridges to the sick. Bridges to the disadvantaged. Bridges to the common people. He was not always successful, particularly with the religious establishment.

His bridge was love ... a love generated by God's incredible grace, which gave him the power to be the person God created him to be. The cross on which he was brutally executed was

his final bridge, a bridge which overcame the chasm between us and God ... a bridge which guaranteed us forgiveness of our confessed sins.

We too can be bridge-builders, to each other and to this hurting world. By the power, the wisdom and the courage available to us through the Holy Spirit, our bridges can be filled with God's love.

Like living stones, let yourselves be built into a spiritual house, to be a holy priesthood, to offer spiritual sacrifices acceptable to God through Jesus Christ.

1 Peter 2: 5

This year it hangs on the wall at St. George's Church, Grafton. People call it the Unity Cross - a wooden cross about two and a half feet tall, filled with a lot of small stones. They are different shapes and colours. Some have painted designs done by creative human hands. Next year it will be in the United Church, the following year, the Roman Catholic Church, and the year after that, the Presbyterian Church.

This unique cross was born as the result of a special worship service for Christian unity, involving the people and pastors of the little town of Grafton and area. The members of each congregation were asked to find a small stone that particularly appealed to them, decorate it if they wished, and bring it to the service.

All the readings, reflections, hymns and prayers focused on a 'spiritual stones' theme. Participants held their stone in their hands, as members of the four congregations shared leadership responsibilities. Toward the end of the service, worshippers came forward during the singing of a hymn and placed their stone inside the raised edges of a cross lying on a table near the sanctuary. Food and warm fellowship followed in St. George's hall.

Later, the stones were carefully arranged in layers to fill the whole cross. A special epoxy was poured over them. When it had solidified, all the stones were bound together within the framed cross. A strong hook was added to the back, so it could be hung on the wall.

Every time I think of that special cross, I have an image of Jesus as the foundation of our faith, binding us all together with his love. His sacrifice was for all who believe in him, not just for a particular grouping of his followers.

The stones are mixed together in the cross, as individual believers united within the cross of Christ. There is no suggestion of uniformity, but simply a statement of unity.

If we confess our sins, he who is faithful and just will forgive us our sins.

1 John 1: 9

Rachel was a music teacher. She gave piano lessons to a number of children and adults, who had varying degrees of skill. Every year, at the close of the season, she arranged a recital for all her students. Each one had a piece of music especially chosen for them, and they were exhorted to practice, practice, practice.

Particular emphasis was given to practicing the last few lines of music. Rachel instructed her pupils to practice the conclusion of their piece at least five times more often than the rest.

This constant repetition made them grumble, to which their wise teacher would reply, "You can make a mistake in the beginning, or even a mistake in the middle; people will forget those mistakes, if you make your ending glorious!"

Almost every day we make a mistake in God's eyes … something we think, say, or do. But God helps us give the day a glorious ending. Before we go to sleep, we admit our mistakes, are truly sorry and repentant, and receive his loving forgiveness.

That's a glorious ending!

I press on toward the goal for the prize of the heavenly
call of God in Christ Jesus.

Philippians 3: 14

On a long week-end holiday, we were visiting some friends for a barbecue. Someone suggested a bocce-ball competition. There were two teams of two players each; everyone else begged off!

This is how it works. We each have two coloured heavy plastic balls, slightly smaller than a softball. A white ball, about the size of a ping-pong ball, is thrown thirty or forty feet away on the lawn. The players then throw their balls, trying to get them closest to the white ball. The first player throws one ball; an opposing player tries to get closer. If that player succeeds, the first team throws again, trying to get even closer. Points are scored for the closest player.

I've seen bocce played in Europe, usually on a hard sand pitch. But we were playing on a sloped, multi-bumped and multi-dipped back lawn. Skill had very little to do with winning. Many well-thrown balls would hit a dip or a bump and go careening off to the left or right. Some would hit the ground and not move forward one inch. Others would land and bounce way up in the air.

On the way home, I reflected about how everyday life is like that bocce game. The pitch is not level and straight. Unforeseen bumps and detours can change our direction. Choices we make can turn out to be wrong. Partners we depend on can let us down. And the world pushes us to be winners at all costs.

Praise God, we Jesus believers are not at the mercy of a mythical 'Lady Luck'. Yes, we will make mistakes. We will take wrong turns. We will seem to be shunted off by detours. But with Jesus at our side and the Holy Spirit to guide us, we will move ahead on the true road of life.

Our goal is to win for the Lord, not for ourselves ... to focus on loving God and each other. All the bumps and curves will not turn us away from being God's people in a world which needs us.

*Finally, beloved, whatever is true, whatever is honour-
able, whatever is just, whatever is pure, whatever is
noble, whatever is pleasing, whatever is commendable, if there is any excellence and if there is anything
worthy of praise, think about these things.*

Philippians 4: 8

Every July first we celebrate Canada Day. These words, that Paul wrote to the first church he established on European soil, are like a flashing beacon in my mind. There is so much in this incredibly wonderful country of ours that is true, honourable, just, pure, noble, pleasing, commendable, excellent and worthy of praise.

To be able to live here is a great gift from God, and we should 'fill our minds with these things'. Our prayers every day should give thanks for Canada, and ask that we have the wisdom to maintain it in peace and unity. And those prayers should include all of our citizens, not just those who are like-minded with our own personal political beliefs.

Above all, we should not abdicate our responsibilities to fill our minds with those things worthy of praise. Canada is God's gift to all of us, not just the power elite or the media moguls or the political pundits or the spin doctors, who would tell us what should be done to suit their own agendas.

The gift is not to us as 'owners' but as care-takers or stewards. So we are called to take care of this land, to preserve it for God's glory and honour, not for ourselves or even for our children.

Then he put the man on his own animal, brought him
to an inn, and took care of him.

Luke 10: 34

Every summer we read about the 'Canada geese problem'. I hadn't thought much about these fabulous flyers since I was at the Church of the Ascension in Port Perry a few years ago. There I was introduced to 'Father Goose', the local resident who used his homemade ultralight plane to lead a flock of geese to their southern winter quarters.

In the process I learned something very special about Canada geese. When one gets sick or shot, it never falls out of formation alone. Two other geese follow the ailing goose down to the ground, often one of them being the mate of the wounded bird, because geese mate for life.

The two healthy birds protect and help the other bird as much as possible, particularly against predators. They stay until the sick bird is once again able to fly, or has died. Then they join another formation flying overhead, adding to the safety and flying efficiency of their numbers.

If there had been Canada geese in the Holy Land at the time of our Lord, I'm sure Jesus would have used them as examples of caring for one another.

Caring means being there for people when they're hurting. Sticking with them when circumstances get tough. Reaching out to them in whatever way they need us. Remembering that we are never alone in our caring … the wisdom and power of the Holy Spirit are always with us.

***Repent and be baptized every one of you in the name
of Jesus Christ so that your sins may be forgiven; and
you will receive the gift of the Holy Spirit.***

Acts 2: 38

Ever since I retired from full-time parish work, I have come face-to-face with a simple, yet profoundly important question, 'Does getting older bring me closer to Jesus?'

What I read and hear seems to push me toward a 'yes' answer. I'm told I have more time for reflection, that the stresses of the earning period are being replaced by the more peaceful delights of the 'yearning period'. I also have more time to relax and enjoy life, because I don't have to prove myself to anybody. I can become involved in good causes and volunteer work. All this is supposed to give me a closer and more loving relationship with my Lord.

There's another side to this question. I'm free to do all the things I've always wanted to do. Free to be me! But who is me? The me I look at in the mirror likes to have things the way they've always been. It doesn't like changes, not even small ones. It responds to life situations in predictable ways. Habits are comfortable, and I like comfort. Values are important, and must be upheld at all costs. Traditions must never be tampered with. None of this sounds like freedom. On the contrary, the combination of the hopes of the future and the baggage of my past tends to make me self-centred. And being self-centred makes it difficult to be God-centred.

Jesus told Nicodemus that he must be born again of water and the Holy Spirit, which is what happened to me when I was baptized. But being born again is not a one-time experience; it's an everyday experience. Life is a journey, not a destination. The apostles received the gift of the Spirit at Pentecost, but that wasn't the final curtain. It was the overture to an incredible life, which day-by-day drew them closer to Jesus, as the wisdom and power of the Spirit gradually worked his wonders in them. Transformation continued during their lifetime.

The same opportunity to have a closer relationship with Jesus is given by the Spirit to all of us ... the child, the teenager, the young parent, the fifty year old and the retiree. Each has obstacles to overcome, if the relationship is to grow. The Holy Spirit, God with us, will always show us how, if we let him.

"I came that they may have life, and have it abundantly."

John 10: 10

Every year the town of Ayr, south of Kitchener, hosts the Canadian Pork Barbecue Championship. Thousands of visitors flood into town for the day and a half event. Each year the people of Christ Anglican Church bake and sell pies for dessert. Between ten and twelve dozen of all kinds, the specialty being fresh strawberry pie, about six dozen of them. The parishioners pick the strawberries. As their priest, I learned very quickly how to pick the juiciest and the best.

One year I went picking with our choir and a handful of servers. Young teen-ager Danny was with us, which was surprising, since he had the reputation of being lazy. We worked in the field for just over two hours, and I noticed that Danny's pail, though slightly smaller than the rest, was full to the brim with large, juicy berries.

The next day the women of the parish hulled the berries and baked the pies. As a special treat for the young servers, they baked a small, saucer-sized pie for each of them. At the appointed time, they all lined up to get their pies. Strawberry was Danny's favourite, and he was positively drooling as he dug in for his first mouthful. As he sank his fork into the flaky crust, he cried out in dismay. Beneath the top layer of berries and whipped cream was a soggy mass of green mush.

Lazy Danny had fooled around in the field and, thinking that his pail would get lost in the shuffle, had filled it with plant leaves, topping it off with a layer of big leaves and berries. The ladies had discovered it and baked his special pie to teach him a lesson.

Many people earnestly want to experience the 'fullness' of God's love in their lives; love which comes as a gift, freely given. Initially, it's easy to accept this gift. But to experience its fullness, we have to work at developing our relationship with him. That requires

prayer, regular scripture study, being involved in a Christian community and actively reaching out to share his love with others. God always does his part. He simply asks us to do the same.

Now to him who by the power at work within us is able
to accomplish abundantly far more than we can ask
or imagine,

Ephesians 3: 20

A few years ago, after the men of my Anglican Church had been beaten at a tug-of-war contest by the men of our local Lutheran Church, I was bemoaning the loss to the sergeant in charge of our regional police detachment. He told me about some experiments conducted by his unit, after they had lost their championship in the police games.

Using a special 'pull meter', they measured the force exerted by each member of their team. Then they measured the force exerted by the whole team; the team result was 1½ times more than the sum of the individual team members.

In science, they call this phenomenon SYNERGISM, which I am told means that the total exceeds the sum of the parts. 2 plus 2 doesn't always equal 4 ... in synergism it could equal 5 or 9.

That's what it's like with our faith as a Christian community. Praying, worshipping, learning and working together can bring incredible results! But when you add the power and wisdom of the Holy Spirit to both our individual and community efforts in Jesus' name, we can truly say, "Glory to God, whose power, working in us, can do infinitely more than we can ask or imagine." (*Book of Alternate Services, page 214*)

SYNERGISM plus the HOLY SPIRIT - an unbeatable combination!

May you be made strong with all the strength that comes from his glorious power, and may you be prepared to endure everything with patience,

Colossians 1: 11

I was in the bathroom shaving, when the phone rang. Audrey said, "Will you take it? I'm in the kitchen."

"I can't. I'm covered with shaving cream," I said.

A short pause. Then she said, "It's for you."

"Take a message," I shouted.

"It's long distance," came the reply.

"I can't talk with shaving cream all over my face," I insisted.

"It's person-to-person," she said, as she handed me the phone.

The ensuing conversation was important, and I'm thankful to my ever-patient and persistent wife.

With modern technology, it's easy not to answer. Telephone answering machines, call-answer services and other ways of avoiding direct response make it simple to turn off the world. Even if it's long distance. Even if it's person-to-person.

The danger is that we will try to put our spiritual life on hold as well. To turn off God!

Fortunately there is no machine or service that can keep God away from us. He's patient and he's persistent. And when he calls, it's always

person-to-person, and he does it every day. We can refuse to listen, but he keeps on calling.

And when we finally pick up God's phone and answer him, life is changed forever. Full of peace, full of joy and full of wonder.

*And the King will answer them, "Truly I tell you,
just as you did it to one of the least of those who are
members of my family, you did it to me."*

Matthew 25: 40

I had been ordained less than a week, and was in my first parish, when a call came to tell me that one of my parishioners, Ken, was very ill in the hospital. Because of my inexperience, my visit with him there was more social than pastoral, but he asked me to bring him communion the next day. I did - another 'first' for me.

When our short Eucharistic service was over, Ken said, "I have never before received communion except in church." I asked him why he had wanted me to bring the sacrament to him, and after a moment's hesitation, he replied, "Somehow I knew that was what God wanted me to do."

Ken died soon after, and I conducted his funeral. Still another 'first' for me.

Much to my surprise, there were so many people at the funeral home to visit with the family that there was a line-up at the door. At the service in the church, we had to use all our extra chairs to accommodate the crowd.

I had not had a chance to know Ken very well, so I spent some time with his family and friends, trying to find out what kind of a person he had been. I couldn't count the times people used the words 'honest' and 'fair-dealing' when they spoke of him.

Ken owned a gas station and home heating oil delivery service in town. They told me how he would make sure every repair job was properly done. How he would deliver oil on a stormy winter night, because a family was freezing. How dozens and dozens of his customers were given service without payment during the Depression of the Thirties, because he knew they couldn't afford it. How he shoveled snow from

the walks and parking lot of the church for many years, without sub-mitting a bill. How he was always able to spend quality time with his loving wife and adoring children.

I can hear him say, after a few moment's hesitation, "Somehow I knew that was what God wanted me to do."

How do we respond when we know, deep inside, that's what God wants us to do?

And live in love, as Christ loved us and gave himself up for us, a fragrant offering and sacrifice to God.

Ephesians 5: 2a

A few summers ago, Audrey and I drove up to Minden. We took part in a fundraising dinner and auction run by St. Paul's Church to pay down their renovation debt. Just south of Minden on Highway 35 is the small town of Norland. The highway runs quite close to the Gull River.

As we came around the bend down the hill and into the town, the car in front of us braked hard and came to a stop, as I did behind it. A woman got out of the car, and beckoned me to get out, too. She asked me to hold up the traffic coming after us, and said she would stop it coming in the other direction. When I asked why, she simply pointed. Standing on the side of the road farthest from the river was a mother duck with five little ducklings.

With traffic stopped both ways on this very busy highway, the entourage calmly and slowly crossed the road and went down the bank to the river. A number of other people had stepped out of their cars, and we all stood there quietly as mother and young ones waddled across. No horn-honking, no yelling, no road-rage. Just beautiful smiles on everyone's faces.

Some folks would say we were all pretty crazy to take such a risk, stopping in the middle of a highway in cottage country on a Saturday afternoon. But we did, and there were no accidents, no bumped fenders. The Lord looked down with love on his people.

Every day we are faced with opportunities to help somebody in need. If we reach out to them, the Lord will look down with love on us. And if there is a risk, so be it. Jesus gave his life for us. Can we do any less than help others in his name?

*"**Whoever has two coats must share with anyone who has none; and whoever has food must do likewise.**"*

Luke 3: 11

A very saintly bishop prayed to God many times to be able to see for himself what heaven and hell were really like. God said that the next time he went to sleep his prayer would be answered in a dream.

In a beautiful celestial palace, St. Peter ushered him into a large hall, where he saw people seated at a banquet table. Spread out before them was a sumptuous repast, with the most delectable foods anyone could desire. But not a morsel was being eaten. The bishop looked in astonishment at the seated people. They were emaciated with hunger, and they moaned constantly for food, even though it was right in front of them.

"They're obviously starving," said the bishop. "Why don't they eat the food on the table?" "Look closely," said St. Peter. "See, each person has both arms strapped straight out from their body. No matter what they do, they cannot get any food into their mouth." "Truly, this must be hell," said the bishop.

St. Peter escorted him into another banquet hall, where there was another table laden with delicious and choice foods. Everyone seated at this table was well fed, full of laughter and joy. These people also had their arms strapped straight out in front of them, Confused, the bishop asked St. Peter, "How is it that they are so well fed, since they can't feed themselves?" "Look closely," said St. Peter. Then the bishop realized that each person was feeding another. "Truly, this is heaven," he said.

We are blessed to live in a beautiful land of plenty. Even so, at least  five million of our fellow Canadians live below the economic poverty line. Equally as many live below the spiritual poverty line. Hell comes from thinking only of ourselves. Heaven comes from caring about and caring for others. Jesus asks us to share our material possessions and to share his love.

A great number of people would also gather from the towns around Jerusalem, bringing the sick and those tormented by unclean spirits, and they were all cured.

Acts 5: 16

I grew up in Montreal. As an Anglican from birth, going to Sunday School, Boys' Choir (no girls way back then), Young People's group, Cubs and Scouts, I spent time every week at the Church of St. Columba in N.D.G. This neighbourhood church was well known for its very large and active healing ministry, under the guidance of the rector, Canon Norman Peterson, and a layman, Dr. Albert E. Cliffe.

The theme of the ministry, which drew hundreds to its services and healing chapel, was 'Let Go and Let God'. The meaning of this theme escaped me for many years, because my spiritual journey was in its embryonic stages. I am still learning and growing, but some light is now shining through.

Let Go and Let God means:

- allowing God to be the centre of my life;

- being open to God using who I am ... my roots, my culture, my talents and my life in the world ... to do his will for me;

- giving of myself to others in love, not taking for myself;

- being supportive of the gifts of others, and encouraging them to use them to God's glory;

- caring for those in need, without controlling or manipulating their lives;

- reaching out to protect the disadvantaged, while helping them to face their own realities;

- opening my mind constantly to the message of scripture and the good news of Jesus as redeemer and friend;

- working co-operatively with those around me for the growth of the kingdom;

- not being afraid to share my spiritual journey with others and help them come to Jesus;

- learning from past experiences, so that I can live for today and grow for the future;

- trusting God completely.

Hear my cry, O God; listen to my prayer.

Psalm 61: 1

I was having a bad day. A really bad day. Every phone call I made gave me a busy signal or 'please leave a message and I'll get back to you'. My sermon notes for Sunday were a hodge-podge of ideas, lacking a focus. Even my coffee was cold. Nothing seemed to be going the way I had planned.

A little while later, I made a pastoral call to take the Holy Eucharist to Selma. She was crowding ninety, and although she lived in her own apartment, was to all intents and purposes a shut-in. I knew she was in constant low level pain, but she always welcomed me with a smile.

Despite having to use a walker, and with increased arthritis in her hands and knees, Selma kept busy doing three things - reading the Bible, talking with God in prayer and making needlework samplers with spiritual messages. She had been making them since she was a girl, always designed by herself with Bible quotations she had chosen. Her daughter told me she had probably given four or five hundred samplers to family, friends and the church over the years. Each one was lovingly created by hard work, tender care and much prayer. Her favourite verses were Psalms 46: 10, John 3: 16, Galatians 5: 22 and 23, John 1: 14, Micah 6: 8, Luke 18: 1 and Philippians 1:3.

Prayer was at the centre of Selma's life. She prayed while she was needleworking. She prayed making a meal and washing up after it. She even prayed while taking a shower. Most of all, she set aside a block of time, three times a day, to talk with God and lift up people in need to him by name.

Just before we began the Eucharist together, she said something so profound that I wrote it down in the elevator on the way to my car. "When your life is filled with scripture, prayer seems obvious. And when you are absorbed in prayer, bad days easily disappear."

The rest of my day was full of hope, peace and joy.

*The child grew and became strong, filled with wisdom,
and the favour of God was upon him.*

Luke 2: 40

His name was Bob. He was a successful, independent businessman, with whom I worked as a consultant of a large company. He loved the outdoors, and was part-owner of a Christmas tree farm outside Pontypool, north of Toronto. Our family had just moved into our first owned home and it needed a lot of landscape improvements.

Bob suggested one day that, if I needed a few trees, he could spare some from his farm. Having only seen young trees in nurseries and garden centres, I had images of pine trees about one-and-a-half to two feet tall, with their roots in a ball of soil in a pot or bag.

Early the next Sunday morning, Bob's car stopped in my driveway, and he came to the door, carrying a small paper bag. In it were three Scotch Pine saplings, about eight or ten inches tall. No soil around them, but the bag was soaked with water. Seeing the surprise on my face, Bob said, "Don't worry. I'll help you plant them way far apart and tell you how to take care of them." Which he did.

That was sixty years ago. The trees grew healthily. Even after we had moved away from that house, we would occasionally drive by to view their progress. Today they are beautiful pine trees, over twelve feet high.

Our spiritual journey is like those Scotch Pines. Faith starts out as a seed planted by the Holy Spirit. To grow, it must be nourished. The trees got their nourishment for growth from the goodness and strength of the soil, the refreshment of water and the life-giving rays of the sun.

We receive our nourishment for growth from the goodness and support of the people around us, the refreshment of the stories and messages of scripture and the life-giving rays of the Son of God, directed to us through that same Holy Spirit.

The Lord your God is in your midst…he will rejoice over you with gladness, he will renew you in his love; he will exult over you with loud singing.

Zephaniah 3: 17

Harold was in a serious car accident. As he lay in the hospital in a coma, he dreamed he went to heaven. An angel sat at a table before the entrance.

"Who are you?" asked the angel.

"I'm the man who was in a bad accident yesterday," answered Harold.

"I didn't ask what happened to you, but who are you?"

"I'm the principal of the local public school."

"I didn't ask about your work, but who are you?"

"I'm married to a wonderful woman, Rachel."

"I didn't ask who your wife was, but who you are!"

"I've got three terrific children."

"The number and character of your children don't matter. Who are you?"

"I'm an active member of the Anglican Church in our community."

"Did I ask about your religion? Who are you?"

After a few more questions, Harold realized that he had failed the test given by the angel. He awakened from his coma and recovered from his injuries. He was determined to find out who he was, not according to the labels the world would give him, but in the eyes of God.

Through prayer, he learned that God didn't want him to be a somebody, or a nobody. He just wanted him to be the man he was created to be. The man God loved. The man who loved God in return. All the rest was the result of who he was.

*Contribute to the needs of the saints; extend hospitality
to strangers.*

Romans 12: 13

I t was September 1942. I had just started my first year at McGill University, and it was two months before my seventeenth birthday. Because so many young men had left to join the services, the bumper crop of wheat in Saskatchewan was in danger of not being harvested. The Canadian government put out a call to all male university students, asking them to volunteer to go to the farms for one month and bring in the wheat. Those who went would receive a return train ticket, room and board on a farm, payment for their work and a special study dispensation from the university.

So I went, as did hundreds of others. Four of us spent a month with a wonderful family outside of Montmartre. None had ever been on a farm before, so the five a.m. rising and the daily twelve hours of hard work, sometimes in cold and windy weather, were experiences we would remember for a long time. We not only survived, we thrived. And we brought the harvest in.

Before getting on the train at Regina, I had wired most of my wages to my dad, keeping enough to buy food on the way to Montreal. We had to change trains in Winnipeg, but when I went to get on the new train, I found to my dismay that my wallet, with my money and my train ticket, had been stolen. They refused to let me board. I was stranded in the station with no money.

I persuaded a clerk to let me phone home collect and arrange for my dad to wire me what I would need for another ticket and food for

the rest of the trip. It was early evening, and the money wouldn't arrive until the next morning, so I curled up on a bench to wait.

At midnight, the railway police closed the station, and I found myself on the street with my dunnage bag. A short time later, an older man in a steward's uniform came out and saw me. Having heard my story, he went back into the station, used the phone, and came out again to say that he and his wife would put me up for the night. The next day, they gave me breakfast, and made sure I got my money from Western Union and boarded the train. Their names were Elijah and Sarah, and I will never forget them.

Trust in the Lord with all your heart, and do not rely on your own insight.

Proverbs 3: 5

The story is told of a highly successful man, who believed that everything he had was a gift from God. He was a widower with a grown-up son. Because of his Christian belief, he kept very little of the money he earned for himself. The rest, which was by far the majority, he gave away to the poor and the disadvantaged.

His son was among those who found it difficult to make ends meet, so the man gave him just enough to keep bankruptcy away from his door. Meanwhile, he helped other people who found themselves in dire need, usually through organizations that could give immediate and effective assistance.

One day a friend asked him why he gave so little to his son and so much to others. "You could help your son so much more," he said, "if you would give less to strangers." "Yes, I could do that," was the reply, "but if I gave my son everything he asked for, he would probably forget the importance of relying on the Lord. He would look to me as his saviour, rather than God. If that happened, I would not really be helping my son at all."

In the world in which we live today, where 'me first' and 'I can do it' are paramount, it's easy to delude ourselves into thinking that what we do determines our future as human beings.

That kind of self-sufficiency, which leaves out God, leads to pride. And

once pride takes over, there's no room for God. The Lord cannot do *his* work in our lives, if our egos keep him out.

As the great theologian Harry Emerson Fosdick said, "We need to work as though everything depends on us, but pray because we know that everything depends on God."

Like good stewards of the manifold grace of God, serve one another with whatever gift each of you has received.

1 Peter 4: 10

There is an ancient story about a blind man and a badly crippled man setting out to walk from one village to another. The path they had to travel was windy and hilly, full of narrow hairpin turns, rock-strewn passes and terrifying precipices.

The blind man begged the crippled man to guide him along the treacherous terrain. "How can I do that," exclaimed the lame man, "when I am scarcely able to drag myself along?" Then, after a moment's reflection, he added, "But if you were to carry me, I could guide you and warn you of what's ahead. My eyes will be your eyes and your feet and strong body will replace my crippled legs." Replied the blind man, "With all my heart, I agree; let us serve one another."

In our parishes, we are all together as God's people in a community of faith. We have different gifts, different skills, different cultural bases, different schedules and different amounts of time to serve the Lord, apart from our family and work responsibilities.

But we are all fellow citizens and members of the family of God ... one body ... united with Christ and with each other. Let us serve one another.

Let us pray together, share our resources together, spread the Good News into the world together. We will be a church overflowing with excitement and power. In a world full of suspicion, hostility, hatred and oppression, we can be a model of God's love as a servant church, witnessing to God's kingdom among us.

Jesus said to them, "Come away to a deserted place all by yourselves and rest awhile."

Mark 6: 31

For thirty years before I became a priest, I earned a living in the sales and marketing of insurance. My responsibilities included a lot of travel across Canada, putting on seminars and conferences. As a result, I became familiar with some of the social and food customs of the various regions across our beautiful country ... Newfie screech, fish chowder, breaded schnitzel, steak with wine and mushroom sauce and many others.

Back then, many service clubs, particularly in the Montreal area, used to have oyster and beer fêtes to raise money. Am I safe to admit I don't like raw oysters? Especially when you have to pry them open yourself?

Despite all my avoidance tactics, I occasionally had to succumb to one of these questionable gourmet adventures. And there I met the unopened but empty oyster shell! After I asked all my oyster-shucking friends, "How come?" one aficionado told me to look for a tiny hole in the shell. Voila! There it was. Subsequent research led me to the whelk, a small sea creature with an appendage that works like an auger. With it, the whelk bores into the oyster shell and then, little by little, sucks out the oyster.

Our complex, highly technological, me-first world is full of 'whelks' - insidious little seemingly harmless attractions, or distractions, which lure us away from developing our relationship with God. As someone said to me the other day, "I feel as if I'm being bombarded on all sides by the world. Everyone and everything wants a piece of me."

Family, friends, work, interest groups, advertising, TV, newspapers, even the church, invade our minds every day. When do we find time for God? The answer, as always, is to look to Jesus. As he walked the Galilean countryside, preaching, teaching and healing, he was constantly surrounded by the crowds, wanting more and more.

He knew that he couldn't do God's will unless he spent time with God. So he made time. He removed himself from the hectic busyness of life, found the 'still dews of quietness', and opened himself to God.

We must do the same. Each day we must be quiet and be with God for a time. Only then can we turn away the 'whelks' of the world, who would suck spiritual strength out of us.

So the disciples went out and proclaimed that all should repent. They cast out many demons, and anointed with oil many who were sick and cured them.

Mark 6: 12,13

In a Bible discussion group the other day, the question was asked, "What is the difference between the life of a non-believer and a life committed to Jesus?" Several answers were given, but the question stuck with me. I embarked on some research. From the Gospels, I tried to make a list, in today's words, of what Jesus expected of his disciples.

1. To be physically with him in his ministry.

2. To give up your former pattern of living.

3. To listen and learn from him.

4. To have a new and closer relationship with God.

5. To have a new relationship with other people.

6. To live a life of self-giving love.

7. To recognize and accept who Jesus really was.

8. To give him absolute trust.

9. To give him absolute obedience.

10. To be free from personal ambition.

11. To stop striving for material possessions.

12. To be truly grateful for God's gift of grace.

13. To stop believing you reach heaven based on merit.

14. To follow only the basic rules of the Ten Commandments.

15. To witness that God's kingdom is here now.

16. To give up all bias and prejudice against others.

17. To repent and receive God's forgiveness.

18. To accept women as equal members of the fellowship.

19. To forgive other people with love.

20. To reach out to the poor and disadvantaged.

21. To share all you have with others.

22. To care for the sick and needy.

23. To make the fellowship a model of the kingdom.

24. To serve God by serving the world.

25. To stand firm in the faith, even when it is painful.

Less than halfway through the Gospels, I stopped. What can you add to the list? And how do we shape up?

"I will pour out my Spirit in those days and they shall prophesy."

Acts 2: 18

The result of the outpouring of the Spirit is found in Acts 2: 41: *Many of them believed the message and were baptized, and about three thousand were added to the group that day.*

On that day, the day we call Pentecost, Peter and the other eleven apostles began the work of the church - twelve ordinary men doing extraordinary things.

Pentecost is the birthday of the Church, and we often add new members to our faith community by baptism, as part of our celebration. The numbers may be different, but the individual results may be the same. Someone 'proclaims the message', and little children or adults join the church. Often they are too young to understand what is happening to them, but make no mistake, the outpouring of the Spirit does take place.

And the Spirit is not only poured out on the newly baptized, but on every one of us who is willing to be transformed by this power. There may not be a 'noise from the sky like a strong wind blowing' nor 'tongues of fire, which spread out and touch each person', but we can all be filled with the Holy Spirit, and, like the apostles, we ordinary people can do extraordinary things.

As Peter said *... for God's promise was made to you and your children - all whom the Lord our God calls to himself.* He calls us. We are his church. Each day we can add to our numbers by ... proclaiming his message ... in words and deeds.

But Jesus said, "Let the little children come to me, and do not stop them, for it is to such as these that the kingdom of heaven belongs."

Matthew 19: 14

It was the family service on Christmas Eve. The church was almost filled, with lots of children. Some regular attenders, with some visitors and occasionals. We sang the traditional carols. The scripture readings were merged into one story, and presented by parishioners in an exciting narrative. There was joy, expectation and exhilaration, with an underlying foundation of serenity.

After the Passing of the Peace, I sat on the chancel steps with the children. On one side was a stable. Without much prompting, the children helped me tell the story. As each character was presented, a child would place the figure in the stable. Not the Wise Men and camels; because they hadn't yet reached Bethlehem.

Our conversation focused on Christmas as a birthday celebration, and we talked about when they had a birthday. There was a party, with gifts, games and a birthday cake. Gifts were presented to Jesus by the Wise Men, even though they arrived late for the party. I explained that we can't give gifts to Jesus, but, as a symbol of our love, we give gifts to the people we love, and children receive gifts of toys and games at Christmas.

What about birthday cake? At the end of our worship, the children would receive a piece of Jesus' birthday cake (an iced cupcake with a birthday candle) to take home. When they woke on Christmas Day, before they opened their gifts, they were to light the candle, say a prayer of thanks for Jesus, and then eat the cake.

I said, "OK?" There were lots of nodding heads, but one loud, "NO!" from a five-year-old girl. When the laughter subsided, I asked her if she ate her cake the day before her birthday, to which she replied, "Mummy hides it from me." I asked her

if she would wait until Christmas Day as a favour to Jesus, and she nodded her head.

A few days later, her mother phoned to tell me that their family Christmas dinner was very special that year, because her young daughter had insisted on starting it by lighting the candle on Jesus' cake and saying a prayer.

Then one of them, when he saw that he was healed, turned back, praising God with a loud voice.

Luke 17: 15

As a boy growing up in Montreal, I looked forward every year to the Christmas holidays. particularly the days after the twenty-fifth, until we went back to school in January. My friends and I would make snow forts, toboggan on Walkley Hill, skate and play hockey at the 'Y' and sometimes ski on Mount Royal.

But there was one thing that spoiled the good times. Every day my mother would say the same thing. "Have you written your thank-you notes yet?" It was during the Depression, and I really appreciated any gift I received, but I hated writing thank-you notes. My standard reply was, "I'll do them when I get home tonight." Of course, my 'tonight' always seemed to be put off until tomorrow night … but tomorrow night never came. My mother even got me some special thank-you notes, but they didn't change things.

One Christmas, she forgot the special notes, and didn't keep bugging me about them. So I forgot, too, and threw away my list of gifts. About the middle of January, my Uncle Ian was visiting. He said to me, "Did you like the present I gave you for Christmas?" "Oh, yes," I replied, "I was just crazy about it!" "May I see what you did with it?" he asked.

I was stumped. I could not remember what he had given me. I apologized. "I'm sorry. I guess I didn't appreciate your gift enough to write a thank-you, and now I can't even remember what it was."

He looked into my embarrassed eyes and said, "Do you remember the story you heard at church a few weeks ago? The one about how Jesus healed ten men who had a terrible skin disease called leprosy? Nine of the men ran off to tell the priests. Only one stayed to thank Jesus. To whom did the healing mean most?"

I got the message. "The one who said thank you," I sheepishly replied. "I really am sorry, Uncle Ian." "I know," he said. "I forgive you, and so does Jesus."

The end of this story should be that I never had trouble writing thank-you notes again. But I do, and Jesus still forgives me.

"This is my commandment, that you love one another as I have loved you."

John 15: 12

L eaving a congregation, even when I have only been part of the Christian fellowship in that place for a short period, is a very difficult thing to do. I often arrive after the departure of a much-loved spiritual leader, and I leave just before the new priest arrives.

During my time in a parish, we pray and laugh and learn with each other. We speak openly and honestly when we do not agree, and we cry together when there is sorrow.

I have been blessed in my interim ministry with many fine and hardworking people willing to share the responsibilities of the parish. It would be a mistake to try to name them - someone would be sure to be left out. The Wardens, the office staff and volunteers, the choir, the pastoral care visitors, the lay readers and servers, the Altar Guild, the children and the young people, the teachers and helpers in the church school, the men and women involved in a wide variety of groups, the custodian, are all vital to the life of a congregation.

Some are part of an organization with a name and specific duties. Others simply do those quiet chores and kindnesses that aren't noticed, but without which we would be the poorer.

Jesus said, "Love one another." I could offer many Bible quotations or entire sermons to remember as I leave, but there is nothing more important to the life of a Christian fellowship than those three words. Love One Another. If a parish community facing change will write them on their hearts, they will see them through anything the future might bring.

I thank all the congregations I have served for the love they have extended to me and to Audrey.

So God created humankind in his own image, in the image of God he created them.

Genesis 1:27

I am a human being. I have lived on earth for four score and ten years. I was brought up by parents with sound Christian values. Regular attendance at church and Sunday School. Confirmation classes in my early teens. But I rebelled at these and wasn't confirmed until I was eighteen. I still hadn't met Jesus. Then a few years later, he met me. That was the real beginning of my journey of faith.

When I reflect on Jesus, I see two things. I get a glimpse of what God is like and a clear example of what I can be like. In Jesus, God shows me a perfect human being, created in his image. In Jesus, God shows me that to be a whole human being, I must follow the two Great Commandments - to love God and to love my neighbour. In Jesus, God shows me a human being who is truly, fully, freely and wholly alive. In Jesus, God challenges me to be the person he created me to be.

If your health is reasonably good, you can be alive in secular terms. But that kind of 'aliveness' is merely existing. You may have a successful career. You may be a loving husband or wife and a good parent. You may be a regular churchgoer and support many worthy causes.

If you have achieved all these as a result of obeying God's will, then you are truly, freely and wholly alive, as God created you to be. Like Jesus, you are living life to the full, as God wants you to.

But if you sometimes do what God wants you to do, and sometimes pay no attention to him, then you are not living life in all its abundance.

God understands this. He knows that life is a battleground, that the evil powers of the world and the demonic thrusts of Satan are constantly seducing our best efforts. He doesn't excuse our failures, but he is always ready, not only to forgive them, but to forget them.

We call that 'hope', which makes our spiritual journey exciting; a journey that focuses on living life to the full in his image.

One thing I do know, that though I was blind, now I see.

John 9: 25

I am told by my ophthalmologist that, in our modern world, it's almost inevitable that we will need his wisdom and skill as we get older. It's not only because we live longer than our ancestors, but also because of the increased glare of lights in our homes, computers and overhead lighting in our places of work, and approaching cars as we drive.

Four years ago I had to have cataract surgery on my left eye. I could see quite well before the operation, but I was told that delay would create serious problems later. Following the surgery and with new glasses, I was able to see a little better, especially for long distances.

Two years later I had the same surgery on my right eye. Another pair of glasses, and again my vision improved slightly. In neither case was there a dramatic major improvement, but I was assured that, barring any serious complications, I would be able to see quite clearly into the foreseeable future.

As I read the story of Jesus healing the man who was born blind, the question arose in my mind, "What helps us to see spiritual matters more clearly?"

- First we have to turn to the source of spiritual sight - an acceptance of Jesus as Lord. That's like a newborn baby opening its eyes for the first time and realizing it can see.

- Then we must take care of our spiritual eyes as we take care of our natural eyes, learning the stories and living the values that Jesus teaches.

- Finally we must turn to the expert in spiritual matters - the gift  Jesus promised us at his Ascension - the gift of the Holy Spirit. He does two things. He constantly nurtures us in new spiritual life by helping us understand what God wants us to do, giving us the power to do it and the courage to move, because with God there is never a risk. And whenever we begin to lose our spiritual sight, he gently restores our vision.

An ophthalmologist for our natural eyes and the Holy Spirit for our spiritual eyes. What a combination!

I am no prophet. I am a tiller of the earth; for the land has been my possession since my youth.

Zechariah 13: 5

I was visiting with Moira in her home, making arrangements for the baptism of her beautiful baby daughter. Even though my parish was surrounded by some of the best farm land in southern Ontario, I only had one farmer in my congregation, Moira's husband, Donald. He grew corn on his own 400 acres and on another 800 acres that he leased. That was the minimum for a profitable farm, he told me.

Donald wasn't much of a churchgoer. You couldn't call him a 'holly and lily' Anglican, because they were usually out-of-town visiting family at Christmas and he was often in the fields at Easter. We would see him in church two or three times a year, so I didn't know him very well.

It was pouring rain outside, and when Don came in from the barn, he was soaking wet. He changed into dry clothes and joined us. When I remarked that it was rough weather to be working outside, he said, as he sat down, "This is Jesus weather." Taken aback by his reply, I blurted, "Why do you call this Jesus weather?"

I will never forget his explanation. "The economy of the Palestine in which Jesus lived was based primarily on agriculture. I know that there were many large farms owned by absentee landlords - today we would call them corporate farms. But there were still a few farmers left like me, believing that God wanted them to hold on and keep growing food for the people. Jesus stood up for them. When it was a dry summer, like it has been for us this year, rain was needed to help the crops grow, and they knew Jesus was praying for rain. I figure somehow he was behind the rain that soaked me this afternoon."

Donald had a faith and an understanding beyond theology. As I left their home, I couldn't help wishing that we'd see him more often in church. He would add a great deal to our fellowship and our belief.

"I will give them one heart, and put a new spirit within them."

Ezekiel 11: 19

I t was the twenty-ninth of December. I had celebrated four Christmas services, had a great family Christmas dinner, taken communion to six shut-in people and struggled through a snowstorm. Lots of love, joy and excitement. But it was tiring. Now all the Christmas decorations had to be taken down and stored for another year - the tree, the bulbs, the lights, the tinsel and the special holiday touches placed around our home.

Usually, Audrey and I do this together, chatting about the festivities we've just experienced. But a phone call changed all that. Her Member of Parliament, for whom she was a Communications Assistant, had some writing that needed to be done right away.

Our decoration take-down session went from being an anticipated pleasure to a challenging chore, because it was all up to me. What's more, as the work progressed, my sciatic back began shooting spasms of pain from my hip to my ankle. It was a real downer!

As I sat down for a short rest, I put on a Bill Gaither CD of gospel music. The second song was "One Day at a Time", which came on just as I was reluctantly re-starting my efforts.

As I listened to the words, I realized that I was feeling very sorry for myself - blaming the church, the weather, the celebrations we'd enjoyed, our MP and even my hard-working wife. My attitude was being unfair to everyone.

I wish I could say that I immediately asked God's forgiveness for my self-centred feelings. But I didn't, and I finished the job in a somewhat sour mood.

It wasn't until later that evening that Ezekiel's prophecy popped into my mind, thanks to the Holy Spirit. I knew that tomorrow would be another gift from God, and that he would "put a new spirit in me". And he did.

Let justice roll down like waters, and righteousness like an ever-flowing stream.

Amos 5: 24

The preacher sat on the floor with the children of the church. On his left hand was a colourful puppet named Peppy. As the preacher tried to use two different voices, we heard the following conversation:

Preacher: Good morning!

Peppy: What's good about it?

Preacher: It's a beautiful day!

Peppy: Only a nut like you would think so.

Preacher.   Now, now! It's great to have all the young folk here, isn't it?

Peppy: You bet! What are you going to talk to them about?

Preacher: I'm going to talk about freedom!

Peppy: You mean when you can do anything you want, any time you want?

Preacher: Not quite. Do you have freedom?

Peppy: Are you kidding? How can I have freedom? I'm a puppet. I say what you want me to say and do what you want me to do.

Preacher: You're right.

Peppy: That makes you a big shot. A God.

Preacher: God's not like that. We are free to live the life we choose.

Peppy: Gee! You're lucky. I wish I had freedom like that.

Preacher: Well, God gives us freedom. But with freedom comes responsibility.

Peppy: I knew there was a catch somewhere.

Preacher: Being responsible means that we can't let our freedom hurt anyone else. By the way, can you sing?

Peppy: Can I sing? I'm the best!

Preacher: OK. Let's all sing together:

God gives me the freedom, freedom, freedom.

God gives me the freedom, freedom to be me.

But freedom's for everyone, everyone, everyone

But freedom's for everyone, or none of us is free.

*Some fell into good soil and when it grew it produced
a hundredfold.*

Luke 8: 8

In the days when trains were the preferred method of travel, a train on a branch line was huffing and puffing through the countryside. Suddenly it lurched to a stop. A passenger jumped to his feet and accosted the conductor. "Why have we stopped?" he loudly demanded. "I'm a businessman, and I have an appointment in an hour in the next town. Surely this old tub can get through a farmer's field without stopping!"

The conductor smiled. "Don't worry, sir. Just a cow on the tracks. We've got to wait her out." A few minutes later, the train began to move, not helped a bit by the frustrated fuming of the businessman.

A couple of miles later, it ground to a halt once again. Before the passenger could complain, the conductor rushed to him and said, "Nothing to worry about, sir. Just a temporary delay. We'll be on our way shortly." Exasperated, the businessman hooted, "What now? Did the cow run on ahead?"

The train did arrive at the next town on time, and the businessman made his appointment. What he didn't know was that the schedule allowed for cows on the track and temporary delays. His fuming and frustration succeeded in doing nothing but make him full of stress and frazzled.

How often do we get frazzled because of our impatience with the way things are going in the church? Not enough families with young children. Few teenagers, if any. Numbers at Sunday worship that go up for awhile, but then drop off as summer

approaches. Offerings that are OK most of the time, but go way down when people take their holidays.

Jesus preached, taught and healed thousands of people. His inner circle was only twelve. The number of true believers was around the hundred mark. And look at the size of world-wide Christianity today.

Small is beautiful, if we use the power and wisdom of the Holy Spirit to make it so. Surely that is the way God has planned it!

*For we are what He has made us, created in Christ
Jesus for good works, which God prepared beforehand
to be our way of life.*

Ephesians 2: 10

A t least three or four times every week, most parish priests receive a phone call or a visit from someone who needs help. Clergy never give a positive response to a phone call, only after meeting a person face to face.

Where the family has no food, they are usually sent to the closest food bank. However, in more than half the cases, the need is for money. Money to buy transit tickets to get to a new job. Money to help scrape together the first month's rent on a new apartment. Money to buy milk, eggs, bread, meat, and other perishable foods that food banks do not supply. Money to fill up a car with gas, so that job interviews can be kept. Money for bus fare to a nearby town, where work is available. And there are many more needs.

As much as possible, clergy try to screen the requests, because there are a lot of con artists out there. In all but a few cases, recipients earn the money by working around the church.

People are hurting. People are homeless. People are in need. Most of them have not been in that position before. They are not runaway homeless or perpetual panhandlers. They are you and me, after being hit by a wave of economic downsizing.

Fortunately, most parishes provide the priest with a Discretionary Fund. Even though the amount is usually limited, without it, these people would have to be turned away. My fellow priests and I are grateful for this outreach into the world.

 Our challenge is to do more. Not only as a faith community in the church, but as individuals, living where hurt is all around us. When you help others in need, you are showing your love for Jesus.

Jesus said to him, "Return to your home and declare how much God has done for you."

Luke 8: 39

Joan and Harry were visiting their daughter, son-in-law and children one Sunday afternoon. Joan was playing a game of Battleship with her grandson, Jeremy. In the middle of one of his turns to play, he stopped and gazed at her intently. "What are you thinking about?" she asked him.

After a long pause, he replied, "You're a Christian, aren't you, Grandma?" "I try to be," Joan answered. "But you never talk about Jesus," said Jeremy. "If you really loved him, wouldn't you talk about him sometimes?"

Not quite sure how to respond to the little boy, Joan said, "You can love someone without speaking of him." "Can you?" asked her grandson. "I didn't know that. You talk about the people you love, like my mom and baby sister, and about Auntie Sally and Uncle John, and even me. But you don't talk about Jesus." "I guess you're right," said Joan. "I don't talk about Jesus, do I?"

"Let's talk about Jesus sometime, Grandma," concluded Jeremy, as he sank her last vessel and started outside to play. Going out the door, he turned and said, "Because I love Jesus, too, and I'd like to talk about him."

We all talk about the people we love. We share our feelings about those who matter to us. What we say tells the world how we feel about them. Where does Jesus fit into our conversation?

As Jesus passed along the Sea of Galilee, he saw Simon
and his brother Andrew, casting a net into the sea - for
they were fishermen. And Jesus said to them, "Follow
me and I will make you fish for people".

Mark 1: 16,17

Having preached and healed for many weeks, Jesus decided the time had come to choose twelve disciples. He would hold a **DISCIPLE OLYMPICS**. When his advertising campaign was completed, applicants came in droves. The competition was fierce, and Jesus was the judge of all the events.

First came the **TEACHING EVENT**. Some had elaborate visual presentations, others long, well-put-together talks. Some told stories. Others used a group process approach. The method seemed more important than the content. There was a lack of heart in their teaching. No winner emerged.

Second came the **HEALING EVENT**. There were long incantations from some, and frantic body movements from others. Loud shouting was used, as well as almost complete silence. No one was healed and there were no winners.

Third came the **PRAYER EVENT**. All the contestants had practiced hard and long. Big words came from some, and religious jargon from others. Some prayers were long and involved. Others were short, with responses. Lofty ideas were followed by spiritual simplicity. But there was no winner. It was all just words, with no sincere relation-ship underneath.

Last came the **WORSHIP EVENT**. The variety was impressive. Full orchestra or one guitar. A soloist or a full choir. Beautiful garments or simple dress. Incense and bells or hand clapping and foot stomp-ing. Lots of gestures and movement or quiet contemplation. Showmanship galore! But no real sense of joy or nurture.

So the Disciple Olympics ended with no winners, no disciples. Tired and disappointed after a long day, Jesus went down to the lake shore to cool off. He saw some men fishing. Not only did they know what they were doing, but they did it with zest and enthusiasm. They would make terrific disciples.

And they did!

*"I will put my spirit within you and make you follow
my statutes and observe my ordinances."*

Ezekiel 36: 27

Shortly before my mother died at the age of ninety-seven, she
bequeathed to me a group of old, leather-bound classic books,
which I had enjoyed reading as a child. I knew that my daughter,
who is a teacher, thought they were something very special. So every
Christmas we would wrap up two or three of them and put them under
the tree as a gift for her.

A few days after Christmas one year, she phoned, quite excited. A copy
of Tennyson's 'Idylls of the King' had fallen open at a page where there
was the imprint of a rose petal. When she put the page up to her nose,
she could catch the scent of roses.

The book was over seventy-five years old. There is no family history to
tell when or why the rose petal was placed in the book, but I'm sure it
represented a very special memory to the person who put it there. And
memories are what give us a rich heritage today.

As Anglicans, we have been worshipping our Lord in some parishes for
many, many years, celebrating our joy at being his people. We are a community of love, in which we try to think, speak and act in the way of God.
It is an intimate place, a place of true belonging, fashioned for us by God
and filled with the presence of Christ. Thousands have lived in God's
house before us. As we live in it today, we hear his voice saying, "Do not be
afraid. Come and follow me."

We are all included in this joy ... our forebears of
yesterday and our descendants of tomorrow. No
one is excluded. It is not a joy of frivolity, but a deep
and inner peace, which encompasses all our hopes
and fears, problems and opportunities. It's a joy that
comes from being free to be fully human and fully
alive, created to be in a loving relationship with God
and with each other.

Someday, our descendants will remember the heritage we leave. May the imprint of our faith be to them as the sweetness of the scent of the rose petal.

Since you are eager for spiritual gifts, strive to excel in them for building up the church.

1 Corinthians 14: 12

Rodney was a farmer. He had lived on the same farm all his life, having inherited it from his father. It was a good farm with fertile soil, and Rodney and his family, with much hard work, were able to live reasonably well. But Rodney wasn't happy. He felt there was something better for him, a larger and more modern farm, that would make him set for life.

More and more he found things wrong with the farm, until finally his wife, Rosemary, could stand it no longer, and said, "Why don't you sell it, then, and buy a bigger and better place?" So Rodney went to his real estate friend, Phil, and gave him all the details about his present farm and an idea of what he was looking for in a new place.

Eagerly, Rodney started looking through all the real estate publications, hoping to find what he wanted. A few days after his meeting with Phil, he saw an ad in the paper that fitted his needs completely.

It was a large farm in an ideal location, hundreds of acres of fertile ground, proper drainage, the latest in modern farm equipment, healthy stock, well-kept barns, high yields on crops, no excessive debt or mortgage, and a solid old farmhouse that had been completely modernized.

With mounting excitement, he showed the ad to Rosemary and then called Phil to arrange to see the place. When he heard the details, Phil said, "Rodney, that's the ad I just put in, describing your own farm."

Rodney made the mistake of focusing on what he didn't have, what he didn't like. In the church we often tend to do the same thing. It's far better and wiser to focus on the good things, the incredible gifts  God has given us. We'll find that the pluses more than outweigh the minuses; that we can grow in faith and have a stronger and more loving Christian community, if we build on what God has already given us.

The Lord God is my strength and my might; he has become my salvation.

Isaiah 12: 2

For as long as I can remember, I have loved music. Any music that has a melody which can be recalled and sung long after its first hearing. That includes the classics, opera, blues, ballads, country, gospel, hymns.

When I was six years old, my parents could not afford a real piano, but they bought me a cardboard piano and helped me learn the notes and keys. Later, I took lessons. I loved the piano. I was supposed to practice eight hours a week. Practice makes perfect, I was told. So, whenever it didn't interfere with baseball, hockey, football, tennis, and swimming, I practiced.

But I had a problem with practicing. I had a good ear for music, and could learn a new piece quickly. So after playing with the music in front of me a few times, I would practice from memory. What I remembered might have a few notes missing or a beat wrong. And I played it perfectly, but I was really playing it perfectly wrong. Practice did not make perfect - it only perfected my mistakes.

When I finish an interim period, the parish begins a journey with a new spiritual leader. If they are not careful, this journey will be like practicing a piece of music from memory. They'll do more of what they have been doing, in the hope that they will become better Christians.

Their new spiritual leader can help them experience God's love in new and exciting ways, with the Holy Spirit to guide them. This guidance involves a willingness to change, to accept God's love, a love so profound that no sin, no shortcoming, no selfish act of ours will turn off his forgiveness, if we truly repent. We must commit ourselves to God's plan, pay attention to God and not to ourselves.

Today I can play the piano, but I can't sight-read because of my old bad habits. I listen to the music a number of times and then try to play it by ear. I'm the loser, because I enjoyed the self-indulgence of easy-to-play music.

As I leave a congregation, my hope for the people is that they will concentrate on 'God's notes', and let the music of their faith flow from those glorious sounds. They will be playing God's tune, and Practice will make them perfect.

So Moses made a serpent of bronze and put it up on a pole; and whenever a serpent bit someone, that person would look at the serpent of bronze and live.

Numbers 21: 9

There is a fascinating story in the Book of Numbers, which takes place during the travels of the people of Israel in their exodus from Egypt into the Holy Land. The camps of the Israelites became infested with poisonous snakes. Many were bitten and many died. The people finally realized that the snakes were a punishment for their sin of doubting and turning away from God. They went to Moses, crying out in repentance, and asked him to pray to the Lord to remove the snakes.

Moses prayed for the people, and God answered by telling him to make a bronze snake and put it on a pole. Thereafter, anyone who was bitten could look up at the bronze snake and live. Through Moses, the Israelites learned that, if they took that which hurt or bothered them and lifted it up to God, they would be healed.

I still remember the first Sunday in the year 2000, which was the start of a new millennium. Considerable hype had been given to the arrival of this supposedly special event, thought to be disastrous for computers. However, nothing happened to justify the fears caused by unfounded rumours and predictions. Was it special to God? I don't think so. Every day is special to him, just as is every person. None more, none less. Our doubts and fears are as precious to him as were those of the desert-wandering Israelites.

We don't have a snake on a pole, but, through Jesus, we can do as they did. We can take our mistakes, our sins, our turning away from God, lift them up to God in prayer, and trust him to heal us. Whenever any one of us makes a wrong choice or takes a wrong turn in our life through doubt, impatience, fear, lack of trust or selfishness, and we admit our sin, God will always show us a way out. Even when we stray, God knows where we are, and he is able and eager to put us back on his path, which is the right path.

Rejoice with those who rejoice, weep with those who weep.

Romans 12:15

Ten year old Amanda was sent to the store by her mother with a list of items to purchase. She was also given very strict instructions to come directly home after she had bought and paid for the purchases.

To the distress of her anxious mother, it was nearly two hours before Amanda returned home. "Where have you been all this time?" scolded her mother. "You were supposed to come right home!"

"I'm sorry, Mom," the little girl replied, "I know I'm late. But I met Jessie on the way. She had just broken her bike, and I had to stop and help her fix it."

"How could you help her fix her bike?" demanded the mother. "When yours is broken, your dad fixes it."

"I know I couldn't really help her fix it," Amanda responded. Then, in a soft, gentle voice, she said, "but I sat down with her and helped her cry."

 Often we fail to reach out to help someone, because we don't know what to say or do. Whenever this happens, do two simple things. Pray for them and be with them. And the Lord will show you the way. Sometimes a loving friend to sit with us is all that is needed.

"I have come that they may have life, and have it abundantly."

John 10: 10

In a questionnaire I completed the other day, there was a section in which I was asked to list my 'recreational pursuits'. Examples were given - sports, arts, outdoors, collecting - and the directions told me to be quite specific. Subconsciously, I had the feeling that if I couldn't write down a fairly good list, I wasn't measuring up to expectations.

As I filled in my answer, which was short, I thought about the label 'recreational pursuits'. The dictionary defines 'pursuit' as the act of pursuing, chasing after, or striving for something. This suggests the need for a special effort to be successful in achieving a particular goal.

But when I listened to the Toronto Symphony Orchestra the other day, I didn't have any sense of 'chasing after', just absolute delight in the sounds of the music, which stirred me deeply inside. Even when I used to play competitive club tennis, the thrill was in doing my very best, not in ultimate victory. Winning occasionally just made playing even more exciting.

Upon reflection, it seems that whenever I begin 'pursuing' something in my leisure-time activities, they stop being recreational and become compulsive behaviour. The result is to destroy the real purpose of the activity, which is to bring more wholeness into my life.

I have become convinced that the word 'recreational' should properly be hyphenated to 're-creational'. Surely a vacation, a holiday trip, a game of golf, a morning's fishing, should remove us from the busyness of doing things and help to re-create us as the persons God created us to be.

Let there be no more 'recreational pursuits'. Let's simply experience the re-creation of those elements of being that result in fullness of life.

And the King will answer them, "Truly I tell you,
just as you did it to one of the least of those who are
members of my family, you did it to me."

Matthew 25: 40

Jeff was in church almost every Sunday, faithful and generous in his offering. At work, he was praised for his skill and commitment. He and his wife were a great couple, whose children and grandchildren adored them. He didn't belong to any service club or civic association. An avid gardener, he didn't participate in the town garden club.

Whatever a proposal was, he was against it. He would always take a position opposed to the general consensus. He wouldn't sit on any church committee, because he said they were all talk and no action.

We had a major special event in the parish for the year coming up, and we needed someone who could make it happen in a dynamic way. After announcements in church and discussion among wardens and key leaders, no volunteer had surfaced. Jeff's name was mentioned and discarded, because of his reputation as "Mr. Negative".

In my prayers, the Holy Spirit brought up Jeff's name, so I finally gave in and asked him to accept the task. His immediate response was No - too busy - and our special event would be a waste of time. I told him that God had selected him for the job and I wasn't going to argue with God. Would he talk with God in his prayers? The next Sunday he said he would do it.

Jeff had a hard time finding a team to work with him. But he persevered, and got a Task Force together. I heard about many points of disagreement among the team. I also learned that Jeff was able to be sensitive to other people's concerns and good at building consensus.

 When it was all over, and tremendously successful, not only did the congregation have a positive attitude toward the future, but many lives had been spiritually nurtured. I

had lunch with Jeff, and he said he had discovered many things about himself and his faith.

• The result of criticism is far worse than whatever you are criticizing;

• Using others' ideas as building blocks is better than knocking them down;

• Working as a team results in higher goals and better results;

• Starting each meeting with prayer puts everything that follows in perspective.

What did I learn? To really listen to the Holy Spirit.

Sacrifice and offering you do not desire, but you have given me an open ear.

Psalm 40: 6

I had an MRI the other day. Our wonderful family doctor wanted to know what was wrong with my left knee. She hoped it was just a loose cartilage, which I'd had in my right knee a few years before. An X-ray was not conclusive, but an MRI would certainly provide an accurate diagnosis.

My waiting time was only two weeks. At the appointed hour, I was given clear instructions by the technician: (1) put the earplugs he handed me firmly in my ears, because there would be a lot of loud noises, (2) lie absolutely still for twenty minutes, because any movement would destroy the results of the test. Then I was placed on my back and power-slid into this enormous machine, which looked like part of a Star Trek set.

There was no pain. But for someone who can't normally sit still for more than a minute, following the second instruction was one of the most difficult things I have ever done. I prayed for strength and self-discipline, and managed to make it through without a twitch.

The noise was a different matter. Despite the earplugs, it pounded away at different decibel levels and varying cadences. I couldn't turn it off. I couldn't escape it. It went on and on until the test was over. A few times, I wanted to yell, "Turn it off!"

God is not a huge sci-fi machine, subjecting us to stress-creating rigidity and the pounding roars of noisy commands. He's exactly the

opposite. He's forever trying to help us bring calm to our troubled minds and peace to the constant noisy demands of the world around us.

Unfortunately, we often turn our backs on the power of his love. We refuse to enter into his presence and be still, so that we can have a dialogue with him. We put 'earplugs' in our minds and spirits, so we are unable to hear him when he talks to us.

Thankfully, an MRI only lasts twenty minutes. Even more thankfully, God never stops reaching out to us.

*"But you will receive power when the Holy Spirit
has come upon you, and you will be my witnesses in
Jerusalem, in all Judea and Samaria, and to the ends
of the earth."*

Acts 1: 8

The renowned violinist, Fritz Kreisler, was always on the lookout for well-crafted violins. One day he came across a beautiful Guarnesius. He listened to its lovely mellow but sprightly tones, and was so captivated that he was determined to have it for his next concert tour.

Unfortunately, in the few days it took to bring together his resources and make a substantial offer, the instrument was sold to a private museum. "That divine voice doomed to silence under a glass case in a collector's museum was a tragedy that rent my heart," wrote Kreisler. Undaunted by his lack of success, he went back to the museum and repeated his offer at every opportunity.

His persistence finally moved the collector to take the violin from its locked case, hand it to Kreisler, and say, "Play." The master tuned the violin and then played as if his life depended on it. Incredible melodies and tones floated upward from its resonant sound chamber.

A few minutes later, moved almost to tears by this performance, the collector stopped him with a motion of his hand, and said, "I have no right to keep it in a case. It is yours, as a gift from me. Take it out into the world and let it be heard."

There are countless men, women and children in our community who

have never met Jesus. They need the power and beauty of his message and presence in their lives. With the Spirit of the Lord behind us, we are called to be his messengers, to "take it out into the world and let it be heard".

"This is my commandment, that you love one other as I have loved you."

Every generation seems to produce a few extraordinary people like Mother Theresa. Her life of self-giving love embodied this command of our Lord, and was given world-wide recognition in the media. Yet everyday hundreds of thousands of men, women and even children, because of their love for Jesus, share that love with others in unsung and unassuming ways. Nothing stupendous. Nothing extraordinary. Nothing that would create a headline in tomorrow's newspaper.

Mother Theresa put it this way, *"Few of us can do great things, but all of us can do small things with great love."*

I participated in a memorial service for one such lover the other day. For decades he was a loyal and active member of a small inner-city congregation, and his death will certainly mean that a lot of small but important activities will have to be taken on by somebody else.

But he also meant a lot to the wider community. The group of retired workers from his former employer will miss the compassionate care he gave to their group and to the families of those who had died. Cards, phone calls, gifts, personal visits - all were part of his contribution to their welfare.

The chaplain from the local hospital paid glowing tribute to the years he spent as a volunteer pastoral care visitor. Hundreds of patients welcomed the warmth and love he spread as he visited them over many years. The staff, parents and children of the local day care, which he enthusiastically supported in their founding years, had many stories to tell of the countless projects he undertook on their behalf.

It has been said the big cities are places where you can be isolated, anonymous and unseen in a sea of humanity. It's hard to love your neighbours when you don't know them. But

when nearly fifty families in the community where he lived spontaneously met and collected a sizeable gift for his widow in thanksgiving
for his life as their neighbour, you knew that this man had passed on to
them the love that Jesus had given him. He loved God and he loved his
neighbours, in whatever part of his caring life he met them.

"Comfort, O comfort my people" says your God.

Isaiah 40: 1

The word 'comfort' and its derivations, appears eighty times in scripture. Comfort against pain, comfort in suffering, comfort in grief, comfort when oppressed, comfort facing death, comfort for individuals, comfort for groups, even comfort for a whole nation. Mostly, comfort is given by God, but occasionally it is from one person to another.

Dictionaries use descriptive words like 'relief, well-being, ease, support, strengthen, soothe, cheer.' But almost without exception, they refer to individual physical conditions. Mention is seldom made of social, psychological, or mental afflictions. Any thought of spiritual comfort is conspicuous by its absence.

All of us have experienced life situations in which we needed to be comforted. Whether the need is created by physical pain, emotional stress, or social and economic uncertainty, real peace of mind can only come with the touch of the healing hand of God.

Fortunately, in every parish I have served, there has been a group of Lay Pastoral Visitors who have shared this healing ministry with me, bringing comfort to those in need – supporting, strengthening and nurturing their spirits.

Comfort from these dedicated Christians comes in countless forms. Some make daily phone calls to brighten the day of a lonely shut-in. Some drive a parishioner to church every Sunday. Others help with shopping or transport for medical appointments. Casseroles are prepared and delivered. Many make home or hospital visits, where a smile, warm conversation and a prayer bring special comfort. Most parishes have visitors who carry flowers from the altar to shut-ins after worship on Sunday morning. Whatever the helping hand, people are not only cared for and prayed for, but strengthened for the task of daily living.

Remember Pastoral Care Visitors in your prayers. And if you believe that God is directing you into this special ministry, answer his call and do something about it. There is training available ln almost every community both from the church and local hospitals.

So let us not become weary in doing what is right; for at the proper time we will reap a harvest-time, if we do not give up.

Galatians 6: 9

It was over 40 years ago. The store manager of the supermarket was very angry!

"You can't put those things in there!" he yelled.

"Why not?" we said.

"Because it's against the law," he exclaimed.

"What law?" we asked.

"It's a criminal offence," he declared stoutly.

"Oh?" came back our answer.

"You're defacing private property," he said.

"Show us where we're hurting your oranges," we retorted.

By now, other customers were getting interested in what was happening, so with a loud snort he walked away. This scene was repeated many times over a few years – in grocery, wine, liquor and convenience stores. We were placing small cards listing the products from South Africa that our General Synod had asked us to boycott. We scattered them in any bin or shelf where there was one of these products. It was a small witness, which anyone could do. And thousands of people in Canada did it.

The boycott was only one of many non-violent protests. Others included shareholder meetings of corporations with South African investments. Many church and public personalities spoke out. Countless articles were written in hundreds of publications. Everyone involved, in almost every country where dissent was not squelched, was committed to the elimination of the injustice and oppression of apartheid. And many years of persistent and faithful

DON'T BUY SOUTH AFRICAN PRODUCTS APARTHEID MUST BE STOPPED NOW

witness were required. Finally, this insidious cancer of human degradation became just a memory.

The groups and individuals whose commitment made success possible were a huge coalition of all kinds of interests and purposes. Despite their differences, they were single-minded on this issue.

And the church, directed and supported by the power of the Holy Spirit, was in the forefront of the action. We did it then, and we can do it again – wherever a cause of injustice needs concerted action.

This is the day that the Lord has made; let us rejoice and be glad in it.

Psalm 118: 24

It was winter. There had been a blizzard the night before. Now it was Sunday morning and we had to drive 30 kilometres for our regular celebration of the early Eucharist at my church in another town. A phone call to the regional police told us that the country roads we would have to drive had been ploughed, but there were many icy spots.

Less than a third of the way there, we hit black ice and ended up in the ditch. Neither Audrey nor I were hurt and the car wasn't damaged at all, but we couldn't get out of the ditch. What to do?

I walked half a mile to Dave's house. He was a young member of my later congregation and in the car painting business. I knocked on the door and woke him up. When I explained the problem, he immediately got dressed, drove me to our car, picked up Audrey, and drove us the rest of the way to the church. We were only a few minutes late for the service.

At the conclusion of our worship, one of the wardens told me that my car was OK and was parked outside. Dave had used his tow truck to pull my car out of the ditch and bring it to the church. We drove carefully back to our other church and Dave and his family were there to worship with us.

Because of Dave, disaster became a celebration. Whether God sends us rain or snow, sunshine or dark clouds, sweltering heat or freezing cold, it's how we perceive the day and what we do with it that counts. The bad weather didn't stop us from driving to church. The bad weather didn't stop Dave from coming to our rescue. God gave us the day and it was up to us to make the most of it in his service.

Our prayers that day were full of thanks-giving, for God and for Dave. And when I went outside after lunch to shovel the snow drifts around the rectory, I couldn't help singing some of my favourite hymns. It was a day of rejoicing!

Jesus Christ is the same yesterday and today and forever.

Hebrews 13: 8

About every five years we buy a new car, because the old one gets weary from the strain of pounding the asphalt for 250,000 kms, and the yearly cost of keeping it in rideable and safe condition is close to its blue book value.

Our latest was an Oldsmobile. We were moving on up. And it was a great car. But six months later GM announced that it would no longer build the Olds. I remembered having gone through three Pontiac 6000s (another great car) and they discontinued it. All in the name of progress. Each year the old models are replaced by new models – claiming that they are better and have the latest in newly discovered technology. Some people call this planned obsolescence. But we're creatures of habit. We buy Canadian and we stick to GM. There's a brand loyalty of ownership in each car we buy

As a pastor, I try to visit within two weeks any person or family that worships with us for the first time. Some of them have a loyalty of ownership because they have been worshipping Anglicans in another location. Some of them feel a void in their spiritual journey and hope that participating in our fellowship will fill that void. Others are church shopping – looking for a Sunday experience with which they are comfortable and will add something uplifting to their lives. And still more are there because it's their duty – a baptism, a wedding, a funeral.

The most common reason for not becoming a regular worshipper is "I didn't get anything out of your service." And they go elsewhere – or go nowhere.

Surely the true reason for going to a Christian church service is to meet Jesus Christ in the worship experience. He is present in the worship of every Christian group, regardless of its name. And you meet him not from looking for something you

can get from the experience, but from your participation – by giving of yourself as you sing, listen and pray, Loyalty of ownership comes when you meet the Lord. That's when you know you belong. And when you belong, you don't go elsewhere.

There's no planned obsolescence!

"So now go. I am sending you to Pharaoh to bring my people the Israelites out of Egypt."

Exodus 3: 10

The Egyptian king had decreed that every newborn Hebrew boy should be killed. Through the courage of his mother, one child was saved and adopted by the king's daughter. His name was Moses. When he was grown up, he saw an Egyptian kill a Jew, so he killed the Egyptian. The king ordered him killed. Moses fled into the Land of Midian. He settled down there, married Zipporah, one of Jethro the priest's daughters, and had a son.

One day, while tending his flock in the desert he saw a bush on fire, but it wasn't burning. Then God spoke to him out of the bush. **"Moses, Moses."**

"Here I am." **"Take off your sandals. You are on holy ground."**

"OK. But what do you want of me?" **"The Egyptians are treating my people the Jews cruelly. I want you to go to Egypt and tell the king to let my people go."**

"I can't do that. If I go back, the king will have me killed." **"No, he won't. I also want you to lead the people to a land I am giving them."**

"Even if the king doesn't kill me, I'm nothing to the Hebrew people. They won't accept me as their leader." **"Yes they will. Just tell them that I sent you."**

"They'll want to know your name." **"I am the Lord, the God of their ancestors."**

"Suppose they won't accept that answer and refuse to believe me. Then what?" **"Throw your staff on the ground."**

"Wow! You turned it into a snake." **"Pick it up by the tail."**

"It will bite me." **"Just do it."**

Moses did. And that was the beginning of the Jews' rescue from slavery.

Having a conversation like that seldom happens to most of us. Our talking to God is usually a monologue. We do all the talking and take no time to listen. Real prayer is a dialogue in which God says something too.

*Then they came to Capernaum, and when he was in
the house, Jesus asked them, "What were you arguing
about on the road?" But they were silent, for on the
way they had argued with one another who was
the greatest.*

Mark 9: 33,34

In addition to being a great teacher, preacher, healer and storyteller, Jesus was a great organizer. He took twelve ordinary men, and built them into a fellowship of disciples. The planning and logistics of their three year ministry, accommodation, food, money, meant that each was given specific responsibilities.

And, being human, each one believed that his contribution to the ministry was the most important. "Without food and drink, we'd be useless as disciples." "We have to have somewhere to sleep, and it's my job to arrange it." "Getting people to come and listen to the master is the core of our ministry and I do it." "You can talk all you like, but without money, which I handle, nothing else will happen."

In the church that Jesus founded, these same discussions continue to take place today. Talk of the value of our contributions to ministry still takes place. Between denominations. Between parishes of the same denomination. Between one congregation and another. Even within a group in the same congregation.

Whether it be in a Parish Council, Advisory Board or other body, there are often heated discussions as to the value of various ministries and traditions.

"A good choir is crucial to meaningful worship." "We need a Youth Director. The young people are the church of the future." "Pastoral visits to the sick and shut-ins are the essence of the Gospel." "Many people in the world are disadvantaged. That's why we need to focus on outreach." "Our children are not being taught enough about our faith." And so on….and so on….and so on.

For over thirty years I was an active Anglican layman in my parish, in Diocesan and General Synod and on their committees. After my ordination as a priest, people said that I must feel good about being able to do 'real' ministry. My reply was always the same. "God called me to serve him as a layman, and that was real ministry. He calls me to serve him as a priest, and that is real ministry. Neither is more important than the other".

*Then our mouth was filled with laughter, and our
tongue with shouts of joy.*

Psalm 126: 2

T here are times when a group of Christians gathered for worship
needs a peaceful calm, with opportunities for prayer, listening
and meditation, that puts them in touch, individually and collectively, with the Lord. Many of us have experienced such spiritually
uplifting occasions. In the midst of serenity, our hearts are warm with
joy and our spirits smiling with delight.

But there are also times when voices are raised with joyous gusto, singing
melodies that are familiar with words that have real meaning. Some prayers
are full of awe and majesty, while others aggressively challenge us to real
ministry in a hurting world. The proclamation of the word in scripture
and in sermon nurtures and informs our faith and makes it come alive
for our everyday lives. Then the celebration of the Eucharist transports
us back to the Upper Room with the Lord in our midst. Our hearts are
singing and so are our voices; our spirits are shining and so are our faces. At
the dismissal, we are walking on a cloud of glory.

Regretfully, there are times when the tunes are unsingable and the
words are meaningless jargon. The scriptures are read in a wooden
monotone and the sermon is a jumble of disconnected meanderings.
Prayers are recited by rote, without any reference to life today. Even the
great prayer of thanksgiving in the Eucharist is rattled off like an
express train. There is no joy, there are no smiles, no delight. The minds
of most of the worshippers are somewhere else.

There can be joy and delight in the stillness of knowing God is among us,

as we prayerfully meditate on His word. There
can be joy and delight when we raise our voices
in glorious prayer and praise. But surely there
is no place for boring, uninspiring, and spirit-
deadening worship. Every worship experience
in the church should put us directly in touch
with the Lord. Through him we will always
find joy and delight.

"For I will restore health to you and your wounds I will heal", says the Lord.

Jeremiah 30: 17

It was a sunny Sunday afternoon. We were relaxing after a busy morning in church. The phone rang. It was a friend of our older son, telling us that he had had an accident on his bicycle and was in the emergency room at North York General Hospital. Riding on a bike path, our son had fallen while making a turn, and the end of the handlebar had jammed into his side. Jumping into the car, we rushed to the hospital, where we heard the worst. His spleen had been ruptured and his abdominal cavity was full of blood.

He was on a gurney, about to be taken into the operating room for surgery. I stood beside him, placed a hand gently on his shoulder, and said a silent prayer. I asked God to be with him and bring him back safe and sound to us. As I did, I felt a tremendous surge of power flow down my arms and fingers. The surgeon who was to perform the operation had her hand on his other shoulder, and she looked at me with startled surprise. Obviously, she too had felt that surge of power.

The Lord was with our son that day. He was also with the surgeon. The operation was successful. Some may cite this as an example of 'faith healing'. But there were instances of healing by Jesus when there was no evidence of faith, just a need for help.

I choose to call what happened to our son 'divine healing'. Divine because the power of God was directly present in that operating room. Divine because the God-given skills of the surgeon provided the necessary and practical skill that was required to correct the cause of the near-fatal injury.

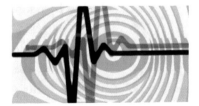

Was there a miracle? I say yes. A double-barreled miracle! Praise the Lord.

***"Ask and it will be given you; seek and you will find;
knock and the door will be opened for you."***

Luke 11: 9

H is wife was one of my wardens. He came to church every so often, particularly when one or other of their two sons was serving. And whenever we had a work party at the church, he showed up with the right tools and the right attitude. Working side-by-side with him, we became friends, and found something we had in common – both of us had worked in the marketing of insurance for many years.

One evening after a meeting, I stopped at their house to drop something off. Accepting an offer of coffee, we were sitting at the kitchen table, and I said to him:

"When you're in church, I notice you don't come up for communion. How come?"

"I can't. I've never been baptized."

"I'm surprised. Is there a special reason why?"

"Not really. I guess I just never got around to it."

"We're having a service of Baptism early next month. Why don't you be part of it?"

"You know, that sounds like a good idea."

It was a short conversation, simple and matter-of-fact. But for both us, it was a faith generating experience. There were smiles on both our faces as we realized that a wonderful thing had just happened. Later,

we had some further discussion about the meaning of baptism. Then he was baptized along with two babies. And he was an ardent supporter and contributor to our parish life until he died three years later from a heart attack.

Research tells us that over 70% of the individuals who come to worship in a parish as 'newcomers' have a family or friendship connection with someone who is already a member. They were invited to come with that member. No lengthy theological discussion. No enthusiastic evangelical presentation. Just a simple invitation.

That's real evangelism.

*Let us therefore no longer pass judgment on one
another, but resolve instead, never to put a stumbling
block or hindrance in the way of another.*

Romans 14: 13

I was new in the parish. One evening I received a phone call from the funeral home in a nearby town, saying that a family had requested that I conduct an Anglican funeral for a gentleman in his early seventies. He had occasionally attended our church.

Arranging to meet the family a half-hour before friends were to visit at the funeral home, I was taken aback when I entered the viewing room. On one side, standing or sitting were about ten people, On the other side, about the same number. Neither group paid any attention to the other. I could sense rampant hostility. The tension in the room was so strong you could almost cut it with a knife. The widow, supported by her sister, wandered from one side of the room to the other, obviously in great anguish. Getting the two sides together to discuss the funeral arrangements was almost impossible.

I learned from the sister that over ten years ago, the two sons had a falling out over a business deal. Since then, they had shunned each other. They would not visit in their parents' home if they knew they would be together. Christmas celebrations were separate. The grandchildren didn't know each other. The parents had tried to bring peace between them, but to no avail. It was sad and painful.

The scripture readings I chose for the service were 1 Corinthians 13: 1-8a and John 15: 9-12. They were read by a person from each side. I also asked someone from each group to say some words of remembrance and thanksgiving. In my homily, I noted how much family members had talked about the love their parents had for each other and for their children and grandchildren.

When I visited the widow a few days later, she said that, in the midst of her grief, she experienced great joy. When the family gathered at the house after

the reception, her two sons hugged each other. There were tears. Forgiveness was asked on both sides and forgiveness was given. Thanks to the Holy Spirit who made this happen.

For I am not ashamed of the gospel; it is the power of
God for salvation to everyone who has faith, to the Jew
first and also to the Greek.

Romans 1:16

When I was in late high school and university, I spent many hundreds of hours as a lifeguard and swimming instructor – most of them connected with the YMCA. My professional qualifications were mostly earned as a Boy Scout at Camp Tamaracouta, north of Montreal. When someone was in difficulty, in a pool or a lake swimming area, you did one of two things. You used a pole or life preserver to pull them to safety. This worked if they were able and willing to grab it when it was given to them. But if they couldn't, or wouldn't, you just dove in and pulled them to safety yourself. You never used the moment of crisis to give them swimming lessons. That may have come later. The objective was simply to save them from drowning.

It's been my experience that God uses both of these skills with us. He employs many different ways to bring us into the safety of his loving arms - preaching, teaching, healing, worshipping, the personal witness of other people - any means through which we can be guided into a personal relationship with him and a belief in Jesus as our Lord and Saviour. And if that doesn't work, he can directly intervene in our lives, as he did with St. Paul, so that there can be no doubt who he is and how he wants us to live.

Whichever way he touches me, I'm saved. Like the person in the water, when I'm in trouble, drowning in my own self-interest, he can bring me back to life. Not a life determined by the powers of the world.

 Not a life directed by Satan. Not even a life based on my own needs and desires. He saves me so that I can be truly alive as the person God created me to be. And when I need to be saved, he doesn't teach me how to be a good Christian. He just reaches out and brings me into the circle of his love. Christian teaching comes later.

That's what we call salvation – being saved to be ourselves, That's the most exciting experience we will ever have. That's when you begin to receive the richest blessings you can ever imagine.

But you are a chosen race, a royal priesthood, a holy nation, God's own people, in order to proclaim the mighty acts of him who called you out of darkness into his marvelous light.

1 Peter 2: 9

Our Bible study group was discussing the second chapter of Peter's first letter. We had established to everyone's satisfaction that, through the twin concepts of covenant and election, the author was reflecting an early Christian understanding that they, the church, were heirs to the promises made to Israel. This sense of identity and excitement resulted in a conviction that God and his Spirit were present and at work in their fellowship. As a people touched by God, their lives were expected to be a living testimony of worship and service in his name.

There was no disagreement in the group about the need and importance of worship. Part of worship (or worth-ship) was taking the time to nurture their faith and create a more intimate relationship with God through prayer, meditation and Bible study. But it was almost as if the group was split into two rival camps when the discussion focused on what was meant by 'service' on behalf of God. On one side were the evangelists, the proclaimers. And on the other were the outreachers, the demonstrators.

Using Matthew 28: 19-20 as their bulwark, the evangelists saw their service as messengers of the Good News of Jesus Christ. Their function was to proclaim the glad tidings of the church to those who had not heard them. God had a plan of salvation for the world, and the church had a special responsibility to make that plan known to as many people as possible. Bringing persons to Jesus was the Number One job.

The outreachers based their Christian service on Matthew 25: 31-45. Jesus' whole ministry was full of caring for people. He spent his time with the poor and the disadvantaged. So we demonstrate our faith in action – by striving against poverty, injustice and greed. Volunteering at a food bank, homeless shelter, hospital auxiliary, supporting food and medicine for children in third world countries – all these and more are what we do in the service of God.

God gives many different gifts to his people, none more important than another. Those who have the gift of proclamation should use it to spread the Good News. Those who have the gift of demonstration should reach out to those in need. And each feeds the other.

*So they went out and proclaimed that all should
repent.*

Mark 6: 12

"If you forgive the sins of any, they are forgiven them."

John 20: 23

Many people are surprised that an Anglican priest is trained to
hear private confessions. Yet in a third of the parishes I have
served, I have been asked to administer this priestly function.
Some requests came from regular worshippers; others from fairly new
members. On two occasions a minister from another church asked me
to hear it from a member.

Private confession/absolution is not just talking about personal problems with your priest, although psychosocial listening and discussion
often take place before the confession. It is a carefully constructed
'liturgical experience' in which the priest wears a stole as an ordained
proclaimer of the gospel rather than a family therapist. The liturgical act occurs when the priest determines that a formal experience
is appropriate for the health, peace of mind and growth in faith of
the confessor.

This is not in any sense just a general confession. The sins for which
absolution is requested must be declared in clear detail so that the
burden of guilt and shame can be removed. I once refused absolution
because a sincere and specific confession was not given. It was a difficult thing for me to do.

On one occasion, a young man just turned 21 confessed that since his

early teens he had been shoplifting in convenience
stores – small items, none of substantial value, and
from many locations. At the altar on his knees, he
recounted in detail what he had done, repented his
actions, and openly asked for God's forgiveness.

Before absolution was given, he declared that his
restitution would be in two forms; First he would
seek help from a trained therapist. Second, he

would donate $100 a month for six months to the local Community Service Association. Liturgical absolution removed his burden of guilt and shame. Six months later, he had done his penance, had refrained from shoplifting, and was continuing to see a therapist.

The Kingdom of heaven is like a mustard seed that
someone took and sowed in his field; it is the smallest
of seeds, but when it has grown it is the greatest of
shrubs, and becomes a tree, so that the birds of the air
come and make a nest in its branches.

Matthew 13: 31,32

We decided we needed a couple of plants at the top of the driveway of our home in Florida. We settled on two large pots, each with a beautiful plant. They stood about twelve inches high and had shiny, dark green leaves. They looked great! They had grown to about twenty inches when we went back up north,

Seven months later, as snowbird returnees, we drove up to the house and found both the pots with huge cracks in them. Fortunately, they were held together by long strips of duct tape, courtesy of a good neighbor. The plants had grown to over three feet tall, with extra branches and roots so big they had split the pots wide open. When we removed the tape, the pots ended up in pieces, but each plant had a solid ball of roots and soil. They were still quite healthy.

I dug deep holes on either side of the driveway and replanted them. They continued to grow and were nearly five feet tall by the end of the winter. Even with regular pruning by a gardener we hired for the summer, by the time we returned they had to be transplanted again. This time they were located away from the driveway because the roots had begun to heave up the corners of the asphalt. Today they are still healthy and stand ten feet high.

When I remember this experience, what comes to mind is that as the

plant grew and had to be replanted, the solid ball of roots and soil also continued to increase in size.

Faith is like that. The more we are open to the Holy Spirit, the greater is our capacity to grow into the person God created us to be. And the more we grow in faith, the greater is the solid ball of our trust and love for the Lord. New shoots are constantly springing forth that make us better able to listen to God and accept his guidance and commandments with delight.

I found out later that my two plants were a form of rubber tree.

With righteousness he shall judge the poor, and decide
with equity for the meek of the earth.

Isaiah 11: 4

T he Huron Hunger Fund is said by some to have originated this prayer. The Girl Guides claim it as their special prayer. In 1959, World Refugee Year, the Primate's World Relief and Development Fund gave it prominence. It originally had only four lines. A few years later, I added a fifth, about freedom. Then Audrey wrote a second verse. Finally, I put it to music. Unfortunately, people say two verses make it too long, so only the first verse is commonly used.

I have used it as a grace on countless public occasions and carry copies of it with me, because people inevitably ask for it. I am told it has been prayed in many parts of Canada, the United States and other countries around the world. It may be liturgically incorrect, but in every parish I have served, it has been used as the "prayer over the gifts" when the offering is received, replacing the ones that are prescribed. In some parishes, the people pray it together at that point in their worship.

Here it is, in its entirety.

For food in a world where many walk in hunger,

For faith in a world where many walk in fear,

For friendship in a world where many walk alone,

And for freedom in a world where many walk in chains,

* We give you thanks, we give you thanks,

We give you humble thanks, O Lord.

Teach us to share our food with those who hunger.

Teach us to share our faith with those who fear.

Teach us to share our friendship with the lonely.

Teach us the way to peace in all the world.

* Lord, give us courage, wisdom and love.

Give us the strength to do your will.

* *These lines are used when the prayer is sung.*

Just then some men came, carrying a paralyzed man on a bed and they were trying to bring him in and lay him before Jesus.

Luke 5: 18

T hey came from all the towns and villages as Jesus healed the sick. Daniel, Aaron and Saul were arguing with their friend Jonathan. They wanted to carry him to Jesus so he could be healed. His legs were paralyzed and he was unable to walk. But the crowd around Jesus had filled the house and spilled into the courtyard.

"There's no way you can push me through the crowd," said Jonathan "They want to get close to Jesus too. Forget it. Maybe he will come this way again."

"Don't give up so easily," scolded Aaron.

"There must be a way to persuade the crowd to let him through." said Daniel.

"I've tried to think of a solution, but I've come up blank." said Saul.

"Let's ask people to move. They see Jonathan is lame," said Aaron.

"They want healing themselves," replied Jonathan sadly.

"Couldn't we yell FIRE so the crowd scatters?" suggested Daniel.

"That's a crazy idea," retorted Aaron. "The crowd would beat us up."

"If we can't go around the crowd. Why not go over them?" said Saul.

"How are we going to do that?" they all chorused in surprise.

"We'll get a ladder, climb up on the roof, remove some tiles to make a hole, and then lower Jonathan slowly down on his mat, using ropes at all four ends," replied Saul.

"It won't work!" came cries of frustration. "He'll fall off the mat!"

"It's better than doing nothing," said Saul. "How about it, Jonathan?"

"To get close to Jesus, I'll risk falling off my mat," he answered. "Let's do it."

It wasn't easy, but in their concern for their friend they made it happen. Jonathan was healed by Jesus. He walked away, cheered by his three friends.

How do we face the serious illness of a friend or family member? Do we despair because we can do nothing to help?

Or support them? By being present with them? By sharing our love and care? By praying for skill and wisdom from the health care practitioners? By asking the Lord to use his healing powers? Hopefully, by doing all of these and not giving up. Because God is always with us in our love and concern for others.

The Lord is my Shepherd, I shall not want.

Psalm 23: 1

Please read the psalm before going any further.

I n Hebrew it takes a mere fifty-seven words. In the NRSV English translation, the tally is ninety-eight words. Whole books have been written, in dozens of languages, trying to understand the unfathomable riches of these few words. Yet the reality of the twenty-third psalm is not only in its beautifully crafted words, but in the incredible way it influences, and even changes, the lives of ordinary people.

- People who are afraid can be given courage.

- People who are grieving can receive comfort.

- People who are in doubt can be guided into the right direction.

- People who feel worthless can be filled with hope.

- People who are stressed can find peace of mind and spirit.

- People who are angry can learn how to deal with their anger.

- People who feel imprisoned by their life situation can be directed to real freedom.

- People who keep wanting more and more material things can learn to be grateful for present gifts.

- People who are lonely can trust that God is always with them.

- People who lack meaning in their life can begin to understand that they can be co-creators with God.

The reassurance that shines like a beacon through each phrase in this psalm points increasingly to a belief that, regardless of what is happening in our lives, someone walks with us, sharing our burdens with love and care. We will never have to handle the peaks and valleys of life alone. We can look to the daily miracles of God's universe. We can cherish the model and the saving friendship of Jesus. We can tap into the wisdom, power and hope offered to us through the Holy Spirit.

The Lord is my Shepherd

And when we say or do something that in reality denies God's love, we can still move back into his circle of care through the greatest miracle of all - his forgiveness.

Under it every kind of bird will live, in the shade of its branches will nest winged creatures of every kind.

Ezekiel 17: 23b

O ur apartment building is on the top of the Scarborough bluffs in Toronto. From our balcony facing east, we overlook the Guild conservation area, and Lake Ontario is to the south. Because we are on a corner of the building, we have another balcony facing north. Every spring pigeons try to build their nests on the balconies. The weather is not yet warm enough to use the area as an extra summer room, so the balconies are uninhabited.

Twig by twig, pigeons build their nests. Our neighbours shoo them away, but they are very persistent. They keep coming back and they're messy. For some reason they favour some balconies more than others. Our balconies are favoured ones. Most years, we return from Florida in time to get rid of the nests before any eggs have been laid. Not this year.

On our large balcony, there was a nest almost completed, but without any eggs. On our other balcony, there was a completed nest with two pale blue eggs and a pigeon stoutly standing guard. What to do? I didn't want to leave them there until they had hatched and learned to fly. By that time the balcony would be unusable. Some of the neighbours had solved the problem by destroying nests and eggs. I didn't want to do that.

My younger son came to the rescue. He carefully picked up the nest with its eggs, placed it in a small box, took the elevator downstairs, and with a ladder, placed the contents firmly in the branches of a

tree. While he was doing this, the parent pigeons protested, but after a day they seemed content with their new nesting place.

This event reminded me of an experience in my parish ministry. A group within the town were working hard to arrange to build some new homes which would be affordable housing for a number of families. However, the NIMBY (Not In My Back Yard!) syndrome had energized the homeowners in the adjacent properties to exert pressure on the local councilors to deny approval of the project. To counteract this pressure, some of the churches in town banded together, and a fairly sizeable group of us picketed the council chambers, complete with signs. Although it didn't happen right away, the houses are now finished and families have moved in.

Who says a God-led church can't make a difference.

*May the Lord direct your hearts to the love of God and
to the steadfastness of Christ.*

2 Thessalonians 3: 5

There is a legend attributed to the former Canadian aircraft carrier H.M.C.S. Magnificent. I suspect it goes back long before her time.

It was a particularly stormy night off the Nova Scotia coast, and the 'Maggie' was steaming at a good speed towards her home port of Halifax. The howling wind had whipped up giant waves, so the Captain was in command on the bridge. Between the gusts of spray foaming up from her bow, he noticed a strange light rapidly closing on his ship from the port side. He ordered his signalman to flash a message to the unidentified vessel. *"Alter your course ten degrees to starboard."* Within seconds came the reply. *"Alter your course ten degrees to starboard."*

Being the Captain of the largest ship in the Canadian navy, he snapped a second order. *"Alter your course ten degrees - I am the Captain."* Without hesitation, the reply beamed back. *"Alter your course ten degrees - I am Ordinary Seaman Brown."*

By this time the light was growing larger and brighter. The Captain was getting angrier by the second. *"Alter your course - I am an aircraft carrier!"* he quickly signaled. Just as quickly, the reply came back. *"Alter your course - I am a lighthouse."*

All Saints Sunday is one of the days the church sets aside for baptisms. What better time could there be for baptizing children as followers of Jesus Christ? Not that they will become instant saints. But with the help of the Holy Spirit and the committed support of parents, god-

parents, family and the parish fellowship, they will grow in faith and spread God's love in the years ahead. They will follow the right course.

Each day, we seek God's forgiveness for our weakness as followers of the Lord. Our repentance includes a promise to alter our course, to do better. And we try. And even when our efforts fall short, forgiveness is ours.

Baptism Sunday is a special day when we can all renew the promises made at our own baptisms, and covenant with God and each other to become better followers, better saints.

But those who wait for the Lord shall renew their
strength, they shall mount up with wings as eagles,
they shall run and not be weary, they shall walk and
not faint.

Isaiah 40: 31

I hadn't been in my first parish very long before we had a serious discussion at the breakfast table one Saturday morning. Every Sunday we had to drive from New Hamburg to Ayr and back to share worship with my two congregations. The distance was thirty kilometres, over two-lane, paved country roads. They were good roads, but somewhat windy and hilly.

I was always in the driver's seat. Frankly, my mind was full of the worship ahead - the hymns, the prayers, the sermon, the children's story and song. Although there had been no accidents, I was not a safe driver.

Gently but firmly, Audrey suggested that it would be better if I had the thirty minutes each trip to relax and meditate on the worship experience for which I would be the leader. I didn't need to try to match the concentration of driving on a country road to the adrenalin that flowed in my mind and body before worship. She would be the chauffeur on Sundays and relieve me from unnecessary stress. She doesn't have a special cap, but she has been our Sunday chauffeur ever since.

The word "chauffeur" comes from the French, and was originally used to describe the stoker, the person who kept the fire burning so that steam pressure could be built up and maintained. He was the man in charge of producing the heat so that boilers and engines could do their work.

In modern day usage, the chauffeur is someone who drives another person to their destination. A good chauffeur is one who knows the right route to follow to get there.

For Christians, the destination is to have a closer, more loving and obedient relationship with God, through Jesus. If I decide the route to follow, it's usually full of detours, wrong turns, potholes and wayside distractions, all of which take me away from my destination. With God as a real "chauffeur", the life-giving power and guidance of his Holy Spirit will keep me on the right road.

Just as the stoker-chauffeur generates power so that the engine works, so will my "God-chauffeur" enable me to do my work in the world - to spread his love and care to others.

For it is time to seek the Lord, that he may come and rain righteousness upon you.

Hosea 10: 12b

There are 168 hours in a week. On average we spend ...

- 52 hours (31%) in sleeping;
- 40 hours (24%) in working, if not retired;
- 12 hours (7%) in eating;
- 10 hours (6%) in personal hygiene and dressing; and
- 10 hours (6%) in home cleaning and maintenance

We are left with 44 hours (26%) each week of conscious active life to devote to any purpose or activity we choose. Retired people or persons not caring for children, not self-employed or not employed outside the home for wage or profit can probably double that figure.

How much of this time should we give to our relationship with God? If we use the Old Testament concept of a 'tithe', then we should devote 10% of our *total* time; that is, 16.8 hours or 1,008 minutes to God.

If we use a more modern Christian concept of a 'tithe', 10% of *net* time after the essentials, then we would have 10% of what's left after sleeping, working, eating, cleaning and personal hygiene. That's 168 hours minus 124, 10% of which is 4.4 hours or 260 minutes.

Regardless of which method of calculation you use, 90 minutes for Sunday worship and 20 minutes a day for prayer and Bible study only adds up to 230 minutes a week, or 4 hours. So, for the working person, there are still 40 hours or 2400 minutes for recreation and ministry to others in need. Double that time for retirees.

Surely it's not appropriate to say, "I have too little time." If we don't devote enough time and energy to God, it's due to poor planning, wrong priorities, or both.

"Take my yoke upon you and learn from me, for I am gentle and humble of heart."

Matthew 11: 29

I was at Centenary Hospital for some tests, sitting in a small, over-crowded room, waiting for my name to be called. There were legs everywhere - chair legs, table legs, human legs, even some crutches. Plus the usual array of purses and backpacks. Any movement required either stepping around or stepping over. And just about everyone had a card or a piece of paper or an envelope in their hands.

Into this sea of humanity came a white-haired old man, moving very slowly, using a walker. Alone, no one with him. Stress written on his face. He went up to the glass-fronted wicket and said something to the woman behind it. A short conversation ensued, during which you could see confusion and consternation on the old man's countenance. Then I witnessed a miracle of healing!

The woman smiled at him and came out from behind her barrier. She asked some of those in the waiting room to move their legs and belongings. Then she ordered a young man sprawled in a chair to get up, took the man by the hand, and gently led him to the seat. Squatting in front of him, she spoke softly for a few minutes. She left and made a phone call, returning once again to talk with him.

During all her conversations, she was smiling. The more she talked and listened, the more his confusion disappeared and his expression relaxed. Finally, he was smiling, too. Distress was replaced by peace, despair by hope. I couldn't help smiling myself, and when I looked around the crowded room, almost everyone else was smiling.

I believe that this kind of caring happens countless times every day across Canada. I call it a love-experience. But there are thousands more people who should be receiving God's message of love and compassion. That's up to us. If we see them through the eyes of Jesus, their need of the moment will

shine out at us like a beacon. Most of these needs are not for physical healing, but are like the old man and the hospital lady. Our response is to reach out to them in love, offering them peace and comfort in their distress. We don't have to explain it. Just do it. And there's no risk, because Jesus is with us.

All who cleanse themselves of the things I have mentioned will become special utensils, dedicated and useful to the owner of the house, ready for every good work.

2 Timothy 2: 21

During my upbringing in Montreal, I had only been an occasional skier, and always with secondhand equipment. Then at 40, pushed by my younger son, I acquired some good boots, skis and bindings and learned downhill skiing. Two years later, I was quite proficient on intermediate hills, but rarely attacked the steep, big-mogul hills at places like Mont Tremblant in Québec.

At my son's request, I joined him in taking first-aid training and on-hill practicing, and ended up as a newly-qualified Ski Patroller. We selected Devil's Elbow near Peterborough in Ontario as our home base, because it was only an hour's drive from home. It was an exhilarating experience, but physically demanding. We would go up the lifts and down the hills about fifty times in a day.

One day it was cold, windy and snowing. Powder snow - great for skiing. About to go up on a lift, my Patrol Leader called me to help him. A teen-age girl had fallen and injured her leg on the cross-country trail.

We grabbed a rescue toboggan. It was slow going, because our ski equipment was meant for downhill, not cross-country. About two kilometres away, we found her. She was in pain; her ankle had twisted in the binding when she fell. We put her on the toboggan, stabilized her leg and made her warm with a blanket. We tried pulling the toboggan wearing our downhill skis, but it proved almost impossible. So we removed them, strapped them to the side of the toboggan and walked back, pulling her with our legs sinking into the soft snow up to the knees at every step. The unexpected had

happened, and we were ill-prepared. The following week there were two pairs of snowshoes in our patrol shack.

Time and time again, Jesus was faced with the unexpected. Ten lepers, a man lowered down from a roof, Lazarus already dead in a tomb, and many more. He responded with care because he was prepared. He knew that God had given him the wisdom, power and courage to meet every situation. Trust, built through prayer. We can have that same trust and be prepared for whatever life places before us.

"You will receive power when the Holy Spirit has come upon you, and you will be my witnesses in Jerusalem, in all Judea and to the ends of the earth."

Acts 1: 8

Every Sunday morning, we have children's time to help the younger members of the congregation feel that they belong to the parish family. The best time for this to happen in an Anglican (Episcopal) church is for them to come in from their own program during the Peace; following that they have their own special few minutes. Then they stay with their parents for the Eucharist.

I have enjoyed this part of our liturgy with as few as three children and as many as thirty. It has been a process of learning what to say and how to say it. The 'what to say' has two simple rules; keep it short and have a simple message. The 'how to say it' has no rules; you either like to be with children or you don't. If you don't, you need to find somebody in the congregation who can communicate with the children.

Children like to sing, so a song that fits the story theme is a real plus. God has blessed me as a banjo player and children's songwriter. I have written over a hundred songs that can be used for a variety of special days and life values. Here's one example:

I show the children a sketch of what Jesus might look like. With a little coaxing, they can see that in the picture Jesus has no eyes, ears, mouth, hands or feet. Since Jesus is no longer physically with us, he relies on us to do his work in the world. He is with us in spirit, so we can be his eyes, ears, mouth, hands and feet.

This is the song that goes with the theme.

Refrain:

I can be Jesus wherever I go,

Whatever I do, whatever I say.

I can be Jesus each day of my life.

That's what he wants me to be.

Verse 1:

I can be Jesus' hands **

I can be Jesus' feet **

Be his eyes, be his ears,

Be his mouth to speak **

Verse 2:

Reach out to those in need **

Care for them every day **

Give myself, don't hold back.

That's how I'll follow his way **

Each * means one clap. Doing this in unison makes the children giggle!
The children love it and remember the message. So do the adults.

"But those who drink of the water that I will give them will never be thirsty. The water that I will give will become in them a spring of water gushing up to eternal life."

John 4: 14

There are many ways to travel on water. Leaving out large ships, we ordinary folk skim the waves on a variety of vessels. If you like noisy speed, you can bounce around on a sea-doo. If you prefer more power, you can skim in a powerboat with twin 75HP outboards. You can get a bigger thrill by being towed behind that powerboat on water skis - using two boards or a slalom single.

Using the wind to provide power on the blue is an ancient form of water travel. If you're young and healthy, wind-surfing adds thrills to this time-proven system, but that doesn't really work for a senior with back trouble and wobbly knees. Regular sailing on a boat is much more peaceful. I learned to sail at Scout camp, in a gaff-rigged, mainsail only, 14' dinghy with a drop centerboard. I've since knifed through the waters with friends on boats from 16' to 35'.

Then there's muscle power. Rowing a whaler or cutter with a team of Navy matelots or providing arms and hands to propel a rowboat across a northern lake are two extremes. They can both move the boat forward, backward or in circles.

But my favourite form of water locomotion is the CANOE. Not the kayaks used in white-water sport, which scare me just watching them. But in early morning or evening, in a vessel invented by our aboriginal brothers and sisters, when your forward motion breaks the calm surface of a mirrored lake.

Somehow, in that tranquil setting, aches and pains generated by the exertion of arms, shoulders and back don't seem to matter. All the dried-up spaces in my persona begin to be replenished by the love which end-lessly flows from our Creator. Busyness and

hurriedness disappear. My mind, usually clogged with things to do, has a simpler and yet more powerful focus - on God's care and purpose for my life.

Life back in the city can be like that peaceful canoe ride, if we give God a chance to make it so.

Trust in the Lord with all your heart, and do not rely on your own insight.

Proverbs 3: 5

The weather forecast was 'sunny with cloudy periods and a 30% chance of rain'. So, in putting together a family barbecue, we had to have a Plan B. What would we do if it rained? But would our mindset have been different if the forecast had read 'sunny with cloudy periods and a 70% chance that there will be no rain'?

The tendency to focus on the negative rather than the positive is often present in a Christian fellowship. We hear:

- *We tried a stewardship campaign a few years ago. It didn't change our envelope giving and it antagonized some of our best people.*

- *A part-time youth minister doesn't work. We've had three different ones in the past four years.*

- *Outreach is important, but we have to take care of our own needs and commitments first.*

With Jesus, there is no 30% chance, not even a 70% probability. With Jesus, through the power and wisdom of the Holy Spirit, there is always a 100% guarantee. If we really listen to the Lord and trust him, there is never a need for a Plan B. Here are a few examples:

- A small country church, with fewer than a dozen worshippers in the winter, is booming in the summer with cottagers and a thriving children's program.

- A worship space was shut down as unsafe. With proper planning and committed faith, reconstruction was completed and the six-figure debt paid off in less than five years.

- Two churches in a small town defied the demise of Vacation Bible Schools and ran a very successful program. It's still going, but now there are four participating churches.

- Over two tons of non-perishable food was brought in, sorted and delivered to the local food bank on Harvest Sunday.

- Over 10% of a parish's annual budget is allocated to community outreach.

There are countless examples that could be given. Every week, in our diocese, a church community trusts the Lord and undertakes a project, when other people say, "It can't be done!" And with the Holy Spirit's guidance – it is accomplished successfully.

**As God's chosen ones, holy and beloved, clothe your-
selves with compassion, kindness, humility, meekness
and patience.**

Colossians 3: 12

In a big city like Toronto, it's often quicker, cheaper and more efficient to
take public transportation, rather than to use your own car. So that's what
I sometimes do - join the million plus who daily board the TTC bus or the
GO train to reach their destination. I've seen many cases of bad manners
and careless behaviour. But I've also seen equal numbers of caring attitudes
and helpful actions.

The other day I was sitting in the middle of a bus travelling to the
subway station. It stopped to pick up some passengers. A group of
noisy young people, one carrying a boom box playing loud heavy
metal music, barged on and congregated at the rear of the bus.

Waiting to get on was a young mother. A small boy about four years
old was holding on to her left hand. Her right hand was on the upper
crossbar of a heavily-laden stroller, in which was seated a little girl, who
looked to be about two years old. The challenge for the mother was not
only to get her small son up the two steps into the bus, but somehow
to get the stroller up those same steps. Then to open her purse and pay
her fare. Not impossible, because she had probably done it many times
before, but certainly stressful.

Before I could move to assist, a teen-age girl two seats in front of me
jumped up and rushed to help. She took the little boy's hand and guided
him up the steps. Then she stepped off the bus, took the front end of
the stroller and helped the mother lift it up into the bus. With a smile,
she held the boy's hand until his mother paid her fare. Everyone then
sat down on her seat again. Spontaneously,
most of the people on the bus clapped.

Many hundreds of books have been written
and thousands of sermons preached about
Jesus' commandment to 'love your neighbour as yourself'. This girl brought the

commandment to life. For that moment, because of her caring action, the world was brighter for one human being.

Each day of our lives we are given opportunities to do the same thing - to make the world brighter for one human being.

"I will lead the blind by a road they do not know, by paths they have not known I will guide them. I will turn the darkness before them into light, the rough places into level ground. These are the things I will do, and I will not forsake them."

Isaiah 42: 16

As we were going through the marriage preparation program, I was continually struck by the life differences between the young couple I would soon marry. Ed was an apprentice tool-and-die maker in a local factory, very skillful with his hands. He rode a motorcycle, and it was his pride and joy. He was always tuning it up and polishing it until it sparkled. I found him easy to talk to, outgoing and intelligent, but not academically inclined. His solutions to the questions raised during our sessions were short and to the point.

His bride-to-be, Sharon, was the opposite. Her innate shyness made it difficult for her to express her feelings and opinions. She was always immaculately groomed and dressed, in contrast to Ed's perennial jeans and t-shirts. She loved music, and had been a loyal member of our church choir since her high-school days. Ed had no church background whatsoever.

Sharon was diabetic, and had been since early childhood. After their marriage, even though she knew there could be serious complications, she wanted to give Ed a child. Much of her pregnancy was spent in and out of the hospital, but her courage was undaunted. She gave birth to a little girl by Caesarian section. Ed's beautiful daughter was strong and healthy. Sharon was now completely blind, and would be so for the rest of her life.

Ed's love for Sharon and his inner strength of character shone through immediately. He spent countless hours renovating their home to ensure that Sharon could be a mother and wife with as little difficulty as possible. His unfailing support was matched by her dogged determination not to let her disability stand in the way of building a caring and loving family.

A year after their wedding, it was an honour for me to baptize their golden-haired daughter before a full church, a beaming Ed and a smiling Sharon with her seeing-eye dog. At her request, we sang the short praise song, 'God is so Good'.

The Lord is exalted, he dwells on high; he filled Zion
with justice and righteousness;

Isaiah 33: 5

I had often asked myself, "Which comes first, wisdom or knowledge?" Then Marian, a woman in her fifties whose husband had just died, helped me learn. Her mate of thirty years had been a good provider and a faithful and caring man. Unfortunately, in retrospect, he had been too caring.

When I visited her at home a few days after the funeral, Marian looked like a lost soul. As we chatted, she kept turning over a set of keys in her hand. I finally asked her what the keys were. She said, "These were Bill's keys. One is for the house, one is for the car, one is for his desk in the den and the last one is for the safety deposit box in the bank." With tears in her eyes, she added, "and I really don't know what to do with any of them. I'm completely lost without Bill."

They had no children, and Bill died without a will. Marian couldn't drive. She knew nothing about their financial affairs, nor anything about the maintenance and upkeep of their home - insurance, taxes, service people, etc. She had no idea what was in his desk or in the safety deposit box. No wonder she was in stunned despair! After we prayed together for God's help, I left to take care of some promises I had made to her.

I asked a woman lawyer whom I trusted to call her, which she did. One of Marian's friends who had a solid head on her shoulders agreed to spend a considerable amount of time helping her sort out her affairs. And a member of the prayer group invited her to come to their meetings.

Marian continued to worship in church every Sunday and I visited her from time to time. On one of my visits about six months after Bill's death, she looked quite wonderful. We prayed together, and then she said, "I know you asked some folks to help me through what seemed to me to be the end of the world. And it did

help. But what really helped was that I started talking to God and listening to him. I realized that, although I knew I had to start living independently, I was never alone. God was always with me. He continually kept showing me that I had a lot of life to live and a lot to give to others."

You have known the sacred writings that are able to instruct you for salvation through faith in Christ Jesus.

2 Timothy 3: 15

I asked the eighteen participants in the parish Bible study group to write down their favourite passage from scripture, and not to consult their Bible in doing so. Without hesitation, they all did. Then I asked them to note the specific book, chapter and verse. Fewer than half of them could. Finally, I asked them to compare what they had written with the words in their Bibles, using my Concordance to help locate the passages. In every case, there was very little difference.

Each person was asked to tell the group why the passage was their favourite. Here are a few of the ones I remember:

- **There is joy in the presence of the angels of God over one sinner who repents.** *Luke 15: 10 ...* chosen by an older man who was a recovered alcoholic.

- **Go therefore and make disciples of all the nations, baptizing them in the name of the Father, the Son and the Holy Spirit.** *Matthew 28: 19 ...* the favourite passage of the Chair of the Evangelism Committee.

- **While I live, I will praise the Lord, I will sing praises to my God while I have my being.** *Psalm 146: 2 ...* selected by our church organist.

- **Be still, and know that I am God.** *Psalm 46: 10 ...* words that gently touch the busiest woman in our parish.

- **He has sent me to bring good news to the oppressed, to bind up the brokenhearted, to proclaim liberty to the captives, and release to the prisoners.** *Isaiah 61: 1* ... the logical choice of the Chair of our Parish Outreach Committee.

- **Do not let your heart be troubled. Believe in God, believe also in me.**

John 14: 1 … the choice of a single mother with two school-aged children.

- **There shall be showers of blessing.** *Ezekiel 34: 26* … the special message for a retired schoolteacher.

God not only works, but he speaks to us in mysterious ways - ways that meet our need.

This is the message we have heard from him and proclaim to you, that God is light and in him there is no darkness at all.

1 John 1: 5

P eggy's Cove, Nova Scotia, has a lighthouse, a lighthouse that has a long history of guiding sailors away from its rocky shores and into a safe harbour. It also has an incredible series of sculptures carved in rock by the well-known Maritime artist, William de Garthe. Thousands of people flock to this Canadian landmark every year to have their picture taken with the lighthouse in the background.

A while back I read a story about another lighthouse; a different kind of 'lighthouse', connected to All Saints Episcopal Church in Bakersfield, California. As the result of a challenge from a visiting evangelical preacher, they believed that God was calling them to be a 'lighthouse' to the people in their community.

Their vision was a beacon which would warn of the dangers of the rocky shores of life and draw people into the safe harbour of fellowship with Jesus. Their ministry was to be the power which made the beacon shine.

Outreach was the first thrust of this ministry. They offered the use of their facilities to community groups free of charge. 10% of their annual budget was allocated to outreach projects, many of which were simply financial support of community programs. When they needed to build a new church, 10% of the money raised was given to a Community Fund which helped build or renovate community social/recreational/ educational facilities. Particular emphasis was focused on disadvantaged individuals.

As their numbers grew, more and more of their money and energy was committed to family, children's and youth activities. At the same time, they didn't neglect Bible Study, spiritual growth and faith formation programs.

Every church or Christian fellowship is located in a community which needs a 'lighthouse ministry', a beacon of Jesus' love. How is yours doing?

The fruit of the Spirit is love, joy, peace, patience,
kindness, generosity, faithfulness, goodness
and self-control.

Galatians 5: 22

It was a Summer Holiday Day Camp program with three churches participating. A solid week of fun, games, songs, Christian value stories and handicrafts. The overriding theme for the week was human behaviour, based on Galatians 5: 22. Each day the focus was on two of the Fruits of the Spirit, with the final one, self-control, on the last day.

For each of the Fruits of the Spirit, the children were helped to suggest what the opposite behaviour was from their own experience. The results were indicative of how children think:

the 'opposite' of generous was mean

the 'opposite' of kindness was nasty

the 'opposite' of faithful was jealous

the 'opposite' of love was hate

the 'opposite' of joy was sad

the 'opposite' of gentle was angry

the 'opposite' of peace was fight

the 'opposite' of goodness was bad

the 'opposite' of patience was now

We then asked them to give examples of the 'Fruits of the Spirit" - I only remember three:

'gentle' - stroking your cat as she purrs

'generous' - sharing your chocolate
bar with your best friend

'joy' - taking home a good report
card from school

We selected two handicrafts. One was a mobile, using symbols of each of the nine Fruits of the Spirit, making two each day and doing the final assembly on Friday. The other was to make a placemat encompassing the nine symbols and the tongues of flame denoting the Holy Spirit.

The leaders challenged me to write a song that fit the way we had organized the week. By Friday the ninety children had sung two new verses and the chorus each day, finishing off at our final campfire by singing the song for their parents and neighbours.

Here is the song. For purists, the sequence follows the program, not the Bible.

THE FRUITS OF THE SPIRIT IN ME

Refrain:

The fruits of the Spirit in me,

The fruits of the Spirit in me,

O Lord, let me live

Both in words and in deed

With the fruits of the Spirit in me.

Acting with **KINDNESS** in all that we do,

Making the Spirit our guide.

Helping each other, no matter the cost,

And trusting that God will provide.

FAITHFULNESS means we must learn to obey,

Listen and follow God's will.

Then we are free to be truly alive,

With power and grace we are filled.

GOODNESS means more than just not being bad.

Let's give our help all the time.

Pass on the love of the Lord in our hearts,

And that's how our goodness will shine.

PATIENCE is hard when our life's in a mess,

Failure is all that we know.

Turn to the Spirit, make use of His power,

In service to others we grow.

Treat other people with **GENTLE** respect.

Life can be fragile and worn.

Each one is precious, a gift from the Lord.

Let's give them our tender concern.

Often we follow our selfish
desires,

Hurting our friends when
we do.

Call on the Spirit and gain

SELF-CONTROL,

And freedom to really be you.

JOY is much more than just
laughter and fun;

It gives us warmth deep inside.

When we trust God and his
wise loving care

We know that he walks by
our side.

There is a longing, a need to be
still,

Conquer our anger and fear.

If we will rest in the Spirit,
there's **PEACE,**

And worries will all disappear.

As a foundation for everything else,

LOVE is the greatest of all.

Giving ourselves with no
thought of return,

We follow the Lord and
his call.

PHONETIC MELODY

Refrain:

S, M M M M R D R

S, F F F F M R M

M S S S S

F M F F F F

M R M M M R D T D

Verse:

M F S S M D R D R M

F L F M S M R

S D' T L S F M F S D

T, L, F M R D T D

You shall eat your fill and bless the Lord your God for the good land that he has given you.

Deuteronomy 8: 10

C anada is a land of plenty - 'plenty' meaning that we have sufficient resources of every kind to maintain a comfortable quality of life for every person. Yet in most towns and cities in this wonderful country there is a FOOD BANK. In the larger cities there are many of them, well used.

Each month hundreds of thousands of men, women and children make use of them. Countless millions of dollars of non-perishable food (and sometimes perishable food too} ends up on the tables of needy individuals and families. This miracle happens through a distribution system of voluntary donations and volunteer workers.

Almost all Food Banks were started by local community churches, and the majority of donations and workers still come from some church connection.

Many times our governments at all levels have promised to end poverty. But it's still here and growing, because we don't acknowledge a crisis as long as we have Food Banks.

What would happen if every Food Bank pledged to close down on a particular date - say seven years from now? We have proved in the past that we can mobilize to accomplish impossible results at a time of national emergency, for example, the Second World War.

If every church, temple, synagogue and mosque relentlessly prodded our governments, it could be done – poverty in a country of plenty would be on the way to disappearing.

Like good stewards of the manifold grace of God,
serve one another with whatever gift each one of you
has received.

1 Peter 4: 10

I was walking on the beach at Siesta Key in Sarasota, Florida. A young boy suddenly yelled and ran with something in his hand to his parents. It was a quarter (25 cents). Such excitement!

About a mile further along the beach, I saw a man with some sort of instrument attached to a long handle. It was magnetic and he was using it to identify metal objects in the sand. When I asked how he was doing today, he said "nothing". But over the years he had hauled in hundreds of coins, rings and other jewellery, plus an assortment of nails and sundry metal objects.

I couldn't help reflecting that the life of a Christian is like searching for objects in the sand. We pledge ourselves to serve God in the world. But much of the world doesn't want to be served. I define 'serving' as helping someone in need or telling people what Jesus means to you.

Some of us respond like the little boy – serving is not part of our every-day life, although it might occur by happenstance. Others are like the man with the magnetic instrument; we try and serve by 'helping' and 'telling'. But there are days when neither happens. There are days when our efforts bring no results. There are days when our efforts are refused.

There are also days when our reaching out makes life a little better for a needy neighbour, or brings someone into God's circle of love through getting to know Jesus. Overall, if we are really committed to serving God in the world, we will be suc-  cessful in drawing people 'out of the sand', because God is a powerful magnet which never stops working.

Then they sent to Jesus some Pharisees and some Herodians, to trap him in what he said.

Mark 12: 13

Jesus has been challenging the religious establishment. They counter-attack by framing questions that will trap him with his own words. They do it in public, to disgrace him before the people.

Palestine is occupied by the Romans, so they ask him, "Is it or is it not lawful to pay tribute to Rome?" They understand that coinage is a mark of power. The greater the areas in which a coin is in use, the greater the power of the person whose name or face is stamped on it. The coin is his personal property.

The Romans imposed three taxes on Palestine; a 'ground' tax of 10% of the grain and 20% of the wine or fruit; an 'income' tax of 1%; a 'poll' tax of one denarius for every male 14 to 65 and every woman 12 to 65 - this was the most hated and was called 'tribute'.

The Pharisees believed that the question placed Jesus in an inescapable dilemma. If he said "no", the Romans would arrest him. If he said "yes" he would be called a coward by the people. His answer was to pay the coin to the Roman Emperor whose face is on the denarius, recognizing their occupational power, but nothing more.

Christians have always had a dual responsibility. We have an obligation to be good citizens of the country in which we live. But we are also members of God's Kingdom. Sometimes these obligations clash, because God's way opposes the country's way. The only choice for the Christian is to work patiently to bring about God's way.

For the past 2000 years most of the positive changes in human existence have been the result of Christians following the teachings of Jesus. It starts with one or two speaking out, then developing into an unstoppable movement over time. God's Kingdom is present, but not fully achieved. It's our job, with the help of the Holy Spirit, whenever possible, to make it happen.

Those who live according to the flesh set their minds on the things of the flesh, but those who live according to the spirit set their minds on the things of the spirit.

Romans 8: 5

King Benjamin lived a very godly and abundant life, full of love, joy and peace. He was able to do this because he had a magic ring, which he said gave him the Fruits of God's Spirit, as described in the Bible in Galatians 5:22. He had three sons, and promised each son privately that he would inherit the ring at his death. He then went to his jeweller and had two rings made, identical to the original.

When King Benjamin died, each son inherited a ring. All three believed that his ring was the original. They asked the courts to decide, and the judges ruled "… that none of the rings could be proved to be 'magic'. However, we will know who possesses the magic ring when we see in the future the life each son lives."

We possess a 'magic ring' called the Holy Spirit. Each one of us formally received the Holy Spirit at our baptism into the church, which is the body of faithful who follow Jesus as Lord and Saviour. This Holy Spirit, working with our own spirit, gives us the wisdom, the courage and the power to live the way that God created us to live.

We do not limit the Holy Spirit, who can be given by God at any time, but at every baptism the whole congregation promises God that we will support the new Christian in the journey he or she is about to share with us.

We will see the results of the 'Fruits of the Spirit' in our lives each day, as we follow our Saviour, one day at a time. We can see them now, in the lives lived by countless faithful Christians:

LOVE – JOY - PEACE – GENTLENESS – KINDNESS–FAITHFULNESS–GOODNESS – PATIENCE – SELF-CONTROL.

Then I heard the voice of the Lord saying, "Whom shall I send and who will go for us?" And I said, "Here am I; send me."

Isaiah 6: 8

I n 1983 I was the Marketing Vice-President of a fraternal insurance society, with a five year contract to clean house and rebuild the sales organization. Three years later the Board of Directors decided to stop selling insurance - meaning I was out of a job. Headhunters were looking, but nothing interesting had surfaced.

To keep in shape, I did a 10K bicycle ride four times a week. One day while taking a rest and reflecting on my situation, God told me to be patient. Something was going to happen. A few days later, while I was having a glass of wine with my parish priest, he said to me, "Morse wants to see you." Morse was Bishop Morse Robinson, a long-time friend, with whom I had served as a layman on the National Program Committee of the church for ten years. I had lunch with him and my life was changed.

He told me that it was about time I paid attention to what God wanted me to do – to take the necessary studies and be ordained as a priest. After much prayer and protesting, and the support of my wonderful life partner Audrey, I said 'yes' to God, and had eight exciting years as a parish priest. During that time I was able to earn a Master of Theological Studies degree at Wilfred Laurier University. There were very few days when I felt that God wasn't supporting me in my ministry. The Holy Spirit was at work, using Morse and many of my parishioners to support and guide me.

There's a postscript to this story. When I retired to Toronto, my contacts with Morse were Christmas cards. Sixteen years later, while serving as a snowbird assistant priest at St. Wilfred's Episcopal Church in Sarasota, Florida, I accepted an invitation to preach at St. Mary's Church, north of Tampa.

At the conclusion of the service, one of the worshippers shook my hand with a smile on his face. It was Bishop Morse Robinson, who was visiting family for two weeks, and had never worshipped at St. Mary's before. He said, "I see God hasn't finished with you yet." And he hasn't!

Then he said to his disciples, "The harvest is plentiful,
but the labourers are few; therefore, ask the Lord of the
harvest to send out labourers into his harvest."

Matthew 9:37,38

There were twelve of them, ordinary men with no special qualifications by ordinary reckoning, who became apostles of Jesus. With the loss of Judas Iscariot, who betrayed him and was replaced by Matthias, and later Paul, they changed the world.

One of them was Simon, called Peter. He was a fisherman, plying his trade on Lake Galilee, energetic, knowledgeable, successful. Also very impetuous, argumentative and prone to becoming excitable.

Another apostle, Judas Thaddeus Labbeus, called Jude, was the opposite of Peter. He was quiet and unassuming, known as the steady one: faithful, loyal, and ready to endure the taunts of the Pharisees, not giving up when things got tough. Two men, as different as black and white. Compare them:

Jude – dependable	Peter – impetuous
Jude – laid back	Peter – excitable
Jude – patient	Peter – volatile
Jude – steadfast	Peter – hot blooded

In both Jesus saw something special which he needed for his team. A special gift they didn't even recognize.

Each one of us has a 'special gift', often one we don't realize or fail to acknowledge. Whatever it is or wherever we are situated in life, it is given to us by the Lord to serve the world in His name. That makes us disciples and apostles, like Jude and Peter.

When Jesus turned and saw them following, he said
to them "What are you looking for?" They replied,
"Rabbi, where are you staying?" He said to them,
"Come and see."

John 1: 38,39

I was sitting on the lanai in our Florida home, reading a book. My wife Audrey came in and said, "The tap in the kitchen is leaking." I replied, "I fixed it last weekend." "Well, it's leaking now" she answered. "Are you sure you turned it off tightly?" I asked. "Yes! And I used both hands" came the patient retort. Disregarding my skeptical look, my bride of many years said very gently, but positively, "Come and see." I did. And she was right. There was more than a little drip … we needed a new washer.

Jesus was on a drive to recruit new members for his team. In a conversation with two prospects, he asked a question. "What are you looking for?" When they seemed interested, he said, "Come and see".

A question and an invitation. The same principle I followed in business when I was recruiting individuals for sales. First, a question focusing on his or her hopes for a life career; second, an invitation to explore the opportunity I was offering.

Publicity and advertising can make a church visible in a community. Studies show, however, that most new worshippers are recruited by someone they know – a friend or family member - someone who recognizes their need for something or someone different in their life. The

question is asked by someone for whom Jesus has already made a difference in his or her life; someone who will, in friendship, extend the invitation to "Come and see. Let me introduce you to Jesus."

A question, followed by an invitation - coming from the Lord - through you.

Finally, be strong in the Lord and in the strength of his power. Put on the whole armour of God, so that you may be able to stand against the wiles of the devil.

Ephesians 6: 10,11

In his letter to the church at Ephesus, St. Paul exhorts his fellow Christians to struggle against the spiritual forces of evil, the wicked forces of the world which corrupt us, using the imagery of 'armour'.

When we think of armour we picture something physical or material. Paul's perception is different. Look at his list: the belt of Truth, the breastplate of Righteousness, the shoes of Peace, the shield of Faith, the helmet of Salvation, and the Sword of the Spirit. None of them can be experienced by any of the five senses.

To be human, to be a person, to know my real identity, I must move beyond the physical to the spiritual. To be the real me, God must be part of my life. If he isn't, I can exist as a physical being, but not as a real person.

The Holy Spirit gives me a connection to my creator, a connection I can make through knowing Jesus. The more that relationship blossoms, the more I can be the person God created me to be. I can ignore the connection, deny it, leave Jesus out of my life, but the God-connection is still there. God will never break it.

Nourishment for my physical body is necessary. It's basic to my survival. But the living bread which God offers me through Jesus is the nourishment I need to live an abundant life. It's not a one-day bread, but a lifetime meal. If it gets stale and moldy, it's because I let my day go by without eating. Just as I need physical nourishment, I need spiritual nourishment.

Through a daily relationship with Jesus, God involves himself totally in my life. That's when I'm wearing 'The whole Armour of God', one day at a time.

When the day of Pentecost came, they were all together in one place. All of them were filled with the Holy Spirit and began to speak in other languages, as the Spirit gave them ability.

Acts 2: 1,4

In 1940 I was fifteen years old and in High School in Montreal. In addition to school, sports and scouts, I belonged to a musical group called 'The Four Flats'; Jim on drums, Paul on guitar, Wally on flute and clarinet, and I played ukulele and harmonica. Mostly we played for our own enjoyment, but occasionally we were asked to play at church concerts or the YMCA. For free – we were not good enough to charge a fee!

Our crowning achievement was on the program at the Snowden Theatre for a Red Cross drive. Through practice we learned that, with our unorthodox assortment of instruments, it was essential that we listened to and supported each other. If we weren't together, we really were 'The Four Flats'.

Jesus was a great teacher, preacher and healer. He was also a great leader, who recruited and trained twelve disciples. Together they did all the practical chores necessary for making their travelling ministry possible. After his death and resurrection, his team, with Matthias replacing Judas, carried on his work. 2000 years later there are over three billion Christians in the world.

In every church or fellowship there will be leaders. But the really successful ones are where there is a committed team of members, dedicated to building up God's Kingdom.

At the conclusion of every service of Holy Communion, Canadian  Anglicans say the following Doxology "Glory to God, whose power, *working in us*, can do infinitely more than we can ask or imagine, in the church and in Christ Jesus!" The power of The Holy Spirit and a team of believers working together – WOW!

"This is the bread that comes down from heaven, not like that which your ancestors ate, and they died. But the one who eats this bread will live forever."

John 6: 58

Children's birthday parties are always exciting and noisy affairs. Most of the participants are school friends or neighbors' kids, with perhaps a sprinkling of brothers, sisters, cousins. Adult birthday parties are different. They are either family affairs, or recognition by a group of friends or interest-related members.

Activities at both these parties vary, but there is usually one common denominator, a birthday cake. Sometimes they are made in-house by Mother or a baking friend. More and more they are bought from a bakery. The best ones are mouth-watering creations with lots of sugary icing – and I love icing.

If you view your slice of cake as just a combination of flour, sugar, butter, eggs, baking powder and whipped cream, it's not a birthday cake. It's just something to eat. It becomes a birthday cake when it points beyond its ingredients to a celebration of warmth and affection within a group of people. The reality of the experience is the celebration, not the cake.

All of life is like that. Reality is much more than what we can see, touch, hear, taste and smell. However important physical or material things may be, I can't make sense of the world, and my presence in it, by those qualifications alone. Likewise knowledge, reason, imagination, words, actions, feelings may result in worldly existence, but not real life as our Creator intended.

Regardless of our religious or atheistic beliefs, each of us is born with a spirit. And the development of that spirit will determine the kind of life we experience. From the beginning, the Spirit of God tries to meld with our own personal spirit so that life may be the way God created it. The influence of that melding, the spiritual dimension, decides who we are. That's reality.

"You are the salt of the earth, but if the salt has lost its taste, how can its saltiness be restored?"

Matthew 5: 13

For over forty years our family has had a wonderful doctor. She's busy, as all General Practitioners are. But when you are in that little room, she takes skill and knowledge, wraps it around with wisdom, understanding and warmth, and tells you what to do. Every so often she warns us against having too much sodium in our food intake.

In Jesus' time salt was highly valued, because of three special qualities – purity, preservation and flavour. PURITY with its glistening whiteness, from the power of the sun and the vitality of the sea. PRESERVATION, because without refrigeration, it was the only thing which kept food from going bad. FLAVOUR, as it turned otherwise bland dishes into a pleasurable food experience.

When Jesus told his disciples they were the salt of the earth, they understood his teaching. The value of salt is measured by what it does. So the value of a disciple is measured by his or her words and actions in proclaiming God's Kingdom to the world.

Faith in Jesus is to life as salt is to food.

Purity in salt is revealed by its whiteness, without any form of blemish. In Galatians 5:22 St. Paul gives us a pretty good idea of purity in human salt.

Salt is never complete unless it mingles and influences other ingredients - faith is a gift to be shared and a gift to be proclaimed - that's preservation.

The disciple radiates sparkle and vitality, joyful living in the world - that's flavour.

Purity, Preservation, Flavour, the marks of a true disciple.

"Comfort, O comfort my people," says your God.
"Speak tenderly to Jerusalem, and cry to her that she
has served her term."

Isaiah 40: 1,2

Many centuries ago the Jewish nation had been destroyed because their leaders had played power politics and lost. All but the poorest had been sent as prisoners to Babylon, 1500 kilometres away. For three generations they were exiled in a place most of them despised. They longed to go home, languished in despair. Tomorrow would be as dismal and hopeless as today.

Then Isaiah, a messenger from God, brought light and hope to their darkness. To a people full of gloom and doom, he made a bold declaration, a promise from God of a better tomorrow. A few years later, no longer in captivity, they were back in their homeland. Through God's intervention, hope had become reality.

Psychologists today tell us that once our primary drive to survive is satisfied, we have four basic human needs (in order of importance).

- we need to know we belong - to someone or somewhere

- we need to have a sense of personal worth or value

- we need to have security, an anchor to tether our lives

- we need to have a purpose or cause, a meaning for existence

The Jews in Babylon lacked all of these, until God acted.

You and I know people like that – tomorrow will be as hopeless as today. They need God to intervene and God expects us to be his Isaiah for them, the bringer of Good News.

It's not that easy, because the world around them is like the world of the Babylonian Jews – no hope, everything stacked against them. The answer is to pray for them and for yourself, that God will show you the way to offer caring and helpful assistance.

And the one who was seated on the throne said,
"Behold I am making all things new."

Revelation 21: 5

I was in a mall to buy a new watch strap. All the stores had their Boxing Week Specials, with the word 'free' in their displays, like 'Buy One - Get One Free'. From my thirty years in the marketing business, I know the incredible influence words play in the sale of a product or service. The words 'sale' or 'free' usually bring results in the short term.

But the most powerful word for long-term benefit is NEW. It inspires the seller and is like a magnet pulling buying interest from prospective customers. Often 'new' means a change in size, or quantity, or packaging, or an update to an existing product - not anything really new. But with creative use of words and graphics, an advertiser can make something ordinary into something we must have.

Each Boxing week many of us reflect on our life situations, after which we make promises or resolutions for positive changes in our lives. In doing this, we can easily seduce ourselves into a newness that is only a matter of packaging, or quantity, or image to others, or a minor tweak to our lifestyle. There is no improvement in substance, no betterment in the person God created us to be. Nothing really different, just a rehash of our old selves.

Experience has taught me that my resolutions for change will be a fantasy if I plan to keep them only through my own efforts. A New Year is a book with my name on it and 365 blank pages. Each day will decide whether I have followed God or my own needs and desires. Each day will be a change in the package I present to others or in the

person God created me to be. Once a day is over, the page for that day is finished. I can't go back and change it.

So my best promises for each New Year must be simple – to try to make God's way, my way – ONE DAY AT A TIME.

Then our mouth was filled with laughter and our tongue with shouts of joy.

Psalm 126: 2

A friend recently told me that she enjoyed "A Word from Father Roy" in the parish bulletin each Sunday and she gave a copy to a neighbour who was homebound. "However," she added, (I hate howevers!) "it would be nice to have some humour once in a while." (A disclaimer – no one laughs when I tell a joke!) So to defeat her 'however', here are two jokes I came across the other day.

Adam had taken to staying out late at night. Eve was suspicious and upset. "You've been running around with another woman" she charged "How can that be?" Adam responded. "You're the only woman on earth." Later that evening, Adam fell asleep, only to be awakened by Eve poking him in the ribs. "What do you think you're doing?" he asked. "Counting your ribs," she replied.

The rule in the monastery was strict silence. But every five years a monk was allowed to say a very few words to the abbot. After his first five years of silence, Brother James said to the abbot "Food cold." Five years later he said "Bed hard." At his fifteenth year he told the abbot "I quit." "I'm not surprised." replied the abbot. "All you've done is complain since you got here."

If they didn't make you smile - remember – I said I couldn't tell jokes.

As Jesus entered a village, ten lepers approached him.
Keeping their distance, they called out, saying, "Jesus,
master, have mercy on us." When he saw them, he said
to them, "Go and show yourselves to the priests." And
as they went, they were made clean.

Luke 17: 12 to 14

Many years ago I participated in a research study, documenting how communities responded to a major disaster. As a budding sociologist, I did on-the-spot coverage of two huge fires and two major floods. In every event, during the crisis period, people of all social and economic status, faith, cultural group and colour worked together. The mayor and the janitor, the CEO and the young mail clerk, side by side, not only fighting the cause of the disaster, but reaching out to help its victims. But when the immediate danger was over, the normal power systems, centres of influence, community structures and prejudices began to take over.

In one Gospel story there was a group of ten lepers – nine Jews and one Samaritan; an unusual combination, because for over five centuries the Jews had hated the Samaritans. But as lepers they shared the same pain and isolation, so it was natural for them to support each other.

Then Jesus healed them. The unity of common despair disappeared. The age-old prejudices took over, the Jews rushing to have their priest declare them no longer unclean, leaving the Samaritan to fend for

himself. He was the only one to say thank you to Jesus. The Jews were physically healed, but the Samaritan was made whole - healed in body, mind, spirit and soul.

How often do we let our prejudices, usually the result of our upbringing, blind us to the many gifts that other people and groups can bring to the betterment of our common life? In a crisis, we may stand together, but when it's over, we return to the status quo.

It could be different. We could say thanks to God for the calm after the storm, and then continue to stand together, foregoing our preconceived biases.

"But you are a chosen race, a royal priesthood, a holy nation, God's own people."

1 Peter 2: 9

A few years ago I attended a seminar on congregational develop-ment. The leader placed a sheet of white Bristol board on an easel. Then he used a marker pen to put three red dots in the centre, in the form of a triangle. He asked us what we saw. Some said a triangle-some said three red dots - two said The Holy Trinity. Not one of us said a white Bristol board.

He continued by saying that at the time of Jesus, one of the red dots represented the political/religious structure of Israel, occupied by the Romans; a second dot was the Priests, Pharisees, Sadducees and Scribes, the leaders who were responsible for the spiritual life and welfare of the people. Unfortunately, they were so absorbed in their own interests, ambitions and desire for power, that they neglected their responsibili-ties to the people, the third dot.

A parish or congregation could also be symbolized by the three dots; the first being the political/religious structure, including the physical plant; the second being the leadership, elected and appointed in the parish; the third being, the rest of the congregation.

As with the Pharisees, Sadducees and Scribes, there is the ever-present danger of the parish leadership being primarily absorbed in their own interests, ambitions and desire for power, to the detriment of the spiri-tual life and welfare of the rest of the congregation.

He concluded by pointing out that unfortunately, in both scenarios, everyone suffered from 'tunnel vision'. They can see their own dot, but not the white Bristol Board, which is the Kingdom of God in which they supposedly live. Unless the Kingdom is the ultimate and over-riding vision and principle, we will have great diffi-culty being a royal priesthood, a holy nation, God's own people.

That we, being rescued from the hands of our enemies, might serve him without fear.

Luke 1: 74

For ten years my wonderful wife Audrey traveled the world for a Christian charity. She told me that in some countries monkeys are a real pest. The women have learned how to deal with them. They build a strong wooden box with a hole in the middle just big enough for a monkey to put its hand in.

Then they put a large tasty nut in the box. A monkey puts its hand in the box to get the nut. But it can't get the nut and its hand out of the box. So it has two choices: let go of the nut and be free, or stubbornly hold on to the nut and be captured. The result? Over half the monkeys hold on to the nut!

The monkey's dilemma is much like our own. We want to follow Jesus, but at the same time there is often something we want to hold on to that keeps us from being his follower. It's usually our present way of life.

Rather than a 'holding on to' it's a 'letting go' that will bring us closer to God. The old expression "Let Go and Let God" applies. We have to let go of whatever is keeping us from following Jesus and let God in.

Doing that is more difficult than it sounds. My own experience brings up four words:

- Take time to **LISTEN** to God. If you are patient, he'll communicate what he wants, one way or another.

- When you listen and God gives you his message, **OBEY** him.

- **TRUST** him. Although there's no risk, that's hard to believe.

- When the world around you is pushing, God's love and the power of the Holy Spirit seem far away, but **DON'T BE AFRAID**.

When we do listen, and we do obey, and we do trust, and we are not afraid, life can be full of an abundance of love, peace and joy.

Then Jesus cried again with a loud voice, and breathed his last.

Matthew 27: 50

Every so often I read a science fiction novel for pleasure and relaxation, and I watch science fiction drama on television, especially where there are well developed characters.

I once read a story of what happened at the Twentieth Century Fox studios. A science fiction movie was in production, but not without controversy. Some consultants and executives said the plot was weak and childish. The number crunchers argued that the sets were too costly. Robots were featured in the film, and people don't like them. The special effects took too much time to develop and execute.

Worst of all, the word 'war' was in the title, and the peace lovers would publicly object. Finally, after much agonizing discussion, the picture was released. It was an instant success. Star Wars went on to gross $525 million.

2000 years ago a man lived in Israel, a Jewish country under Roman occupation. From a small town, he was a carpenter from a family of carpenters. He didn't own a home, he had no money, he had no formal education, particularly in Jewish law. He was the leader of a small group of disciples, ordinary men, including some fishermen and a tax collector.

He had no official position in the religious hierarchy. He roamed the countryside telling stories, healing thousands. His preaching was considered blasphemy by the established spiritual leaders, with whom he argued constantly. So the men of status and influence had him arrested, convicted by a mock trial, and put to death in a painful way.

His name was Jesus and he and his band of disciples changed the world for the better.

Again Jesus spoke to them saying, "I am the light of the world. Whoever follows me will never walk in darkness, but will have the light of life."

John 8: 12

During World War Two, they gave me a lot of tests before they sent me to an intensive six week course to determine whether I was fit to become an officer in the Navy. Every time I read John Chapter 8, I am reminded of one of these tests.

I was put in a room about 10' by 10' and sat in a chair. It was the only furniture. There were no windows, and the walls, floor and ceiling were painted black. Even the door was black and edged so that there was absolutely no light in the room.

I was shut in there for thirty minutes to experience what real darkness was. I couldn't see my hand in front of me. It was not a happy experience, but somehow I survived. I was told that one out of five people could not last the full thirty minutes.

The world in which we live is full of a different kind of darkness; a noisy, blatant, aggressive magnetism, pulling us away from God. On our own, we are powerless to resist it, and it can become an incipient spiritual blindness. The only weapon we have against it is our belief in Jesus.

A relationship with the Lord shines on all our other relationships. It is a gracious work of God which opens the way to repentance and forgiveness when we fail to follow His way, and instead follow our own selfish way.

 It is a spiritual light which is eagerly and constantly seeking to fill our spirits with the love and mercy of God. This light uses every possible opportunity in our lives to destroy the darkness with its powerful beam. It never goes out. It never needs recharging. On the contrary, it can be a recharger for our own spirit, when our light becomes dim.

The poor man died and was carried away by the angels to be with Abraham. The rich man also died and was buried. In Hades, where he was tormented, he looked up and saw Abraham far away with Lazarus by his side.

Luke 16: 22,23

In the parable of Lazarus and the rich man, Jesus adds the dimension of role reversal. In real life, wealthy and famous people are known by name. The poor and the homeless are an amorphous mass of faceless humanity. In fact, many less expensive foods and other products that the poor can afford are called 'no-name'. In this story, Jesus intentionally does the opposite. The rich man is anonymous and the poor man is named Lazarus, emphasizing the message of caring for the needy and the consequences of ignoring them.

During our winters in Florida, Audrey and I for many years volunteered at a day program for the homeless called Resurrection House. She worked on the computer and I worked in the laundry.

Most days, over two hundred men, women and children receive counselling, job help, laundry, showers, haircuts, medical care, snacks, transportation and housing. They also use the RH address to receive mail, especially pension and disability cheques. One of the crucial services is personal identification. They all have names, but many can't prove it, because their usual means of identification has been lost.

I remember one client named Johnny, a Vietnam veteran with a crippled leg. With help from Resurrection House, he got his I.D. and his Veteran Benefits sorted out, a place to live and a monthly cheque from the VA. One day he came in to help in the laundry and for five years we worked side by side. Then one winter, Johnny wasn't there, having died during the summer.

Johnny was a Lazarus. A group of Christian volunteers gave him his name and a life with meaning and, despite his disability, he reached out to help others.

There are hundreds of millions of Johnnies in the world just struggling to survive. Each one has a name. Each one is a unique human being. Each one is a child of God. Each one is my brother or my sister. We can't help all of them, but with love, care and support, we can help some of them. When we do, we're helping a Lazarus.

"They shall all know me, from the least of them to the greatest," says the Lord, "for I will forgive their iniquity and remember their sin no more."

Jeremiah 31: 34

A t a Bible study one day in the parish, we were discussing how difficult it is to forgive someone who has treated you really badly. Jim, a fourth generation master cabinetmaker, said, "I don't understand how God continues to forgive us, when we constantly do things we know he doesn't like."

Hilda, a ninety-year-old who had lived in town all her life, said, "Jim, if that beautiful dining room table your grandfather made was scratched badly, would you throw it away?" "Of course not" said Jim. "I'd work hard and long to fix it."

"And when we refinished the church pews last year and found some with chewing gum all over and others with initials carved in them," replied Hilda. "did we throw them away?" "They were solid oak and sturdy." Jim exclaimed. "We sanded them down and refinished them."

"Spoken like a true craftsman," said Hilda. "God is like that. He continues to find his creation precious, despite our obvious flaws. He never stops loving us and he's always ready to forgive us if we're truly sorry."

Scripture tells us that the Holy Spirit wants us to be absolutely sure of God's forgiveness. Isaiah puts it that it is so complete that he blots out our wrongdoings – he doesn't even remember them. He takes our transgressions to himself and makes them disappear, if we are repentant. Each time I truly repent, I receive his forgiveness, freely given with a hand full of love.

And he does it ... again ... again ... and again. In the words of an old song "Could we ask for anything more?"

Then Jesus called the twelve together and gave them power and authority over all demons and to cure diseases, and he sent them out to proclaim the Kingdom of God and to heal.

Luke 9: 1, 2

In 1951 Audrey and I had a new baby boy. Despite a university degree, two years in the navy, and five years as a YMCA program supervisor in Montréal, Halifax and Toronto, I was so poorly paid that I couldn't take care of my family. I resigned and became a trainee for an insurance company. From their service department I was on track to be a sales supervisor. But first, I had to prove I could sell.

In my first week, I called on eighty-one people, made seventeen sales presentations, and didn't get a sale. Completely dejected, I met with my manager, who reminded me of the five basic rules of selling:

(1) a person with a good product will always find customers

(2) the law of numbers – if you see enough people, some will give you a hearing

(3) the law of averages – if you ask people to buy, many will say "no", but some will say "yes"

(4) the bee that gets the honey stays away from the hive – you can't make a sale sitting in an office all day.

(5) you have to be patient and you have to persevere – "no" only bothers you if you forget the first four rules

God chose us to be his disciples of today, to spread the Good News of His Kingdom, to invite people to say "yes" to his offer of love. Apply the five rules to our discipleship. If we will let the Holy Spirit be our Manager, we'll make it.

Jesus got thousands more "no's" than "yes's". St. Paul was thrown out of many towns and cities. So don't give up. You'll be in good company.

"You did not choose me but I chose you. And I appointed you to go and bear fruit, fruit that will last, so that the Father will give you whatever you ask in my name. I am giving you these commands so that you will love one another."

John 15: 16,17

Thirteen men who changed the world. Impossible, but true. They were the twelve disciples chosen by Jesus, the prophet from Nazareth, plus Paul, later chosen on the road to Damascus. A motley group. Few people would call them winners by worldly standards.

One of them was Simon, a member of a politically active group called the Zealots. Radically opposed to Roman rule, they were a fervent group of freedom fighters, demanding nothing less than political religious, social and economic independence for the people of Israel. Struggling for the purity of their faith and freedom for the Jews, often to the point of recklessness and personal suffering, they were hostile to anything or anyone connected to the Roman occupation.

Simon was the opposite of another disciple, Matthew. He collected taxes for the Romans and was despised by everyone, particularly because he collected the infamous 'poll tax.' Simon wanted to overthrow the Romans, Matthew worked for them. Simon was a tax hater, Matthew a tax collector. In their own way, both were zealous. Both tended to be hotheads. Yet Jesus selected them as members of his inner group of disciples.

After the death, resurrection and ascension of Jesus, they became part of a team spreading out into the region, teaching, preaching and healing, as Jesus commissioned them to do.

Wherever we Christians find ourselves – small parish - Diocesan committee – house church - or huge cathedral, we are members of that same Jesus team. As St. Paul put it, all with different gifts.

It's those differences, plus the power and wisdom of the Holy Spirit, which can make us successful in building up God's Kingdom, his circle of love.

"And everyone who hears these words of mine and does not act on them will be like a foolish man who built his house on sand."

Matthew 7: 26

I n the complex in which we live in Florida there is a clubhouse. On the front of the building there's a sign. "This building is not designed to withstand a hurricane. In such an event, please follow evacuation instructions." Wouldn't you say that is a warning?

Matthew recounts how Jesus gave this warning. As a carpenter, he not only built furniture, he built houses. Wherever you built a house in Palestine, location was important. You would dig down to solid rock for a solid foundation and you never built on sand. When the rainy season came, the powerful rush of water could blow the sand away and topple your home. Building on rock prevented such a catastrophe.

The moral and spiritual strength of each one of us, says Jesus, is like a house, a house of faith. How it is built determines how it survives the storms of life - doubt, fear, guilt, disappointment.

- Some folks drift through life without any foundation or direction – without meaning or purpose - a house built on sand.

- Some folks let the world give them purpose – personal achievement, status, wealth, power – another house built on sand.

- Some folks make a real effort to have Jesus and the Holy Spirit build a strong foundation for their lives – a house built on rock.

God created me to love him and to serve him in the world. At the end of my earthly life, God will judge me on how I have lived his creation.

Has my house been a circle of love with God at the centre – a house built on rock? Or has my house been a structure with me at the centre – a house built on sand?

He calls together his friends and neighbours, saying to them, "Rejoice with me, for I have found my sheep that was lost."

Luke 15: 6

When you were young, did you play 'hide and seek'? What did you like best - being the seeker or the one being sought? Were you ever in hiding when the game was over, everybody had left, and they had forgotten you? How did you feel? Lost? Abandoned?

The Scribes and the Pharisees chastised Jesus for eating with prostitutes and tax-collectors. They were considered to be bad company, people who were sinners because they didn't keep all the laws of Moses. They were outlaws, living on the fringe. Following tradition, if you broke bread in fellowship with someone, you were publicly accepting that person on your own social level.

Jesus responded to their challenge by telling them a parable. A sheep becomes lost, straying away from the flock, frightened, helpless, unable to find its way back. So it lies down, powerless to get out of its lostness. The only way back for this sheep is if the shepherd finds it.

Sinners are like lost sheep. They are separated from God, and they can't find their way back to him. Fortunately, God is a seeker. Many people spend a lifetime looking for God, to no avail. As the Psalm says, "Be still, and know that I am God." Stop doing all kinds of things to find God. Be still. Open your heart, mind and spirit. You'll find God there.

The shepherd is patient and persistent as he looks for his lost sheep. He starts looking as soon as he realizes his sheep is lost. So it is with God. Whenever we are separated from him, he knows it. He starts looking with patience and persistence, even when we hide from him. He doesn't abandon us, because he's eagerly trying to bring us into his circle of love. He is always a seeker when we are lost.

For everything there is a season, and a time for every matter under heaven.

Ecclesiastes 3: 1

L ife with God has an incredible creative quality within itself. All the things that happen to me - working, playing, eating, listening, writing, loving, crying, laughing; all the successes and all the failures, all the pleasures and all the pain, become part of my relationship with God and with those around me.

- The wonder that comes from the skilled cabinet making at St. Timothy's Church, Agincourt - that wonder comes from God.

- The sheer delight of swimming with a 1200 lb. manatee in Crystal River, Florida – that delight comes from God.

- The joyful listening to the glorious melodies of Richard Rogers – that joy comes from God.

- The sense of belonging to the awesome world of nature with its variety of colour and fabrics – that sense comes from God.

- The relief of having my physical body made healthy by a skilled surgeon – that relief comes from God.

- The love I experience as I share my life with a caring mate – that love comes from God.

- The peace that I see in the eyes of a dying friend – that peace comes from God.

- The absolute conviction that, despite all the suffering, injustice, oppression and greed in our world, God is working for our fulfillment, not our destruction – that conviction comes from God.

Jesus is present in all my living, the good and the bad, the wise and the foolish, the delightful and the distasteful. As part of my life there must be times of quiet, without a set purpose,

time, or even reflection and meditation; times just to be still and celebrate being - those times come from God. If I embrace his presence and his love, my life will be full - one day at a time.

(Jesus said) "If you forgive the sins of any, they are forgiven; if you retain the sins of any, they are not forgiven."

John 20: 23

Christians believe that if we do something against God's will, we create a barrier which disconnects us from God. To reconnect, we have to consciously say we're sorry and repent. In Biblical terms, repentance means a change of mind, a change of heart, a change of will and a change of behaviour. The word 'change' is an active verb influencing everything we think, say and do. Only with change can we ask God's forgiveness, an absolution that he gives freely and completely.

The church provides formal rituals to help us consciously repent, through the General Confession during worship or in a private confession. In both cases, tradition provides for an ordained priest to hear the confession and act as the medium through which God's forgiveness is given.

A few years ago, a single mother with two daughters asked me for a private confession. She had been divorced from her very abusive husband, who took all their common assets and ran off with another woman. She was angry and bitter at him. She also had feelings of guilt and shame, because both families blamed her for the separation.

Even now, eight years later, they constantly criticized the children's behaviour and her poor parenting, leaving her with feelings of inadequacy. Nasty letters about the situation were still being sent. She asked God to help her get over her angry feelings about these family members, specifically naming them, formally repenting and committing to change her relationships with them, if at all possible. She was given absolution for this confession.

However, she was not prepared to forgive her ex-husband for his mistreatment of herself and her daughters. There was no way that she would change that deep-rooted attitude. Without repentance, without a change, she could not receive absolution. A very sad day for me and for her.

In those days Jesus came from Nazareth in Galilee and was baptized by John in the Jordan.

Mark 1: 9

Our Bible study group was discussing Mark 1 verses 4 to 11, when someone said, "I don't understand. History tells us that Jesus was thirty years old when this happened. Why did God wait so long to publicly acknowledge his special presence and ministry, a ministry which only lasted for three years?"

A good question. I don't have any factual answers but I do have some thoughts about it.

- For thousands of years God had sent many prophets, so that his people could understand why they were created. The leaders either disregarded them or killed them. Finally the time was right for Jesus.

- Being careful not to separate Jesus into two people - the human and divine - a certain amount of human existence was necessary before the people would be ready to listen to his message.

- The ministry of his cousin John was a sign that the preparation was over. The world was now ready and so was Jesus.

- To cement this readiness, God publicly identified Jesus as his Son and put the seal of approval on him.

- The symbol of the dove had a special meaning to the Jews, hence its appearance at the baptism of Jesus.

When God calls me to a ministry in his name, surely what happened on the banks of the Jordan should happen to me. When the call comes, it's because God has decided that the world needs my ministry at this moment in time.

The call must be answered. When it's a 'yes', it means I have made a conscious decision to follow Jesus.

God will provide an opportunity for me to be publicly identified as a believer and given his seal of approval. God renews the power, wisdom and courage of the Holy Spirit in me.

***For the creation waits with eager longing for the
revealing of the children of God.***

Romans 8: 19

Sebastian was a spider, known throughout Spiderland as the greatest web weaver of them all. A web was important because it was the spider's home. One day Sebastian decided to make the most beautiful web ever. He worked long and hard.

When he was finished, it was so cleverly constructed that crowds of spiders came to admire it. School teachers organized trips so their spider students could view this amazing creation. Sebastian was happy to answer all their questions, revelling in their attention and praise.

One morning he went to check his web once more. Perhaps a few strands needed to be repaired, or a thread strengthened. No spider was infallible. All was in order until he saw a thread he didn't remember spinning. It was very long, reaching above the web. He checked it carefully and then, without hesitation, bit through what he thought was a useless thread. It broke! And the whole web collapsed like a bubble in cold water. He had destroyed the thread on which his whole world depended.

He fell. He wasn't physically hurt, but his ego, his pride, suffered badly. Sebastian hadn't felt dependent on anyone or anything. He was completely absorbed in himself - his needs, his interests, his desires, and his relationships with the rest of Spiderland. Nothing else mattered.

You and I know people like Sebastian. Their work, their families, their special interests make up their world. They are quite content with their lives, dependent only on themselves, and certainly not on God. There's no place for God in their lives. They don't think of him. It's not a question of putting God first, nor last. He is not even in the game.

What can you, a believing Christian, do about a Sebastian whom you know? Pray about them, regularly, eagerly and sincerely. And if the occasion arises, show your care and love, not by nagging, but by listening, supporting and inviting them to meet Jesus.

"Go, wash in the pool of Siloam (which means Sent)."
Then he went and washed and came back able to see.

John 9: 7

Because of my age, I have to take a test every two years to renew my driver's license in Ontario, an eye test and a written test. For reasons unknown to me, there is no actual driver's test. When I reflect on the word 'test', there seems to be no end. Blood tests, CT scans, ECG, MRI, income tax, voting, non-residence status, claim forms, etc. For some I have a measure of control. Others are in someone else's hands.

John chapter 9 is the story of a man blind from birth and the tests he has to pass. He didn't seek out Jesus. He just happened to pass by when the subject of blindness came up for discussion. The Jews believed that sickness was the result of sin, caused by you, or your parents, or even in your mother's womb. "Why is this man blind?" ask the disciples. Jesus does not answer. He takes immediate action to give the man sight. Now look at the tests the man must undergo:

Test 1: Jesus makes a poultice of clay and spittle and puts it on the man's eyes. He lets Jesus do it, but he doesn't have to.

Test 2: Jesus tells him to go to the pool of Siloam and wash it off – a long and arduous journey for a blind man

Test 3: With his new sight, his neighbours say he's a different man. He insists that he's the same man, but now he can see. When asked how, he says "The man Jesus."

Test 4: He tells the whole story to the Pharisees, who harass him. He says that Jesus was able to heal him because "He is a prophet," a dangerous assertion, because the Pharisees have the power to throw him out of the synagogue. He stands firm.

Test 5: The Pharisees claim the whole thing is a fraud put together by the man and Jesus. Again he stands firm, impatient with them. They chase him away.

Test 6: Jesus finds the man, who kneels before him and calls him "Lord."

This is a conversion story – from unbelief to belief, with tests along the way. When we invite someone to meet Jesus, remember that there's a similar process.

Then he said to his disciples, "The harvest is plentiful but the labourers are few."

Matthew 9: 37

Charlie was a codfish – not one who was satisfied with swimming with his school all day. He liked to go off on his own to explore the sea around him. He wasn't in any danger because his friend Sherman the Shark (of Lagoon fame) protected him.

One day he was swimming close to shore, observing the human creatures on the beach. A teen-age boy was running, stepped in a hole and fell. He lay there in pain.

A jogger checking his watch passed by without stopping.

A woman walked by reading a book.

A father helping his daughter fly a kite ignored him.

A boy on a bicycle nearly ran over him, but kept on going.

Two girls listening to a ghetto-blaster were singing as they sauntered by.

Finally, an old man with a cane noticed him and yelled for people to come and help.

Charlie felt sorry for the boy, but he was shocked at the lack of caring by so many of these humans.

The story of Charlie is not too far-fetched. Incidents like this happen every day in our community, for any number of reasons. Inconvenience - can't be bothered - too busy - don't feel like it - their own fault - day dreaming - what's in it for me? - getting involved is risky - indifference - apathy - prejudice - selfishness - let someone else do it … the list goes on.

If Jesus had been walking on the beach, how would he have responded?

What does it mean to really care about others? It means believing in Jesus and trying to follow his way. Standing up for your faith; not being afraid, because with Jesus there is no risk. Looking at others with the eyes of God, not your own eyes.

This day shall be a day of remembrance for you. You shall celebrate it as a festival to the Lord; throughout your generations, you shall observe it as a perpetual ordinance.

Exodus 12: 14

These were God's orders about the Passover, when he delivered the Jews from bondage in Egypt. The Hebrew and Aramaic words for 'remembrance' are much more than just recalling in our minds an event in history which we've read about. In Biblical terms, remembrance means experiencing the event as though you were there when it happened, and trying to understand what influence it has on your life today.

So when a Jewish family celebrates the Passover with a Seder meal, the special foods, the words, the prayers and the ritual take them back in time and help them feel they are really escaping from slavery. They are actively remembering God's saving grace for his people. That's what Jesus and his disciples were doing one Thursday evening in an upper room in Jerusalem.

Now, two thousand years later, Christians don't celebrate the Passover, but we do celebrate what happened in that upper room. Jesus took bread, and when he had given thanks, he broke it and said, "This is my body which is given for you. Do this in remembrance of me."

Then he took a cup of wine, gave thanks, and said "This is the new covenant in my blood. Do this as often as you drink it in remembrance of me." We call this Holy Communion, the Eucharist, or the Mass.

When we participate in it, we are remembering God's saving grace for his people, for us. We are there. We can experience his real presence among us.

In the early days of television, the Prudential Insurance Company sponsored a program which dramatized an event so that the viewers were actually involved. Jesus being really present in the Eucharist is carrying us back in time, so each of us is there in that upper room as one of his disciples.

"Whoever does not carry the cross and follow me cannot be my disciple."

Luke 14: 27

There's a picture in our office at home of thousands of people gathered in Dominion Square in Montreal in 1995, in support of a referendum to keep Quebec in Canada. Audrey and I were there, with two busloads of people from our neighbourhood in East Toronto. There were hundreds more buses from all over Ontario and beyond, filled with folks who spontaneously decided to make the trip in patriotic fervor.

When I was ten and my brother John twelve, we were avid NHL hockey fans. When the star of the Canadiens team, Howie Morenz, died, a public memorial service was held in the Montreal Forum hockey arena. It was a school day, and we decided to skip school and go. Using our allowance to buy streetcar tickets, we ended up in the top of the arena, where we couldn't see anything.

In both cases, we were caught up in the crowd, swept along by the excitement of the event; like the celebrations when World War Two ended, when the Toronto Blue Jays won the World Series two years in a row, when over one million people attended a Gay Pride parade and fewer than 1% were gay. The sociologists call this phenomenon "collective behaviour."

Jesus was teaching and healing in the Galilee region for three years. Everywhere he went, thousands flocked to hear him. If Jesus was coming, you had to be there. Jesus saw the crowds of excited faces. He knew that his popularity had aroused the religious establishment. Pain, suffering and death lay ahead. He tried to explain to the excited people that, if they wanted to follow him, there was a price to be paid. Sacrifices would be required.

Scripture tells us that of the hundreds of thousands of eager listeners, only about one hundred and twenty became followers of the Lord. The same is true today.

There's a difference between a spectator and a participant, between a hanger-on and an active member, between worshipping every Sunday and dropping in for Christmas and Easter. It's our choice. We can make sacrifices, be different, be a real disciple, or just be part of the crowd.

The Fruit of the Spirit is love, joy, peace, patience, kindness, generosity, faithfulness, goodness, and self-control.

Galatians 5: 22

T his is best expressed as a prayer. God give me:

LOVE - that I may love you as you have loved me, and love my neighbours as you have loved them.

JOY - that I may be happy within myself, and help others to feel the same, knowing that a truly warm smile is always better than a sour frown.

PEACE – that I may never again be restless, worried, nervous, stressed out.

PATIENCE – that I stop fretting at delays, no longer irritable and hurried.

KINDNESS – that I will desire to give rather than get, share rather than keep, praise rather than criticize, and forgive rather than condemn.

GOODNESS – that I will strive to follow Jesus as a model in all my relationships, and not as an example of superiority to others.

FAITHFULNESS – that through all the chances and changes of life I will be true to you, true to my loved ones, and true to myself.

GENTLENESS – that I will be humble and not proud, and never deliberately or carelessly hurt others in any way.

SELF-CONTROL – that no moment of passion or impulse or prejudice will cause me to hurt someone, or inflict feelings of uselessness on others.

Help me to live and use these Fruits of the Spirit in everything I say and do.

May God's Spirit so engulf my spirit that these Fruits will be reflected in all my relationships with others and the world in which I am called to serve.

Amen

Therefore, since we are surrounded by a great cloud of witnesses, let us also lay aside every weight and sin that clings so closely and let us run with perseverance the race that is set before us.

Hebrews 12: 1

There's a story about Jesus having a conversation with the angel Gabriel upon his ascension into heaven. "Master," said Gabriel, "you must be terribly disappointed. The people you came to save humiliated you and finally killed you on a cross. "Well," replied Jesus," they weren't all really bad, just confused and very selfish. But thousands heard my message of love and some of them believed."

"You only had three years of teaching and healing before they arranged for the Romans to crucify you," cried Gabriel. "What a waste of time and energy." "It wasn't wasted," Jesus began to say, when Gabriel interrupted, "What's going to happen to your message now?" Jesus gently answered "I recruited a small band of men, Peter, James, John and the others. They will carry my message to the world."

"Master, they are just ordinary men with little education and training. How can you expect them to do what you did?" came the reply. "They'll be fine," said Jesus. "I trust them." Gabriel persisted, "But what if they forget what you taught them and go back to fishing?" "They'll be fine." said Jesus. "I trust them."

Gabriel almost shouted, "Surely you have made other arrangements? A Plan B or Plan C?" "You don't understand." said Jesus. "I trust my disciples. They will tell people about me and a few will believe. They will tell others and a few will believe. And so on and so on, until the whole world believes my message."

"You're expecting an awful lot from a few humble men." Gabriel concluded. "They won't be alone." said Jesus. "They will have the Holy Spirit with them every step of the way. It may take time, but it will happen." And it did. And it still does. There's no Plan B or Plan C. We are it – today's disciples. Jesus is counting on us and the Holy Spirit, working in us.

*But so you may also know that the Son of Man has
authority on earth to forgive sins - he said to the one
who was paralyzed - "I say to you, stand up and take
your bed and go to your home."*

Luke 5: 24

Some years ago my wife Audrey experienced a sharp pain in her right side. Off to the hospital. Her appendix is going to burst. Must operate, so in they go. Not the appendix, but they remove it anyway. More tests and x-rays. She has a serious kidney disease. She's given medication for the pain and sent home. There's nothing more they can do. It may possibly get worse, so she must have x-rays every month. Audrey prays. I pray. Many family and friends pray for healing.

After the first month's x-rays there's no change. After the second month, our doctor phones. The x-ray technician has made a mistake. Could she please repeat the x-rays? She does. He phones again. Still a mistake. Please repeat the x-rays, but also have some blood tests. Everything is clear. The kidney disease has disappeared. But kidneys do not regenerate. The specialists are called in. They can't explain it. She's absolutely clear. Even the pain has gone. Many prayers have been answered. I call that 'Divine Healing'.

Some people say healing has nothing to do with God. They claim that the story of the paralyzed man walking away is either an exaggeration or a fake. But many of us can remember times when 'divine healing' did seem to take place. Someone was ill, and then they were better. People were healed. Many were healed by the skill and care of medical professionals and we must never forget that their knowledge and skill are gifts of God. But in some, a 'miracle' happened – divine healing. In others it was a combination of professional skill and divine healing.

By the power of the Holy Spirit, we can reach out to someone in need; seldom in big ways, mostly in non-miraculous ways. When we do, whatever the circumstances, 'divine healing' takes place. As Albert Einstein wrote, "We can live as if nothing is a miracle, or we can live as if everything is a miracle."

"I am the good shepherd. I know my own and my own know me."

John 10: 14

I was reading a book on the history of the Jews and came across an artist's rendition of a shepherd around the time of Jesus. Looking out of the window I saw a construction worker, and couldn't help thinking that times haven't changed much. He was ready for work; hard hat, safety boots, yellow overalls, gloves, belt filled with tools.

And there was the shepherd in the picture, leading his flock, ready for work; heavy brown robe, sandals on his feet, a head covering, a girdle holding a pouch with some food, a staff with a crook to keep his sheep from straying, and his two means of protection, a sling, and his rod, three feet long with a knob on the end. Later I picked up a children's book about Jesus. On the cover was a picture of Jesus as a shepherd, in a flowing white robe, carrying a crook, his sheep trudging ahead of him. No girdle, no sling, no rod.

What a shame we have romanticized Jesus as a shepherd to the point where he doesn't represent reality. In his day, the shepherd and his flock were an important segment of the fabric of everyday life. Jesus lived in an agricultural society. In addition, the image of the shepherd was a key element in their faith.

In the Old Testament, God is often represented as the shepherd of his flock, the people of Israel. The Messiah was thought to be a Good Shepherd for his people. When Jesus declared himself to be the Good

Shepherd, it meant that he provided the three basic essentials of a shepherd's job; to know his sheep, to care for his sheep, and to protect his sheep.

We need to remember that the picture of the shepherd is as much about the sheep as the shepherd. Sheep are dependent, needy, hungry, foolish, wandering, getting into trouble. They need the shepherd to know, care for and protect them.

In our world, we are like sheep, and we need Jesus, the Good Shepherd, to know us, to care for us, and to protect us. He does his job, if we are of his flock, every day, one day at a time.

"Anyone who resolves to do the will of God will know whether the teaching is from God, or whether I am speaking on my own."

John 7: 17

There's an old Jewish folktale about Joseph, a merchant, who decided to have an engagement party for his daughter. Instead of a gift, each guest was asked to bring wine to the party.

Benjamin and his wife were invited, and he resented having to bring wine, even though he could afford it. His wine would be poured into a large jug with the wine of the other guests. So he decided to take a jug of water, instead of wine. "No one will notice", he thought, "there'll be lots of wine from the other guests."

When the time for the toasts arrived, everyone was shocked, because all that came out of the large jug was water. Every guest, like Benjamin, had brought water, not wine. All of them believed they could get away with it, because "no one would notice."

Every day we make choices – some small ones, some big ones. That's being human, the result of God giving us the gifts of reason, imagination and free will. In his wisdom, God understood that in order to love him you had to have the right to choose. You can't say "yes" to love unless you can say "no" to love. Without that choice, there can be no love.

Hopefully, we will go through life making right choices, doing good deeds because we love God. But we will sometimes make bad choices and do wrong things, not because we're evil, but because we're human and "no one will notice."

The conclusion of this story is that Joseph forgave Benjamin and the other guests. He provided the needed wine himself, because he wanted the celebration for his daughter to be a success.

Praise God. When we choose our way instead of God's way' and we are truly repentant, God forgives us, and the joy of being human will continue for us, because that's what God wants.

*Jesus said to him, "I am the way, the truth and the life.
No one comes to the father except through me."*

John 14: 6

The Shepherd family lived in Ajax, an 'improvement district' of 4,000 people just east of Toronto. In 1954 it was officially declared a 'town'. As an active resident, I knew my way around town and never got lost.

Today it's over 88,000 people and still growing. I was the Interim Pastor at St. George's church in the town in 2010-2011. If I wanted to visit a parishioner I would ask Helen, the administrator, to Google me a map from the computer, and even then I would get lost, because I didn't know the way.

Jesus warns his disciples that he will be killed, but he will still be with them when they die, in another of God's spaces. One of them, Thomas, says they don't know the way to this other place. Then Jesus makes this astounding declaration, using three of the basic tenets of Jewish faith. "I am the way, the truth and the life."

He's making it clear that we don't have to die to be with God. We can be part of God's Kingdom now. Through the Holy Spirit we can get to know Jesus, and through Jesus, we can get to know God. Moses said, "You shall walk in the ways God commanded you." Jesus says, "These ways are me. Follow me and you will be following God's way, and never be lost."

Jesus didn't say "I will tell you the truth." He said, 'I am the truth." We read in Psalm 96 "Help me to walk in your truth, O Lord." We could make a list of words to describe 'truth', but God's truth goes way beyond our lists. The reality of truth is Jesus. He is the only one who can lead us into the presence of God. He didn't only use words to show us God, he lived it.

In John 3:16, Jesus says "… anyone who believes in me shall not perish, but have eternal life." Believing in Jesus helps me to be the real person God created me to be, to have a life in which I can experience the love, joy, peace and hope which only God can give. Jesus offers me, and you "… the way, the truth and the life", which we can experience now, by following him, one day at a time.

As a father has compassion on his children, so the Lord has compassion for those who fear him.

Psalm 103: 13

It was Tuesday, and a Pentecostal friend said to me, "You're having three special services tomorrow at St. Wilfred's Church. What is this Ash Wednesday you folks make such a fuss about?" A fair question. How would you answer?

Our opening prayer for each of these services includes "... forgive the sins of those who are penitent; create and make us new and contrite hearts." It's the beginning of the church's season called Lent, during which we are to make a special effort to be spiritually prepared for the great celebration of Easter.

There's a legend about a man going to St. Peter to ask God's forgiveness for the bad things he had done in his life. He asked a friend to go with him, who said he didn't really need forgiveness. St. Peter asked them if they really wanted God's forgiveness. "Very much," said the first man. "I guess so," said the friend. St. Peter said, "Go into the field over there and bring back a stone for every sin you want God to forgive and bring them back to me."

They went off. Sometime later the first man came back with two very large stones, so heavy he couldn't carry them, but pushed them along the ground on his knees. He placed them before Peter, utterly exhausted. His friend came back, carrying a bag with twelve small pebbles. "Now," ordered St. Peter, "go back to the field and place your stones exactly where you found them. Then return to me and you will receive absolution."

The man pushed his stones back where he found them. When he faced St. Peter again, he declared his penitence and was forgiven. After a long time, his friend returned and cried out, "It's impossible! I can't put my pebbles back. I can't remember where each one was." Peter replied "So often that's true in life. We do many small things that hurt

God and hurt others and we don't recognize them or think they are important. Easily forgotten, we don't think to repent and seek forgiveness. That's why, if you follow the Jesus way, you will ask God's forgiveness every day, one day at a time."

After his suffering, he presented himself alive to them by many and convincing proofs, appearing to them during forty days and speaking about the Kingdom of God.

Acts 1: 3

I have met many people, some of them practicing Christians, who accept the Bible's description of the crucifixion of Jesus of Nazareth. These same Christian people do not accept his resurrection. They doubt the truth of the event, because it's against the natural order. There were skeptics 2000 years ago and there are skeptics today.

On the other hand, there are a large number of the world's critical scholars, historians, archeologists, Christians and non-Christians, who agree that the following facts can he accepted as 'knowledge-able history':

- Jesus did die on the cross – he was not just unconscious.

- He was buried in a sealed tomb – with guards posted outside.

- His death resulted in his followers hiding in fear for their lives.

- A few days later the tomb was open and the body was not there.

- The body of Jesus was never found.

- The authorities searched for his body to no avail.

- The accusation that the disciples stole the body was never proved.

- No shrine was ever erected as a remembrance of his death.

- On nine different occasions, plus others not recorded, his disciples experienced what they believed were appearances of the risen Lord.

- Experts say that these appearances, to individuals and groups, were too similar to be visions or hallucinations.

- The disciples no longer hid in fright, but boldly proclaimed his resurrection and some of them died for their beliefs.

- After the resurrection, the disciples had the power to heal and many miracles were recorded as happening because of them.

- The Christian church came into existence and Sunday became their special day of celebration, not the Jewish Sabbath.

- Two of the known skeptics, James the brother of Jesus, and Paul, a persecutor of Christians, had appearances of Jesus, and became leaders in the early church.

The scholars' conclusion - the resurrection of Jesus, in a transformed but recognizable body - is the only logical explanation for these historical facts.

Jesus said, "I am the gate. Whoever enters by me shall be saved and will come in and go out and find pasture."

John 10: 9

A few years ago, I served as the Interim Pastor of the Church Of The Ascension in Port Perry, Ontario. To my dismay, the worship centre was a construction site undergoing a complete renovation. The same thing happened four years later at St. Paul, Minden. In both cases, the large beautiful front doors were propped up against a wall. Neither door was fulfilling its function.

The job of a church door is to open the worship centre for the people of God to enter, to worship together and to be nurtured in the faith while they are inside with the doors closed. Then, when worship is over, the doors are opened and the people are sent out to serve the world in God's name. They are blessed as they enter and blessed as they go out.

In the two spaces under construction, there was no open door, no worship, no nurture, and no service for the Lord. But without the doors, worship still took place and nurture swelled forth. Every Sunday morning the Parish Halls were creatively transformed into worship centres. The doors to the churches were not really the doors to the worship centres.

Jesus was and always is, the true door to worship for Christians. He is the lover who invites us into the presence of God. Jesus is the teacher/healer/preacher who nurtures us when we are together in his name. And when our worship is over, he doesn't send us out into the world, he leads us out to serve God's Kingdom, staying with us for the days until we come back together to worship in his name.

That's what being a disciple is all about. That's being what St. Peter described as the 'people of God'. That's why it's important for us to regularly come together in his name.

*If you will only heed his every commandment that I
am commanding you today - loving the Lord your God
and serving him with all your heart and with all your
soul*

Deuteronomy 11: 13

A t the conclusion of Anglican worship, a leader often says these words, "Go in peace to love and serve the Lord." In scripture, 'love' means giving of yourself without wanting, expecting, or asking for anything in return. But what does the word 'serve' mean? Including its derivatives (servant, service) it appears in the Bible 1273 times.

I made a list of today's uses and was surprised. The people who maintain my car are called the 'service department'. In many commercial buildings there is a 'service elevator'. They call military people the 'armed services'. Those who serve the crown are 'in her Majesty's service'. The person who starts a tennis game 'serves' the ball. A waiter is often called a 'server'. To register a complaint you call 'customer services'. Wealthy people have 'servants'.

Christians pray together in a 'worship service'. To follow their worship they have an 'order of service.' To fix my TV someone makes a 'service call'. I can be 'served' a writ to appear in court. In the kitchen I use a 'serving spoon'. I can be compensated for 'services rendered'. My mother had a 'silver tea service'. My sofa can 'serve' as a place to sleep ... you could add many more.

From the above, serving the Lord can include any words or deeds which directly or indirectly bring an individual in contact with the Kingdom of God. So we can use words like work for, promote, minister to, perform duties, give help to, be of use to, manage, start, explain, distribute, make good and many more.

Some 'serving God' activities may seem more important than others, but to the Lord, any words or actions which bring someone into God's circle of love mean that we are 'serving' him.

Then Jesus said to the disciples, "There was a rich man who had a manager, and charges were brought to him that this man was squandering his property."

Luke 16: 1

A Canadian icon, Tim Horton's, was sold to an American investment firm which also owned Burger King. Part of the deal was a promise not to give 'pink slips' to Tim's employees. Two months later, more than a thousand were fired, in the interest of efficiency. From time to time other Canadian enterprises are taken over and the new owners become 'absentee landlords'.

In Jesus' era there were many absentee landlords. Hundreds of small farmers had to give up their promised land because of excess taxes - by the Romans, by King Herod, and by the temple. Men with power and money bought them for unpaid taxes and then hired the original owners as tenants. The result was big farms owned by city people who were only interested in profits.

So Jesus tells a story about one absentee landlord. He has a manager whose primary job is to collect the rent from tenant farmers, usually in produce. A whistleblower tells the owner that he's not receiving his fair share of the rents. There's an audit and the manager is fired.

To get back into the owner's good books and also please the tenants, the manager tells the tenants to reduce their rents, and he makes them sign an invoice for the reduced amounts. The owner praises the manager.

Jesus doesn't condone this behaviour. He uses this story from real life to show how dishonesty and greed on the part of all the characters is really being irresponsible in using the gifts God gives us. The owner was greedy, the manager likewise and the tenants went along with it. A small dishonesty becomes a trap into more and more dishonesty.

We are God's managers, mandated by him to exercise responsible trusteeship over the whole of creation. If we squander what he has given us,

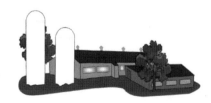

whether it be the environment or our talents, we must answer to God. Once someone uses this stewardship for gain, it easily becomes something that everyone does and creation suffers.

Now there are varieties of gifts, but the same Spirit,
and there are varieties of service but the same Lord,
and there are varieties of activities but it is the same
God who activates all of them in everyone.

1 Corinthians 12: 4 to 6

I learned to play the piano when I was very young. My Grade 3 teacher discovered that in addition to taking classical lessons, I could listen to a melody and then play it by ear.

Our kindergarten class had an assortment of simple instruments and wanted to have a band as part of their musical training. They needed a song or tune to provide a musical background. So a deal was made. Twice a week I would play tunes the children knew so that the band could practice. This continued until I reached High School. By then I had the reputation of being able to accompany people at social gatherings who liked to sing.

It was during the depression of the Thirties and the local YMCA held an outdoor community program called the "Bonfire" twice a week in the evening There were games, magicians, athletic demonstrations, musical groups, etc. and attendance was usually over 2000. There was always a sing-song, led by Johnnie Walker, with me on the piano.

One evening Johnnie wasn't there. He had joined the air force. The Director decided that I would lead the sing song, since I knew all the songs. Louie Charbonneau would accompany me on his accordion. That was a major moment in my life. This shy, overweight young teenager, with a negative self-image and lacking in self-confidence, was offered a new sense of self-worth.

Many times since that evening I have been challenged to do something for which I had no experience and little skill. The Holy Spirit gives me the courage to accept and guides me through the situation. As for that special evening, was the Holy Spirit involved? If the Spirit was, this young teen-ager didn't know it. But now I do.

The Lord upholds all who are falling, and raises up all who are bowed down.

Psalm 145:14

An eagle got caught by an enormous gust of wind, hit a wire and fell to the ground with a broken wing. His squawks were heard by farmer Ralph, who wrapped him up in his coat and took him home. With the help of his wife Nancy, the broken wing was put in a splint.

"What do we do with him now?" she asked. "He's helpless. If we put him back outside, the raccoons and the coyotes will kill him." "We'll have to keep him somewhere on the farm until his wing heals," replied Ralph. "We could put him in with the chickens," suggested Nancy. "They will be afraid of him," said Ralph. Despite his protestations, that's where the eagle ended up.

After a few days, the chickens got used to him. To feed the eagle, Nancy gave him the same corn feed that the chickens ate. After a while, being hungry, with nothing else offered, he ate it. After a week the eagle started to cluck-cluck like the chickens and everyone was happy. Even after the wing was healed, the eagle still lived among the chickens … cluck-cluck-cluck.

One day Billy Bob, a neighbour, was visiting and was amazed at the cluck-clucking eagle. "Why doesn't he fly away?" he asked. "I don't know." said Ralph. "He's often in the yard alone, but he still clucks around."

"Let's try something," said Billy Bob. He took off his coat, wrapped it around his arm, forced the eagle to perch on it and went around the barn into the field. He faced the eagle into the sun. After a short hesitation, the eagle gave a great cry and flew away. The sun had made him an eagle again.

 Jesus can be the sun (son) in someone's life, if a Billy Bob like you introduces him. With Jesus, anyone can be an eagle instead of a chicken. With Jesus, everyone can live the way God created us to be.

For those who live according to the flesh set their minds on the things of the flesh, but those who live according to the Spirit, set their minds on the things of the Spirit.

Romans 8:5

St. Paul makes it clear that you are either for God or against God. There's no in-between. Who is at the centre of my life, God or self? If there's a choice between my desire and the commands of the Spirit, who wins? For Paul, the answer is always the Spirit.

But my personal experience tells me that *sometimes* I follow God and *sometimes* God is left out. I hope that doesn't sound like a typical Anglican compromise, a spiritual cop-out. It's just a description of the reality of the world in which we live.

Sometimes my human nature, with its weaknesses and ego, easily succumbs to the people or things around me. My spirit disregards the Holy Spirit.

Sometimes the opposite happens. The Holy Spirit ignores the barriers in my head and forcibly directs me to speak or act in a 'changed' way.

Sometimes the Holy Spirit is patient. The Spirit works slowly on my spirit so that it takes a long time for me to change. Often I don't even notice that a real change in behaviour has taken place.

Sometimes the Holy Spirit gently and unobtrusively stirs up my heart, mind and spirit, and then waits for me to catch up, to consciously invite the Spirit to play a real role in my life.

The result of all these "*sometimes*" is my life becomes a battleground between the world and the Holy Spirit. Both sides can claim victory. The war is won when there are no more *sometimes;* the battleground disappears and the winner is declared. It can be the world, what Paul calls the 'flesh', or it can be God, through the power, wisdom and courage given to me by the Holy Spirit.

To date in human history there has only been one winner on both sides – Jesus of Nazareth, God's son. That's why having a loving relationship with Jesus is so important.

Then God said, "Let us make humankind in our image, according to our likeness, and let them have dominion over the fish of the sea, and over the birds of the air, and over the cattle, and over all the wild animals of the earth."

Genesis 1:26

Take the brightest, largest, roundest Macintosh apple you can find. Clasp it in your hand as though you were holding the world in which you live. This is the world God gave us to take care of. Remove the core with a sharp knife. At this time it is not our concern.

- Next, cut the apple in a little over half; the larger of the two pieces represents all of the *sea water* we have. We are not taking care of it very well; two examples – overfishing and billions of non-dissolvable plastics thrown into it every year.

- Cut the smaller portion that is left as follows: one third is *fresh water*, which we have been wasting with pollutants such as sewage, chemicals, acid rain, mine tailings, etc. The remaining piece is *land*.

- Cut this piece into four. One piece is mountains and forests, being reduced by clear cutting; a second piece is ice and swamps, being diminished by global warming and dammed rivers; a third represents land covered by towns, cities, factories, houses, roads, etc.

- Take the final small piece, which represents about 8% of the surface of the earth, and trim the skin from it. This skin is all the land on which crops can be grown. Every year we build more houses and roads on it, or overuse it and reduce its ability to grow crops.

It's a fragile earth in which we live, an island home in a massive universe. It is more than our world, it is also God's Kingdom. The

ultimate ruler is God, and he has entrusted us with taking care of it. Not just our little part, but all of his creation.

Call us rulers, call us caretakers, call us managers, call us stewards - the name doesn't matter. What is important is what we do with the sacred trust God has given us.

"But when you give a banquet, invite the poor, the crippled, the lame and the blind."

Luke 14: 13

Seating arrangements at most Jewish feasts were quite specific. Tables were arranged in a three sided square. The host sat at the centre top, the guest of honour on his right, the second honoured guest on his left, and so on and so on back and forth. The further away from the host, the less important you were. Your dress indicated not only how important you were, but also how distinguished your host was.

Legend tells of a teacher who was invited to a banquet by the President of the synagogue. Teachers were poorly paid, so he had to have a second job. The teacher worked in a mill grinding out bushels of flour. This day, when he had finished work, there was only enough time to wash his face and dust off his work clothes as he rushed to the banquet. His seat was about halfway down the table on the right.

Before dinner was served, a servant came and said that the host was concerned that he might feel out of place in the middle of this finery. Would he please wear this very fine dinner jacket? He put it on. When the first course was served, he plastered the food all over the jacket, loudly proclaiming how delicious the food was. The other guests were shocked. The President angrily demanded an explanation. The teacher replied, "When I sat down in my ordinary work clothes, you insisted I wear this beautiful garment. I assumed the garment was your intended guest, so I had to feed it."

We may think that the teacher's actions were improper and offensive to the host. He could have refused the jacket in the first place, even though the offer was an insult to him. Clearly the President treated him as an inferior.

How often are we like that host? How often do we treat people as lesser human beings because they are different? How often do we consciously or sub-consciously rank people,

slotting them into a position below ours, defining them by appearance, behaviour, occupation or racial origin, and then treat them according to the ranking we have given them?

"For I am about to create new heavens and a new earth; the former things shall not be remembered or come to mind."

Isaiah 65: 17

I am writing this 'Word' just before Palm Sunday. Everywhere in the media there is talk about it being the first day of spring. Unfortunately, it doesn't feel like it. Yes, the sun is shining, but the temperature reads minus 3 Celsius. Most of the snow has melted, but I've only seen a few crocuses springing forth. In the forest next door, there are no green leaves budding on the trees. However, meteorologists are saying that winter is over, a new season has started, and there is sprightliness in many people's steps.

Tomorrow, most Christians will go to church pondering the meaning of a parade on Palm Sunday and the beginning of Holy Week, or 'The Passion of our Lord.' This 'passion' tells the story of the cruel execution of Jesus of Nazareth on a wooden cross. There's nothing new about the story. It is history two thousand years old. Yet it touches our very being, a humanity which we share with the man on the cross.

It moves through popularity and excitement to confrontation with established authority, to misguided betrayal by a close friend, to a mock trial, and the use of power to kill someone who is innocent. When we try to relive the story as if we were there, we fail, because deep down we know the tragic ending had a postscript.

The real climax of the story is difficult to understand because it was a celebration – a celebration of how a loving and caring God can make things new; how the death of one of our brothers can make up for all the wrongs we have done and will continue to do, and can enable us to have an intimate and loving relationship with our Creator.

Unfortunately, the events in Jerusalem still happen today in many places. There are still betrayals, mock trials, misuse of power, injustices and even brutal executions. But through the whole of this old story we can renew our faith in the wonder and joy of being able to live in God's Kingdom of love. We may not be happy with spring weather, but with God there can always be spring in our hearts.

Now the Lord came and stood there, calling as before, "Samuel! Samuel!" and Samuel said, "Speak, for your servant is listening."

1 Samuel 3: 10

I grew up in Montreal during the Great Depression, often referred to as the "Dirty Thirties." My childhood had its usual ups and down, but on the whole it was a good time. I give credit to my parents who emphasized honesty and hard work and had strict rules for behaviour. In the area where we lived there were two train tracks, six east-west arteries, three north-south arteries, two bus lines, three street-car lines, few traffic lights and a number of level crossings. Without a car, crossing roads was dangerous. So for our own safety, it was drilled into us – Stop! Look! Listen!

God called Samuel out of his sleep. He forced him to wake up and look at the reality of the life around him. What followed was an encounter with God that changed the whole direction of his life. Samuel had a Stop! Look! Listen! experience.

Stop! Look! Listen! is still a good rule to follow in everyday life. But it's also a 'must' warning about the dangers to our spiritual life, the attractions that the world places in front of us to prevent us from being safe in the arms of Jesus. Stop! Look! Listen! guides us in crossing from one kind of life to another kind of life, in going from darkness to light, from just an existence, to being the truly free and fully human beings God created us to be.

Sometimes God *stops* us in a direct confrontation, a moment when we know God is speaking to us in our stress, confusion, doubts and pain, shining the light of his love on our tunnel vision of self-interest. More often we are *stopped* by the ordinary everyday experiences in which events and people bring God into our lives over time. We *look* at the world through a variety of media and personal relationships

with others, a *look* in which the story and influence of Jesus cannot be dismissed.

Finally, every minute, every hour, of every day Jesus is calling to us, opening our hearts, minds and spirits to *listen* to the joy of knowing him. God stops us from living a self-absorbed life, from the world turning us away from him. When we *listen* to the ever-present call of the Lord, we find a wonderful circle of love waiting for us. Stop! Look! Listen!

"Today I tell you, just as you did it to one of the least of these who are members of my family, you did it to me."

Matthew 25: 40

N o nation has ever had a greater sense of responsibility for their less fortunate brethren than the Jews. By the time of Jesus there was a routine custom. Two designated collectors went around to the market and private homes every Friday morning and took up a collection for the needy, partly in money and partly in goods. No one would refuse to contribute. Later in the day what had been collected was distributed. Those who were permanently unable to support themselves were given enough for two meals a day for seven days. Those who were temporarily in need received enough to carry on with life.

The fund for this distribution was called the 'Kuppah' or basket and was the safety net for the disadvantaged. Unfortunately, if you didn't live in a town or village with or near a synagogue, you were out of luck. You were either helped by a caring neighbour, or you became a beggar.

Today we have a formal, organized safety net through the government, paid by everyone's tax dollars. It's an impersonal system. There are no collectors or distributors with whom there is personal contact. The theory is that the poor should not be shamed before a live person, perhaps a neighbour. On the other hand, taxpayers who supply this safety net do so because they must, not always because they want to. Providing additional support through charitable organizations allows for people's wishes.

When Matthew recounts Jesus telling the story of the shepherd separating the sheep and the goats, his message is very clear. At the final Day of Judgment, we will be assessed according to our response to any kind of human distress, either by increasing the safety net, or helping those who fall through the safety net. He makes it personal by declaring that if a man is homeless and you give him shelter, you are giving shelter to Jesus.

Caring for someone in need is not an option, but a duty. It is part of the essence of our creation. To refuse is to deny our humanity.

Jesus answered, "I am the way, the truth and the life.
No one comes to the Father except through me".

John 14: 6

From earliest times God was so all-powerful to the people of Israel that they never wrote his name, Yahweh, in full; they left out the vowels. When Moses asked God in the burning bush what his name was, the Lord replied, "*I am who I am*. You must tell the people, *I am* has sent me to you."

Centuries later, John recounts that whenever Jesus is asked, "Who are you?" his answer begins with "*I am*". He uses the phrase God used to describe himself. To the degree that John's mind is able, he is trying to reconcile two basic beliefs about Jesus - that Jesus is fully human and also fully divine.

There is the earthly order (flesh) and the heavenly order (spirit). Both exist in all of us. They are what make us human, created in the image of God.

In Jesus, the flesh and the spirit are completely integrated. He is uniquely the carpenter from Nazareth and also uniquely the Son of the Creator God. He is human being/God and God/human being. That is the heart of his consciousness; where flesh and spirit interact with each other in perfect freedom.

As we move through John's Gospel, one *I am* follows another: the Good Shepherd, the Gate, the Vine, the Bread of Life, the Light of the World, the Way, the Truth and the Life, the Resurrection and the Life, each one adding to our understanding of who Jesus is.

But they also affirm that if we live in God's Kingdom, within his circle of love and care, we too can experience an interaction of flesh and spirit. Jesus offers it to us as a free gift. The more we open ourselves to invite the Holy Spirit to bring flesh and spirit together in our lives, the better we are able to actually experience Jesus and know him as *'I am'*.

When they came to the place that is called the Skull,
then they crucified Jesus there with the criminals, one
on his right and one on his left.

Luke 23: 33

I have read and heard the story of Good Friday many times - a story that pits the evils of the universe against the goodness of God – a cosmic battle here on earth for the souls of humanity. It can easily become legendary, but it's not. It's real. Jesus of Nazareth was cruelly executed on a cross, not for a crime, but for declaring and living God's love.

Primarily, it's a story about power; about the flagrant use of power, the fear of power by those who don't have it, the threat of losing power by those who do have it, and the desire for more power by those who have only a little. It's all there at the heart of an important event in human history.

- I see the power of religious zeal. Blinded by the conviction that they were the true spiritual leaders of the people, the Scribes and Pharisees felt threatened by this popular wandering preacher from Galilee.

- I see the power of status and prestige. An ordered and comfortable life was enjoyed by the upper-class Sadducees and high priests in Jerusalem. They could not afford to have Jesus' growing popularity go on any longer.

- I see the power of mystic holiness. The Temple was the centre of the Hebrew faith, administered by the priests, whom the people placed on a pedestal. They needed to get rid of this upstart teacher.

- I see the power of ambition. The puppet ruler Herod Antipas wanted to increase his meagre power and Jesus stood in his way.

- I see the power of military might. The conquering Romans ruled the country with unwavering force.

- I see the power of a coalition. Priests, Sadducees, Scribes, Pharisees, Herodians, and Pilate the Roman Governor, together manipulated charges of blasphemy into a charge of treason.

- I see the false power of the crowd. Enthralled by the excitement of what was happening at their Passover Festival, and incited by the minions of the coalition, the people cried "Yes" to the crucifixion of an innocent man.

The rest is history. Power corrupts and absolute power corrupts absolutely.

Then he took it down, wrapped it in a linen cloth and laid it in a rock-hewn tomb where no-one had ever been laid.

Luke 23: 53

In the previous 'Word', I described some of the realities of power which resulted in the execution of Jesus of Nazareth on a cross. A coalition of groups and individuals, who perceived their power to be threatened, connived together to subject an innocent man to an excruciatingly painful death.

Their worldly power really uncovered a different kind of power, the power of God's love. There is no doubt that with his charisma, his talent with words, his popularity with the people and the support of his group of followers, Jesus could have overcome the power pitted against him and walked away free. But he didn't!

We see him accept the terrible burden placed on him and, as the drama unfolds, a different kind of power surfaces;

- the power of loyal friendship, as he admits his identity to his captors, but successfully invokes the innocence of his disciples,

- the power of self-assurance, as he claims his authority for his mission to his accusers,

- the power of silence, as he steadfastly refuses to debate with those who oppose him,

- the power of obedience to God, as he accepts the inevitability of his death,

- the power of courage, as he refuses to cry out against his pain,

- the power of care, as he entrusts his sobbing mother to a loyal disciple,

- the power of love, as he hangs on the cross and asks God to forgive those responsible for his death,

- the power of hope, as he ends his life with the words "It is finished", not meaning defeated, not meaning over, not meaning mission impossible, but mission accomplished.

*There is no longer Jew nor Greek, there is no longer
slave or free, there is no longer male and female; for all
of you are one in Christ Jesus.*

Galatians 3: 28

I was asked by a young couple to marry them. The bride had been a server in my former parish; the groom had no childhood church connection. They were living together and had bought a house in a new community, which was 100 kilometres from where we were living. Both were university grads with good jobs, a very likable and sensible couple. Her parents were old friends who lived 100 kilometres in the other direction and supported the marriage. The couple had worshipped a few times in a local parish, and the priest was agreeable that I marry them. They participated in a Marriage Preparation program and I had two sessions with them.

They wanted to be married in a garden park which specialized in non-church weddings and receptions, all in the same place. Their answers as to 'Why not a church?' were the usual and honestly provided: new in the community with only a casual church connection; neither of them had been regular churchgoers for some time; most of the family and friends who would be attending were non churchgoers. Going over the marriage service, I made it clear that it would be a Christian celebration. They both said they were Christians (technically they were, because they were baptized), but admitted that for them it meant being just a good person. They agreed that many of the values they lived by could be traced back to Jesus, but that was all.

Rather than see them as wishy-washy Christians, I chose to treat them

as young people with a zest for living, and this wedding as an opportunity for them to know Jesus better.

Faith is a journey, not a destination. We are all on the same journey, and some of us have the good fortune of travelling with Jesus longer than others. 'Travelling" means walking with Jesus as our life-guide and supporter, listening to his directions, asking for advice regularly, not just at a crossroads, accepting his love with delight, and sharing it with our fellow travellers. Being the principal characters in a Christian marriage celebration is surely a spiritually important milestone in that journey. And it was.

In those days John the Baptist appeared in the wilderness of Judea, proclaiming "Repent, for the Kingdom of heaven has come near."

Matthew 3: 1

John was of the House of Aaron, the priestly class. At the age of thirty he should have taken up his duties in the Temple, but he didn't. Instead, he preached the moral standards of God, denouncing the wrong-doings of the people and their evil and sin.

Above all, he preached Repentance, using a traditional Jewish ritual of showing God's forgiveness through baptism, the washing away of sin. The people saw him as a prophet, and there had not been a prophet in Israel for four hundred years. 'Teshubah' is the word for repentance, the verb from the noun 'Shuba', meaning to turn away and turn to.

By worldly standards most of us are reasonably decent people. However, if we match ourselves against the standards of God, as preached by John and lived by Jesus, we usually fall short. Just saying sorry, even though we mean it, is not repentance. True repentance produces in us a deep sense of regret that we have broken our connection to God.

It demands an understanding that we will not be our true selves until we reconnect with God in a genuinely humble manner. Thankfully, God is always ready and eager to continue our relationship with him. Repentance starts with accepting our wrongful condition and being prepared to openly confess to the barrier we have created between us and God.

 It's not enough to say, "I've been bad today." Confession must be specific; we must name exactly what we have done wrong. Then, having humbled ourselves by admitting our estrangement from God, promising not to do it again is also not enough. We must name and accept God's standard of behaviour and agree to change ours to match his. It's a change not only of values, but also of attitude.

A change of attitude results in a change of life, of our thoughts, words and actions, in keeping with God's will for us. We turn away from our present sin, and turn to a life centered on God and not on self, and God forgives us with love and trust. That's true repentance.

*"But I say to you, Do not swear at all, either by
heaven, because it is the throne of God, or by the earth,
for it is his footstool, or by Jerusalem, for it is the city
of the great King."*

Matthew 5: 34, 35

In Federal and Provincial elections in Canada, you might go to vote
and find you are not on the Voter's List. In order to cast your ballot,
you must complete a special form, in which you officially register
all your vital statistics. Then you read out loud, from the form, an
oath, declaring that you meet the qualifications under the Elections
Act. Then you sign the form and you may vote.

At the time of Jesus, there was considerable controversy over the swearing of an oath, with the Scribes and Rabbis hotly debating the validity of
various oaths. In particular, there was much hair-splitting over the proper
interpretation of the third commandment - taking the Lord's name in vain,
and the ninth commandment – bearing false witness. Some considered a
simple "I swear" as sufficient, but many would not accept that. Others
swore "by heaven", others "by earth", some "by Jerusalem". Again, some
accepted, others did not. The result was a variety of oaths commonly in
use, most not considered binding.

Today, oaths regularly are being sworn in one form or another, as a
witness in a court of law, in signing many government forms, even in
making an insurance claim. The majority of them are accepted without
contention as to their legality. In the church we rarely demand an official oath, but what do we swear to in services of Baptism, Marriage,
Confirmation, Ordination? Is a promise different from an oath? How
binding in the Baptism service is the response, "I will, with God's help?"

Jesus took a courageous stand by dismissing the swearing of an oath.

Taking an oath to tell the truth is an
admission that you sometimes tell lies,
and that you don't tell the truth unless
compelled to do so. There is a general
loss of truthfulness in any group or
society which requires the swearing of

an oath. "My followers", says Jesus, "will at all times be completely truthful, and a simple 'yes' or 'no' is all that is necessary."

I think Jesus understood how easily words can be misinterpreted, or taken out of context, or used to stretch the truth. For Him, a yes or no answers to the truth without misunderstanding.

Jesus said to him, "Have you believed because you have seen me? blessed are those who have not seen me and yet have come to believe."

John 20: 29

T he birth of faith is not an easy matter. Although a gift from God, it springs from a human mind, which is full of doubt. It really is the birth of a new creation. To believe in the resurrection of Jesus, we don't have the disciples' advantage. The beloved disciple believed with no evidence except an empty tomb; Mary Magdalene believed because of a spoken word; two believed when Jesus broke bread at a supper; ten disciples believed because Jesus appeared to them.

But for absent Thomas, faith in a risen Lord would come only with difficulty, because so much was at stake. He needed what happened a week later. We don't know why he was not there the first time Jesus appeared. We do know he asked serious questions (John 14: 5) and that he was a man of courage (John 11: 16). His faith had been struck a serious blow with the crucifixion of his teacher and master, but he didn't run away for good, he returned to be with his disciple friends.

I find this story of Thomas very reassuring. There are many times when faith and doubts need each other. It's not a sin to have doubts. Even when our own doubts turn us away from Jesus, or we shamefully completely abandon him, as did the Apostles in those three unforgettable days.

Doubts can happen when we think Jesus has forgotten us in a particular life-situation, or when a non-believer makes life painfully embarrassing.

 Faith can be growing or faltering, strong or weak. It is not a personal decision made once, but a decision which is renewed time and time again in our life journey, a new creation which pushes deeper into a believing heart. Faith and doubts come together when we honestly accept our doubts and give them to the Lord.

Thankfully, there is no risk in our acceptance of doubt. Like a Good Shepherd, Jesus is already aware of our doubts and eager to support us with a loving response. Doubts given to Jesus result in a stronger faith. That's what he meant when he called us "blessed".

In fact, when we were with you we told you beforehand that we would suffer persecution, so it turned out, as you know.

1 Thessalonians 3: 4

Before we set out by car for Florida each year, we check the weather in Michigan, Ohio, Kentucky, Tennessee, Georgia, and Florida. We go on the Internet … not just in Toronto, but all along our route … the same on our return trip. At any other time of the year, the immediate future of the weather in these places is never looked at. Weather forecasts are only important when we need them, otherwise they are ignored.

Many of us are prone to do the same thing with God. In ordinary circumstances, we disregard him, tacitly assuming we can manage well enough on our own. In an emergency we clutch at God, because we know we need him. Even when we turn to him, we often ignore his guidance and support, taking a chance that our personal assessment of the situation hits the mark.

The Apostle Paul preached the Gospel of Jesus in many places, so going on a trip was routine for him. Yet, before he set out, he always turned to God for guidance. God was with him 24/7, as we say today. He led a God directed life, not a "please help me I'm in a crisis" life.

If we only turn to God in a crisis, we are living a 'God rescue me' life, not a 'God direct me' life. Our challenge is to move from God

rescued to God directed. That's where the Holy Spirit comes in, melding with our personal spirit to move us into a God directed life. Hopefully, along the way we will learn that God directed automatically includes God rescued.

"Abide in me as I abide in you."

John 15: 4

I n verses four to ten of the fifteenth chapter of John, the word 'abide' appears twelve times. The root of the Greek word for abide is 'meno', which means to continue in place. We seldom use abide in everyday conversation, yet Jesus overuses it in this teaching to emphasize the importance of having a meaningful relationship with him.

Abide means to 'live with', a mutual relationship between two people, in which both people experience the presence of the other. With Jesus there is a togetherness, so that the Holy Spirit can influence our lives.

We live in a world which is constantly in flux. In all of its elements there is change, so that the environment of one generation is different from that of the next. Some changes are good, some are bad, and the value of many takes time to be determined. Stability in life cannot be assumed as a given.

Responding to a myriad of worldly activities which are changing or evolving demands considerable maintenance, both in effort and attitude. To use a nautical example, your ship needs an anchor so that the changing tides do not crush it on the rocks.

My anchor is God, through Jesus, empowered by the Holy Spirit. He gives me the wisdom, the tools and the courage to cope with the changes that challenge me every day. To be the real me requires that I abide in him and he abides in me.

That's the only way that I can release the God-given gifts that provide meaning and purpose to my very existence. That's the only way that I can experience self-giving love and share it with you. That's the only way I can discern God's plan for my life and be willing and able to follow it each day.

But Jesus said, "Let the little children come to me and do not stop them, for it is to such as these that the kingdom of heaven belongs."

Matthew 19: 14

I n Macleans Magazine in March 2015 an article entitled "God is the answer", said recent research shows that "kids raised with spirituality are safer, happier and healthier in the vulnerable teen-age years."

The article claimed that spiritually connected teens are 40% less likely to abuse alcohol or other substances, 80% less likely to engage in unprotected sex and 60% less likely to suffer depression than adolescents who are not spiritually oriented. Other recent research reveals that adolescents' neurological development is as overwhelming as their bodily changes. The brain's wiring is a work in progress, so there is a surge in spiritual longing at the same time as the surge in unfamiliar hormones.

Finally, although parents play an important part, children develop their own personalities, and are not carbon copies of their parents. Assuming that the church, synagogue, temple or mosque should be involved in creating awareness of spirituality in a child, how does an Anglican parish church respond to all this?

Every parish exists within a local community. If it is to have any influence on the spiritual development of the children in its area, its members must be involved in the life of that community. Once research has been accumulated about the culture and demographics of the community, the parish's allocation of resources of time, talents and money must reflect its commitment to children's spirituality. This means more than Bible pushing, and should include at least:

- a variety of church and community activities from infancy to adulthood;

- a variety of church and community activities especially for teen-agers;

- information and activities for parents, including supportive sharing;

- the use of church facilities - free of charge.

Partnering with other groups is desirable.

He called the crowd with his disciples, and said to them, "If any want to become my followers, let them deny themselves and take up their cross and follow me."

Mark 8: 34

The story is told of a man who loved the colour yellow. He drove a yellow car, lived in a yellow house with a yellow picket fence, and grew yellow roses in his garden. Inside there was yellow everywhere -yellow walls, yellow ceiling, yellow furniture, yellow drapes and a yellow carpet. He slept in a yellow bedroom, in a yellow bed with yellow sheets, in yellow pajamas. Even the lights were yellow.

One day he became ill with yellow jaundice, and was in great distress. The family doctor came to see him and went upstairs to the bedroom. He was gone a long time. When he came down, the patient's wife anxiously asked, "Doctor, how is he?" The doctor replied, "I don't know. I can't find him."

The Christian life is not a small yellow world, a world pre-occupied with self-interest, satisfying our every needs and desires. For some folks the demand "Deny yourself ... take up your cross and follow me", is ridiculous. But for those who believe in Jesus, it's exactly the opposite. It doesn't mean you must be a puppet on a string, or that you obliterate the unique person God created you to be. Denying yourself means making God, through Jesus and the Holy Spirit, the principal motivation in your life ... the ruling passion of your thoughts, words and action ... a true reflection of God's love for you and your neighbours. When you trust and obey him, the glorious, wonderful, living you will shine forth. You will be alive in a world where there will be love in your heart, peace in your spirit, courage in your will and hope in your mind.

There would be no 'cross' if we lived in a world where everyone lived and loved like Jesus. But the powers of Satan and selfish people face us every day. We are forced to make choices, choices for Jesus or choices for the world. My 'cross' is to follow him even though it requires sacrifices, gives me distress, pain or suffering. To follow him is to be Jesus in the world … to be his eyes, ears, mouth, hands and feet … to ask each day how I can serve him … to trust him to take care of me, no matter what the day will bring. That's denying myself, taking up my cross, and following Jesus, every day, one day at a time.

"Very truly I tell you, anyone who hears my word and believes him who sent me has eternal life, and does not come under judgment, but has passed from death to life."

John 5: 24

A group in the parish was discussing the reading for the day, John 5: 24 to 29. I was astounded to hear that everyone believed that 'eternal life' was living with God after you die. Some even believed that 'everlasting life' was the same as 'eternal life'. As I understand it, everlasting life is living as it is now and lasting forever. Eternal life means living in God's Kingdom.

Ordinary life is life in the present reality – physical, mental, social, spiritual living today, a breathing human living on the earth. Life in the future, after the physical body dies, is not just the continuing existence of the soul. You are still a person, your personality exists, you are recognizable, in a state which we don't know, but which scripture assures us does exist.

The reality of our future life is as strong as the reality of our present life. The combination of two lives, the present reality and the future reality, is what Christians call eternal Life, living in God's Kingdom.

It's the whole of our existence, not just life after physical death. Eternal life means full human life, present reality and future reality, in a loving relationship with God, living in his Kingdom, realized in the physical world of present reality and the yet to come after physical death. Jesus made it clear that God's Kingdom is now, when he said, "the kingdom is within you." When it is, you are indestructible. Once you 'are', you can never cease to be.

Eternal Life can be wonderful, full of love, joy, peace, hope. That's one side of the coin. The other side of the coin is judgment at the Last Day. The judge is Jesus, as to whether we have accepted or rejected his self-giving love;

a self-generated and self-deserved reality of who we are and how we have served God in his Kingdom.

Every person can experience eternal life in both realities. Our fitness for the life to come with God in the future reality depends on the here and now. The fuller our life with Jesus now, the fuller it will be in the future.

*After this the Lord appointed seventy others and sent
them on ahead of him in pairs to every town and place
where he himself intended to go.*

Luke 10: 1

Our six grandchildren are all grown up. At a family gathering the other day, they were telling stories and laughing at some of the crazy things they used to take to school for 'Show and Tell'. Their parents chipped in with some of their own prized expressions of this much-vaunted educational procedure. The consensus was that, although it might be a good teaching tool, it was also sometimes embarrassing for them, because the other kids made fun of them.

When Jesus sent seventy 'others' into every town and place, their mission was to 'Show and Tell'. With no experience and very little training, like my young granddaughter at her first Show and Tell, they were charged with proclaiming to the people that the Kingdom of God had come near them, and to demonstrate his presence by healing them of their many ailments. They went out and returned with joy and said, "Lord, even the demons submit to us in your name."

Every Christian is one of the 'others' appointed by Jesus to bring the Good News of God's Kingdom to the people around us. It's a commission to Show and Tell by proclamation and demonstration, to help people experience Jesus. We are bound by our faith to do these two things - to spread his word and to serve his world.

If our hearts are full of God's love, then there is no big deal in the 'Show' part of Show and Tell. By our behaviour every day, people can see and experience Jesus in our caring hearts.

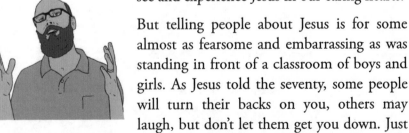

But telling people about Jesus is for some almost as fearsome and embarrassing as was standing in front of a classroom of boys and girls. As Jesus told the seventy, some people will turn their backs on you, others may laugh, but don't let them get you down. Just wipe them out of your mind and keep going.

Although love for Jesus is a personal relationship, it is not a private matter. It must be shared to grow. And who better to tell about Jesus than someone who already walks with the Lord?

Telling is simply sharing, at every opportunity and in your own words, what the love of Jesus means to you.

"By this everyone will know that you are my disciples,
if you have love for one another."

John 13: 35

When you're chatting with a group of neighbours, do you carry a sign saying "I am a Christian?" In the place where you work, are you wearing a pin declaring, "I love Jesus"? Is the cross around your neck covered by a shirt or a blouse? How do people around you know that you're a Christian, a follower of Jesus?

Time was running out for Jesus. The religious establishment was determined to arrange his defeat, imprisonment and even death. The Lord needed something to solidify three years with his disciples, and he didn't present them with a badge, or a pin, or a T-shirt announcing "Jesus is Lord".

He gave them a way of life. "I give you a new commandment, that you love one another, just as I have loved you. By this everyone will know you are my disciples." He didn't take each one of the twelve aside and privately say this. He gave them this commandment as a group.

The commandment to love your neighbour had been around for a long time (Leviticus 19: 18). What made this a new commandment were the words Jesus added, "Just as I have loved you." Jesus had shown his disciples a real 'love your neighbour', one which they had never before experienced.

It was not an idea from scripture you could memorize. It was a lifestyle to be practiced, a way to behave, day in and day out, among themselves

and with the world around them. When they lived that way, it would be the badge by which others could know they were his disciples.

Today, 'love' is a popular marketing and high profit word, like the scantily clad woman who says "I love my new Honda". That kind of love is designed to make *you* feel good inside. Everything points to you.

'Jesus love' is the opposite. It first points to God, then to your neighbour, and finally to yourself. It works in progression – you must love God before you can love your neighbour, and you can't really love yourself until you have loved the first two.

We have gifts that differ, according to the grace
given us;

Romans 12: 6

Brian was a twenty year old engineering student at McGill University. He met Karen who was studying nursing at Royal Victoria Hospital. On a ski weekend Karen hit some ice and fractured her skull, ending up in the Montreal Neurological Institute, comatose, with a grim prognosis of never regaining consciousness.

Her parents and sister lived in Sherbrooke, 150 kilometres away, and could seldom be with her. She was alone, unconscious, with only a few fellow nursing students able to visit her once in a while.

But Brian came whenever he could. Between lectures, study and a part-time job, he was there, sitting beside her, telling her about his day. He played the guitar and sang softly to her.

For two months Karen lay with no response. Then, one day as he was leaving, her eyelids flickered. The next visit, her eyes blinked momentarily. He kept visiting, talking and singing, and slowly, day-by-day, helped by the doctors and nurses, she became more responsive, moving fingers and toes, then hands, legs and arms.

At the end of term, Brian left for a summer job and Karen was given special therapy. In the Fall he was back at McGill and she was able to study nursing part-time. They became good friends, but never really dated.

After graduation, Brian moved to Australia, got married and had two little girls. Karen also married, had a son and was a nursing supervisor in Halifax. They kept up their friendship with letters.

Brian's parents had divorced when he was twelve. He lived with his mother and sister in Montreal. His father moved to Calgary. Before he entered McGill, his mother remarried and moved to England with his sister. He was alone, except for a few friends at his church, friends who understood his pain and really supported him.

He began to know Jesus, experiencing His love in his life. It was that love he shared as he visited an unresponsive Karen, that and his love of music. These two gifts from the Lord were the beginning of healing for Karen.

"A new heart I will give you; and a new spirit I will put within you; and I will remove from your body the heart of stone and give you a heart of flesh."

Ezekiel 36: 26

T he word heart appears in scripture hundreds of times, so it is important to understand its meaning in Biblical terms. It is not just the seat of sentimental life, from which we get such words as heartbroken and heartfelt, nor is it simply an organ in the body which pumps blood.

In its fullest Biblical meaning, both Jewish and Christian, it is the source of all physical, mental, emotional, social, spiritual and moral values and energies. From this heart arise needs, wishes, impulses, desires, moods and conscious feelings. The heart is also the centre of reason, imagination and understanding. Finally, it is the foundation of the will - it considers, plans and makes decisions.

If you are a Jew of Bible times, your heart is the core of your personal life. It determines your personality. It is not only the place where God dwells, but also the place where Satan directs his fiercest attacks. When you sin, for the moment, God is missing from your heart.

It is also the place of prayer. The prayer of your heart springs from the core of your being and thus guides the whole of your life as a human personality.

Read Psalm 91 and listen to these words. God is speaking to your heart. "I will deliver you ... I will protect you ... I will answer you ... I will rescue you ... I will show you my salvation ... and all I ask is that you know me and love me."

It is the Lord speaking to you and to me, intimately, in the language of love, going beyond the mantle of power and protection, passionately showing his care for us, personally and collectively.

We are his people, not just a bunch of unconnected individuals. We can feel the compassion of a God who never stops loving us. He stirs a fire in our hearts, an intense and powerful energy that is the foundation of who we are - what we say and what we do.

A certain woman named Lydia, a worshipper of God, was listening to us; she was from the city of Thyatira and a dealer in purple cloth. The Lord opened her heart to listen eagerly to what was said by Paul.

Acts 16: 14

I n this passage from the book of Acts, St. Paul is speaking to a group of women about Jesus. Among the group is Lydia, a business woman from Philippi. We hear these words, "The Lord opened her heart to receive Paul's message". Who is this woman whose heart was opened? She was wealthy, and lived in Thyatira outside Philippi, where she managed a purple-dye trade. There was no synagogue in the area, because there were few people of the Jewish faith. Nevertheless, they met regularly for prayer at a spot on the bank of the Little Ganges river. Along with Silas and Timothy, Paul went there to tell the women about Jesus.

Lydia was not Jewish, but she had a loose connection to the faith. We don't know why she was there that day, but God opened her heart to Jesus and she and her whole household were baptized. She offered the hospitality of her home to Paul and his party. On the way there, Paul had a heated argument with the owners of a fortune-telling slave girl. Taken to the magistrates, Paul and the others were flogged and thrown in jail.

That night an earthquake released the prisoners. Paul stopped the jailer  from committing suicide, and he was then baptized with his whole family. Next day the magistrates begged them to leave town and they accepted Lydia's hospitality. They spent many days there, teaching and encouraging the small group of new Jesus believers. After their departure, the group continued to meet at Lydia's home. It was to this small Christian community that Paul wrote his Letter to the Philippians.

God was at work during this whole story, sending Paul to Philippi, having Lydia among the women praying, opening her heart to Paul's message, offering hospitality to the visitors, the altercation with the slave girl, the imprisonment of Paul's party, the earthquake, the freedom of the prisoners, the baptism of the jailer, the release by the magistrates, Lydia's hospitality, the birth of a Christian community, and finally, Paul's letter to them. All because God opened the heart of one woman!

Then Jesus took the loaves, and when he had given
thanks, he distributed them to those who were seated;
so also the fish, as much as they wanted.

John 6: 11

The event has many names … a Pot Luck Dinner … a Carry-In Dinner … a Covered Dish Dinner. A group of people want to have fellowship together and they choose a meal as the method. There's no host or hostess. Everyone brings something to share. Regardless of the number of people involved, even if some of them arrive empty-handed, there's never a shortage of food. In fact, there's often food left over.

Every time I attend one of these shared meals, I'm reminded of the Biblical story of the Feeding of the Five Thousand. As usual, whenever Jesus was present, there was a crowd. He had become quite popular, and on this particular day, the crowd was huge. All four Gospels recount 5,000 men, not counting women and children.

After many hours of teaching and healing, people were hungry. A small boy offered his meagre lunch to share and a blessing from Jesus resulted in everyone having enough to eat. The hunger need was satisfied. What's more, there was food left over. Sharing and a miracle were bound together.

Whenever we share, someone's need is satisfied. It may be our food, our money, our material possessions, our time, our skills. Our sharing creates a miracle in someone's life. Sometimes it's a small miracle, sometimes a big one, but always a miracle of some kind.

Your package of Kraft Dinner will fill a child's stomach. Your muscle power and a lawnmower will cut an elderly neighbour's lawn. Your call to a homebound widower will brighten his day. Opening your parish hall with beds will keep a family from winter's freezing cold. Conversation with a teen-ager at a Pot Luck Supper may open

her heart to the joys of meeting Jesus through sharing the bread and the wine at Holy Communion.

Miracles of all kinds happen when Jesus is around.

As God's chosen ones, holy and beloved, clothe your-
selves with compassion, kindness, humility, meekness
and patience.

Colossians 3: 12

Webster's Dictionary describes compassion as "an act of mercy". Including its derivatives (like compassionate), it appears in the Bible ninety-six times. Most of us would agree that we seldom, if ever, use compassionate in everyday writing or conversation.

In Scripture, compassion primarily refers to God's relationship with his people, a people who are usually in rebellion against him. Yet it is number one on St. Paul's admonition to the Colossians about our treatment of each other. He puts together a characteristic of God and a much desired trait of behaviour as essential in all human relationships, to God and to each other.

There's an element of judgment in the compassion of God, a tempering of justice and mercy which overlooks the constant disobedience of the crown of his creation. He cares for us so much that he's always prepared to forgive our transgressions, even when there's no real repentance.

It seems to me that human compassion is expected to go beyond that. It is supposed to remove the element of judgment in our relationships, because judgment can come only from God.

Compassion is an intrinsic part of our human nature, the ability to truly care about those with whom we share a common journey. This means every person on the earth, not just those immediately around us. Through compassion we can think, speak and act with kindness of heart and gentleness of will in any relationship with another, even if we don't like that person.

It's a special gift from a loving and compassionate God that pushes us to deal with each other in ways which are always to the building up of the other person.

I will cleanse them from all the guilt of their sin against me, and I will forgive all the guilt of their sin and rebellion against me.

Jeremiah 33: 8

Tennis is a sport I really enjoy. I loved to play it but finally had to stop because of wonky knees and arthritic fingers. I have watched the top pros of past and present play, folks like Jimmy Connors, Pete Sampras, Roger Federer, Martina Navratilova, Serena Williams and many more. Their skill and their athleticism astound me. But mostly I admire their courage – they never quit. Even when they are faced with three or four match points, they still keep coming at you.

'Just keep coming at you' is a summary in scripture of God's dealings with his people.

- Adam and Eve lost their innocence, and God gave them clothes.

- People were selfish, but God gave them a second chance through Noah.

- God made a covenant with Abraham to make his people a most blessed nation, and the people broke the covenant.

- God renewed the covenant by delivering the people from slavery in Egypt. God gave them Ten Commandments to live by, and the people disobeyed them.

- When Jerusalem and the Temple were destroyed and the people exiled to Babylon, God still didn't quit.

- Generation after generation disregarded the ten basic rules, so God gave them more specific rules they could understand.

- God sent prophets to bring them to their senses when they went astray.

A small group of elites, responsible for the people's spiritual life, became puffed up with pride. God said, "Enough! I will come myself and live with them, so they will know who I am."

And Jesus of Nazareth helped people understand that faith is not just a set of rules. Each one of us is directly responsible for accepting God's gift of love, and enabled through Jesus and the Holy Spirit to experience a loving relationship with him.

All through history, century after century, God has not only forgiven our wickedness, but has forgotten it. No matter how far we stray, how often we turn our backs on him, he never stops forgiving, never stops loving, just keeps coming at us.

"If you continue in my word, you are truly my disciples, and you will know the truth, and the truth will set you free."

John 8: 32

I was invited to preach at the United Church in Scugog, Ontario. It was a special service celebrating paying off the mortgage on their parish hall. They had a big banner hanging up which said "Free of Debt."

By the time of Jesus, the Jews knew something about freedom; freedom from hunger, freedom from slavery, freedom from exile, freedom from political occupation, all freedoms they once had but had no longer.

What does FREEDOM mean to a group of people in a Christian church today? Freedom is a two-sided coin; on one side there is 'freedom from', on the other side there is 'freedom to'.

Here are a few 'freedom froms' that we must face:

- freedom from the slavery of fear – membership declining, shaky finances

- freedom from the slavery of pride – believing that ours is the only and better way

- freedom from the slavery of arrogance – which stubbornly worships habit and tradition and resists change

- freedom from the slavery of prejudice – which looks down on people who are different

- freedom from the slavery of greed – focusing on what the church can do for you, instead of what you can do for the world outside

- freedom from the slavery of guilt - knowing our mission has not been one which has built up God's Kingdom

- freedom from the slavery of the world - which constantly promotes its values and expectations against those of the Lord

- freedom from the slavery of apathy – of not actively participating in the life and mission of the church

- freedom from the slavery of self-interest – making the church a place where ambition and desire for power defeat the purpose of a loving fellowship

- freedom from the slavery of sin – by allowing Satan and the evil powers of the world to successfully push forward any and all of the above.

"I am the vine, you are the branches. Those who abide in me and I in them bear much fruit because apart from me you can do nothing."

John 15: 51

A part from me, you can do nothing. What a claim to make! The portrait of the vineyard, with God as the gardener, Jesus as the vine, and we as the branches, is a clear teaching of how to be a true disciple of the Lord. In the last "Word", I focused on the negative dimensions of freedom, those aspects of church life which deny real freedom to its people.

God the gardener prunes away the 'freedoms from' so that through the Jesus vine, the branches have the freedom to be the church God intended it to be.

Here are some of the 'freedoms to' that we can build on:

- freedom to believe there is no risk in loving Jesus, nothing to be afraid of

- freedom to hear the word of God without worldly distractions

- freedom to learn more about God's purpose for the church and its members

- freedom to experience worship in ways that nurture our faith

- freedom to have a faith which supports and guides our daily life

- freedom to change the darkness of a hurting world into the light of Jesus

- freedom to develop a fellowship built on a foundation of love

- freedom to speak out against anything or anyone that oppresses someone

- freedom to respond to the need to change in a creative and positive way

- freedom to use all our resources of time, talents, money to serve the Lord

- freedom to have the courage to let the Holy Spirit direct our lives

- freedom to present to the world a fellowship of love, peace and joy

- freedom to help others build up their sense of dignity and self-worth

- freedom to express our feelings and opinions without danger of recrimination

- freedom to share our resources with anyone in need

- freedom to accept our failures and move ahead with the Lord

- freedom to love each other as Jesus loves us

- freedom to be fully alive as God created us to be.

***In that city there was a widow who kept coming to him
and saying "Grant me justice against my opponent."***

Luke 18: 3

From our sixth floor balcony, we can see the raccoons romp in from the adjacent forest with their little ones, foraging in the large garbage bins. It reminds me of a time when we visited our friends Dave and Eileen at their summer cottage. One evening we sat in the porch and watched a raccoon calmly lift the lid of a garbage can, tear open a plastic bag and start eating. Dave chased her away. Five minutes later she was back eating. Dave chased her, closed the lid and tied it with some string. Back came the raccoon. Within minutes the string was chewed through, the lid was off, and the eating recommenced. Chased away again. Dave finally locked the garbage can in the shed. The raccoon left.

Jesus tells the story of a widow who pleaded with a judge to hear her case, a civil case involving money. Judges were given considerable freedom in scheduling. They were not well paid, so perhaps he was hoping for a payment under the table. The only weapon the widow had was persistence, and the judge finally gave in.

"God is not like this judge", says Jesus. "He is a righteous judge, champion of the needy and the powerless. He listens to our pleas and takes action."

That's where prayer comes in. Prayer doesn't start with me. It has already been started by God. From the moment of my birth he has been telling me he loves me. If I haven't answered, it's because I haven't listened. I can communicate with you through e-mail, text, or leave a message on your answering machine, but I can't have a conversation with you unless it's face-to-face or on the phone.

God has a permanent line into my life. All I have to do is answer when he calls – person-to-person. When I do, he's listening and inviting me into his circle of love. And within that circle we can have a conversation, because a conversation requires a relationship.

Like the raccoon and the widow, God is persistent. He doesn't stop loving me and he doesn't stop calling me. He listens to my prayers and he always has an answer. It may not be the answer I want, but his answer is always the right one for me.

The wicked draw the sword and bend their bows to bring down the poor and needy, to kill those who walk uprightly;

Psalm 37: 14

Modern day ships, especially submarines, have a variety of defensive mechanisms against an incoming torpedo or missile. One common method is to release a cloud of particles which, through sound or heat, deflect the projectile from its target. This cloud is called 'chaff'.

Our faith in God is constantly bombarded with torpedoes and missiles of a different kind. They have the same explosive force and can destroy our faith. They come from every direction and in many forms and strengths. Sometimes their presence is self-evident; other times they sneak up on us, hidden and unheralded.

Their sources are the wiles of Satan, and/or the behaviour of evil and wicked people. The bullets they shoot can be very powerful and easily recognizable. But there are more insidious missiles, small ones which don't seem to hurt, but can build up over time to weaken or destroy our faith without our even knowing it.

Whatever its source, however it's released, and whatever its form and strength, we need defensive mechanisms to eliminate its threat, some 'chaff' to destroy it before it reaches its target.

- The first chaff is to accept the reality of evil in the world, be aware when it attacks you, and respond with the defenses God gives you.

- The second chaff is not to be afraid, to trust in the Lord to give you the necessary preventive measures.

- The third chaff is to look to Jesus, who had more destructive missiles thrown at him than we'll ever have, and who walks with us every day.

- The fourth chaff is through prayer to obey the guidance of the Holy Spirit as he empowers our spirit to act.

- The fifth chaff is to nurture our faith through Scripture, worship, and service.

- The final chaff is to remember we are not alone; that we share our common faith with many others, and we can be mutually supportive in the battle of faith.

I will sing a new song to you, O God; upon a ten-stringed harp, I will play to you.

Psalm 144: 9

The Psalmist had it right! You can 'Praise the Lord' in many ways, but the most spirit-strengthening method is through music, particularly congregational singing. This includes voice and instrument, and voice only, the emphasis being on togetherness rather than soloism. As a priest and Interim Pastor for over 30 years, here are some axioms which are crucial to any church's liturgical experience.

- Much of our worship focuses on individual worship - listening to scripture, preaching, prayer. Group singing builds fellowship.

- Through a careful selection of hymns and songs, the words being sung further enhance the theme or principal message of the day.

- The emphasis should be on participation. If fewer than half the worshippers are raising their voices, then there is no real togetherness.

- The age, gender, size and cultural background of the congregation must be reflected in the songs to be sung. Old favourites and new Praise songs suit different groups.

- The use of instrumental accompaniment also determines the content and style of singing – organ, keyboard, piano, rhythm band, orchestra.

- The function of a choir is to lead congregational singing. Choir anthems deepen the worship theme and assure their competence to lead singing.

- The opening song brings the people together, the closing song lifts them up with joy as they go out to serve the Lord in the world.

- Some songs are better sung by soloists
  – e.g. O Holy Night.

- The Choir Director must be involved in the selection of hymns with the Pastor.

- Hymn Books are no longer essential. Hymns can come from a variety of sources. When licensed, printed words or a large screen are alternatives.

- New words to familiar tunes bring a new delight to singing. A completely new song can best be introduced by the choir as an anthem.

- Worshippers are strengthened in body, mind and spirit when they come together as a group to share in the joy of praising the Lord in song.

"But I say to you that listen, love your enemies, do good to those who hate you,"

Luke 6: 27

The Bible gave the Jews 613 rules to live by, most of them "do-nots". Centuries of rabbis gave them a vast array of interpretations of the 613. By the time of Jesus, many of their supposed spiritual leaders were arrogantly failing to meet their responsibilities to the people. In addition, they lived in an enemy-occupied nation. So the Jews had much to hate. Then Jesus told them, "Love your enemies, do good to those who hate you." The crowd would have every reason to laugh and shout "That's impossible."

Jesus was not saying, "Don't do rotten things to other people." He was demanding that we consciously and actively do good things to other people.

For him, love was not a single emotion. The love for parents and children is different than the passionate love marriage partners experience, or the affection we have for our closest friends. Jesus does not expect us to have any of these 'love' feelings for people we don't like, disagree with us, or hurt us. The love that Jesus is describing is Agape. It is an active and determined effort not to judge, not to retaliate when hurt, not to strike back when anger is hurled at you, not to be deterred by abuse, hatred, sneakiness, false accusations, not to label people as bad because they are different, not to consciously calculate results or possible rewards in any relationship.

He's also not talking about behaving sensibly and courteously to people we like. There's nothing special about that. No matter how badly people treat us, insult us, lie about us, say mean things about us, Agape commands us to keep all bitterness, jealousy, resentment, anger and envy out of our relationships with others.

Through experience, we all learn that we can't live by Agape based on our own efforts.

We need Jesus power, which comes to us through the Holy Spirit and enables us to take his self-giving love and share it with others. Only Agape can open our hearts to forgive those who hurt us, hold us back from judging others, prevent us from harbouring a grudge, stop us from requiring retribution when suffering an unnecessary loss.

To express it simply, Agape means that in any relationship I will give of myself without wanting, expecting, or asking for anything in return.

That's Agape! That's love! That's the Jesus way!

Wait for the Lord; be strong, and let your heart take courage, wait for the Lord.

Psalm 27: 14

For our cat Misty, waiting is not an acceptable dimension in her life. In the morning, she wants to eat her breakfast at the same time as we do – any delay results in a constant barrage of loud meows. When she wants to go out into the lanai, she moves back and forth between the door and where we are, with the odd little meow to get our attention. A tradition in her world demands a treat every afternoon – when her time clock says now, she sits forlornly at our feet, occasionally putting a paw on one of our knees. For Misty, life is full of anticipation, always fulfilled. Waiting is not acceptable!

Many folks today are waiting; waiting for the monthly cheque from the government so they can buy food; waiting for the doctor's report on the tests they've just taken; waiting for the phone call to tell them they got the job they applied for; waiting for the results of the exam they've just written; waiting in line in the cold for the bus that's late.

In every case there is anticipation, but also apprehension. Unlike Misty's, their anticipation is not always fulfilled, and there is disappointment and sometimes even despair.

But apprehension can be eliminated. If you have faith and trust in a loving God there is no risk, no fear, and disappointment can be softened. There have been many anticipations in my life, and many disappointments, but the Lord has always taken care of me.

Waiting is often inevitable. My family and friends would unhesitatingly agree that I can be very impatient at times, but seldom is there any real apprehension. Despite instant coffee and 'scratch and win', there are few instant solutions to what we need or desire in life, so I have learned to live one day at a time with the Lord. With faith I live with patience, peacefully, without any fear or stress, remembering

that God has done more waiting and is infinitely more patient that I could ever be.

Misty's world depends on me. My world depends on God.

So faith by itself, if it has no works, is dead.

James 2: 17

T he 'Sisters of Mercy' are a religious community dedicated to acts of charity, particularly to those who are unable to fend for themselves. To use the imagery of drowning, they don't shout out instructions of how to swim or what to do. They dive right in and help the drowning person to the safety of the shore.

All around us are people in need, real need, not just a minor thing like a cut finger. It's our mission to go wherever people are lonely, homeless, poor, suffering, disadvantaged in any way. The Holy Spirit gives us the courage not to sit idly by, just giving them something to temporarily ease the pain of their condition.

The call is to remove the cause of their condition as soon as possible. We can only do that if we walk with them in their suffering and rely on the Holy Spirit to give us insights and understanding to recognize the systemic structure and elements that give rise to their condition. In co-operation with other groups and individuals, we can analyze the situation, determine what's really wrong, and do what needs to be done to correct it.

To change any systemic structure which creates disadvantaged and second class citizens requires access to the corridors of power, including the acquisition and use of it. That requires not only understanding how political power works, but the courage to risk getting involved. Unfortunately many of us are reluctant to take that step, partly because of our inexperience, but also because of our fear of being defeated.

Once again, we need to trust the Holy Spirit. By melding the Spirit of God with our own personal spirit, we will have the courage, the wisdom and the power to walk with those in need and become not only Brothers and Sisters in Christ but Brothers and Sisters of Mercy.

*"For to those who have, more will be given, and they
will have an abundance; but for those who have
nothing, even what they have will be taken away."*

Matthew 13: 12

Instinctively, I don't like these words. They seem to make it fine for the rich to get richer, and for the poor to be absolute paupers. But this saying has nothing to do with the economics of today, when 1% of the people own over 30% of the world's wealth, and the other 99% fight for the rest. It's about faith and trust in the Lord.

There were two groups listening to Jesus. The Scribes and Pharisees heard, "You are supposed to be the spiritual leaders of the people, but you are so engrossed in your own status that you are unable to help others in their relationship with God." The ordinary folk heard, "Open your hearts and minds to God. Stop being so lazy about your faith that you relegate it to just a few hours a week."

For us today, there's a similar challenge.

- If you use the gifts God gives, your life will be fuller.

- If you fail to use those gifts, your life will lack meaning and purpose.

- The more you use them, the stronger and more meaningful they will be.

- If God gives you a particular talent, and you neglect it, you will lose it.

- If you have a particular talent from God, even though you use it, you must not let it grow stale, but keep learning how to use it more effectively to serve the Lord.

  - Each time you give in to temptation, it is harder to resist it the next time.

- Every act of self-discipline you exert in responding to the mission of serving God will make you better able to serve him in the future.

- Every time you turn your back on an opportunity to serve the Lord makes you less likely to grasp the moment in the future.

- Every time you open yourself to Jesus, you will experience the joy of his love, and the more you do it, the greater the joy.

- The more you forget about Jesus, the less able you will be to accept his invitation the next time it's offered.

- Strength and courage build a mountain of love and peace. Fear and weakness will dig a ditch of stress and misery.

Afterward Moses and Aaron went to Pharaoh and said, "Thus says the Lord, the God of Israel, 'Let my people go, so that they may celebrate a festival to me in the wilderness'."

Exodus 5: 1

P haraoh, the ruler of Egypt, held the Jews in captivity. Their work as slaves gave him freedom. God had to use a lot of persuasion, but finally the enslaved Jews were set free and started on a journey to their promised land. They were excited, because they were full of optimism for the future, eager to have their freedom result in a new life.

But their hearts and minds needed clarity and certainty about this new life, a clear picture, not only of today, but of tomorrow . And for them tomorrow was not far distant.

Wandering around in the desert, relying on God for sustenance, was not their idea of freedom. So God tried to help them understand a few facts about freedom. He gave them Ten Commandments, the first four dealing with their relationship to him, the latter six dealing with their moral responsibilities to each other.

It was God's way of showing them what real freedom was all about. Unfortunately, their response was negative, and it took them a long time to get to the promised land.

Today, freedom is on people's minds. Governments engage in war to bring freedom to people in other parts of the world. In our country there is a constant debate about freedom.

 On the one hand, our law in Canada, with our Charter of Rights, gives us freedom. Then we enact laws that limit our freedom; we can't murder, steal, cheat, tell lies about others. There are thousands of laws which restrict our freedom, but where do you draw the line between 'freedom' and 'you can't do that'?

God gave the Jews his Ten Commandments, a simple message about true freedom. Most Prayer Books list them somewhere ...maybe we should recite them together more often.

Let us come into his presence with thanksgiving; let us make a joyful noise to him with songs of praise.

Psalm 95: 2

A lady went in to Second Cup Coffee Shop, bought a cup of coffee, sat down at a table for two and prepared to eat some cookies from a bag in her purse. The shop was crowded and a man sat down in the other chair with his cup of coffee.

The lady began reading her newspaper and took a cookie from the bag. The man also took a cookie from the bag. Even though upset, she ignored it and kept reading

She took another cookie. And so did he. Visibly annoyed, she glared at him. He took the last cookie, smiled and offered her half of it. Angrily indignant, she got up, left her coffee and stormed out of the shop in a huff. A few minutes later, reaching in her purse to take out her monthly pass to get on the bus, to her distress she found her bag of cookies.

We can easily fall into the trap of being like the lady with the cookies. I can say that whatever success I've had in life has taken a lot of time, energy and hard work on my part over many years.

With a career, a home, good income, loving wife and children, I've got it made. With continuing effort, it can get even better. I may have had some great opportunities and some help from others along the way, but my reality is that the result was primarily due to my own efforts.

If I forget, even for a moment, the true reality, that God is the foundation of my life, guiding and supporting me every day, then I'll really be just like the lady with her cookies, in a bag, in a purse. Unless I open the purse, take out the bag and let God in, my cookies will grow stale, moldy and useless.

Without God, my life, whatever its seeming success, will be worthless. Only with God can my life have any real meaning. The lady didn't think of sharing; the man did. Whose cookies were better?

> *"Peace I leave with you, my peace I give to you, I do not give to you as the world gives. Do not let your hearts be troubled, do not let them be afraid."*
>
> *John 14: 27*

Half way through most services of Communion we participate in the 'Passing of the Peace.' We greet each other with the words, "The Peace of the Lord be with you. This not saying "hello" or "Have a great day". It's something much more. St. Paul described peace as 'passing all understanding', but that doesn't really answer the question. If you are going to pass the peace, surely you must have some sense of what you're doing.

First of all, I'm passing something to you, and you are giving it back to me. Neither of us can give it unless we already possess it. When Jesus gave it to his disciples, they had some understanding of what he meant.

For three years, wherever he went, there were large crowds, demanding more stories, teaching, healing, casting out of demons. At every town there were people to challenge him, using any tricks to make him say or do something which would get rid of him.

Through it all he was able to maintain his inner serenity. This 'peace' was a spiritual gift which came from his quiet times of prayer. When they embraced this gift, it changed their lives.

If we embrace it, it will change our lives - a change which removes whatever troubles our hearts, drives out whatever makes us afraid, helps us accept the things we really can't change, gives us the courage to change the things we can change and the wisdom to know the difference. It teaches us to count our blessings and give our failures to God .

We will be satisfied with our possessions, making the most of them and never envying our neighbours. We will not only trust God, but trust each other. We will show kindness of heart and gentleness of words and actions to everyone, even when we disagree with them. We will be sensitive to each others needs, and respond to them with genuine love and care.

To possess this 'peace' is to have the Holy Spirit give us the courage, wisdom and power to live in God's Kingdom. So, from me to you, "The Peace of the Lord be with you."

They departed and went through the villages, bringing the good news and curing diseases everywhere.

Luke 9: 6

In my younger days, just out of university and working for the YMCA, I coached a children's swim team and two basketball teams. The swim team had a good time and so did the two basketball teams, and they both won the Y city championship.

I was not a super coach but I had some teen-age boys who loved to go to the gym and shoot some hoops. This was our first team, so melding them into a group that would play together was the real challenge.

There were no stand-out stars on either team, so concentration on fundamentals was essential.

That meant PRACTICE, drill after drill of both individual and team skills – dribbling, shooting, passing, blocking, three times a week for an hour, together, learning to be a team. During practice time, they learned that each team member had some special ability, and using their skills together built the teamwork essential to winning.

Sometimes a good long shooter was needed, sometimes driving to the basket for a lay-up was the key in a game. That meant one player being supported by the rest of the team.

Learning to do that I call PREPARATION. Lastly, games had to be played, which required each player to commit to an all-out effort from start to final whistle.

I call that PERFORMANCE, giving one hundred percent at all times.

A parish church or fellowship is like a team. Practice means learning what is required of a disciple of Jesus – study, prayer, worship, proclamation and demonstration, individually and collectively; how to do the deeds and tell the story of God's love and care for each one of us.

Preparation demands a sharing of faith, time and talent so that each member can make a meaningful contribution to the building up of God's Kingdom. Performance means going out to serve the Lord in the world as members of God's team.

Who's the coach? Jesus, through the Holy Spirit, travelling with us through practice, preparation and performance, supporting and guiding us in every situation. We are the "Jesus Team". We may lose some games, but we'll always win the championship.

He sat down, called the twelve, and said to them,
"Whoever wants to be first, must be last of all, and
servant of all."

Mark 9: 35

People are always debating who was the "greatest" - the greatest Prime Minister (Mike Pearson or Pierre Trudeau), the greatest hockey player (Howie Morenz or Wayne Gretzky), the greatest modern opera (Godspell or Jesus Christ Superstar), the greatest movie (Gone With The Wind or Citizen Kane). I'm sure your choices will be different than mine.

Jesus overheard his disciples arguing about who was the greatest among them. Since each one had a specific responsibility as a member of the team, their evaluation probably included not only the job, but how well it was performed. That happens today in most parish churches, particularly when it comes to the liturgy or the common worship service; old Prayer Book or New Prayer Book, King James Bible or the New International Version, common prayer or Holy Communion, scripture readings or prayers of the people, hymns or preaching, organ or praise band.

Jesus chided his disciples for thinking about their self-interest instead of their mission to proclaim the Gospel. I came across this list, which describes a disciple as a true servant of God:

- A true servant never tries to control or dominate others.

- A true servant does not seek to win favours from others.

- A true servant doesn't seek any form of recognition and discourages it being offered.

- A true servant never forces his service on someone who doesn't want it.

- A true servant does not let the values of the world decide who needs help, because no one is excluded from the Lord's loving care.

- A true servant never sets conditions for help to be given.

- A true servant does not help others in order to get something from them.

- A true servant never criticizes those in need, even if it's self-inflicted.

- A true servant reaches out with understanding, love and care.

Being a true servant is both a blessing and a celebration – a blessing from God and a celebration of life.

For you yourselves know very well that the Day of the Lord will come like a thief in the night.

1 Thessalonians 5: 2

We all know what it's like to have to wait, and it frustrates us. I once took a flight from Toronto to Houston. It was an international flight, so I had to be there three hours ahead of time. Then I began the wait in line system; to go through security, to pass customs, to be accepted by immigration, to check my baggage, to register my ticket, to get my boarding pass. In the meantime, after that was all over, I waited, had a coffee, read a book, talked to a friend, or just sat there.

The early Christians believed that the final Day of Judgment, the Day of the Lord, was going to happen soon, within their lifetime. They were concerned that their brothers and sisters who had already died would miss out on the great event. Not only did St. Paul reassure them, he also exhorted them to be strong in the faith in the meantime.

Today's Christians live 'in the meantime'. The Kingdom of God is here now, but it's not fully realized. In the meantime, we live each day in the truth of our memory and the certainty of our hope. We remember and learn from our own past, we hope for a future expectation, which is life eternal with Jesus. The 'meantime' is the present, suspended between our memory and our hope.

And to a large degree, our realization of future hope depends on what we do at the present moment, in the meantime. We must be careful not to be stuck in the past, or wallowing in dreams of what the future might hold. Living in the meantime is not just biding time. It demands preparation, sensitivity to any opportunities, and readiness to act.

We walk with Jesus every day, not because it may become our last, but because we want to. Yesterday's love-sharing experiences influence today and are part and parcel of tomorrow.

The Kingdom which is coming is also here now, a kingdom of love, caring and sharing. So we live in this wonder-filled kingdom, walking with Jesus, one day at a time, as though the future is already ours.

"The earth produces of itself, first the stalk, then the head, then the full grain in the head."

Mark 4: 28

The other day I saw on television what is called 'time-lapse photography'. It took the whole process from seed to a cob of corn, and reduced it to a few seconds. The effect on my mind was incredible. Beauty was instantaneous. I couldn't wait for it to be in my hands, ripened, cooked, and smothered with butter, ready to eat.

From planting to harvest, growth is a process which takes time. Assisting that growth is a farmer, who can't make the seeds grow. All he can do is plant the seeds properly; in good soil, yes, but he can't create the good soil. He can fertilize it, but he can't create the fertilizer; nor can he create the sun and the rain that's essential for growth.

In fact, neither he, nor we, can create anything. We can uncover, we can discover, we can re-arrange, we can add or subtract, we can even manufacture, but we can't create. The corn seed that was planted had a built-in life-form – a life form which, under favorable conditions of soil, light and water, would make it grow. There's a design and an energy in the seed which cannot be denied. Growth is irresistible, inevitable, regular and constant.

Just as the farmer can't create the plant, we can't create the Kingdom of God. We can only experience it, as God leads and guides us. Just as the corn seed has a life force built in which makes growth possible, we have a life force built in us – a life force which contains the design and the energy to make us grow the way God intended.

All we have to do is connect our spirit to that life force – the life force we call the Holy Spirit.

"Make yourself an ark of cypress wood, make rooms in
the ark, and cover it inside and outside with pitch."

Genesis 6: 14

Whether Noah and his family were real living persons or a legend based on historical fact doesn't really matter to me. Noah is one of my favourite Biblical characters. We don't know much about him. Scripture calls him righteous, blameless, and he walked with God. Of his shipbuilding experience, there's nothing, of his carpentry skills, no indication. Yet God chose Noah and gave him a set of instructions about building a huge boat, an order to which no man in his right mind would pay attention. But Noah obeyed God and followed his commandments.

Thousands of years later Jesus was chosen by God. At his baptism by John in the river Jordan, God said to Jesus, "You are my son in whom I am well pleased", an announcement that he was indeed chosen by God. Three years later, Jesus selected Peter as the leader of his church. He too was chosen by God.

Paul was on the road to Damascus, where he had a commission to persecute the members of the new Christian group. Jesus appeared to him and chose him to be an apostle and tell the Gospel story to the Gentiles.

Each one of us, when we were baptized, was chosen by God. Even if that event took place when we were infants, someone (parents, grandparents, uncle, aunt, friend) was moved by God to present us for baptism. We were chosen.

Noah was an ordinary man, chosen by God. Against all the odds, he followed God's will and built an ark. Mission impossible – accomplished. Peter and Paul, notwithstanding persecution by both Jews and Romans, against all the odds, followed God's will and built a church. Mission impossible – accomplished.

Whatever God chooses us to do, despite our perception that it's against all the odds, if we obey him, mission impossible will be mission accomplished.

A great windstorm arose, and the waves beat into the boat, so that the boat was already being swamped.

Mark 4: 37

Just north of Toronto is 'cottage country', with dozens of lakes, around which people have built their own summer cottages. On a sunny day in July, boaters, fishermen and water skiers enjoy the clear blue waters. And then, with little warning, a storm moves in, forcing everyone to scurry for shore.

Lake Galilee is like that. The wind can funnel down the valley and hit the water with incredible force. So this Gospel story in Mark is for real. The disciples are in a boat crossing the lake when a treacherous storm hits. Everyone is frightened, even experienced fishermen like Peter and Andrew.

Except Jesus. He's sleeping. They wake him up, he drives out their fears and calms the storm. He asks them, "Why are you afraid? Have you no faith?"

So often, when the hectic pace of life wears us out, our faith goes to sleep and fear takes over. Fear can be generated by a myriad of circumstances - failure, rejection, change, insecurity, helplessness, oppression, loss of job.

Since the beginning God has told his people, "Do not be afraid". Yet century after century fear has continued to rear its ugly head. Fear can whip a group or even a nation into a shattered lump, as the people of Israel had experienced many times.

Then Jesus came to destroy fear and replace it with love and trust. Through Jesus and the Holy Spirit, the fellowship of the Apostles, who had hidden in fear during the crucifixion, learned not to be afraid, to trust the God who loved them, and to work to bring others within that circle of love.

As the apostles of today, any parish or group of Christians can keep their faith alive, overcoming any fears by the assurance that if you walk with Jesus, there is no risk, nothing to be afraid of.

When that happens, hearts are touched, faith is nurtured, hope is fostered, intentions are formed, commitments are honoured, gifts are uncovered and used, relationships are celebrated, joy is rampant, forgiveness is asked and given.

When people look at such a group, they see love, peace, joy and hope, a glimpse of God's Kingdom the way it was meant to be, people who are not afraid, but in love.

He was praying in a certain place, and after he had finished, one of the disciples said to him, "Lord, teach us to pray, as John taught his disciples."

Luke 11: 1

She was very ill, in Cardiac ICU, with a tube of oxygen in her nose and machines measuring heart rate, blood pressure, breathing, struggling with her eyes closed. I anointed her, prayed for her, and then began the Lord's Prayer.

After a few words, she suddenly joined me, slowly but surely, only missing a word or two when her breath wouldn't come. Together we finished with the Amen. Her eyes were open and there was a faint smile on her face. I could see that the 'peace of the Lord' was with her.

I've had that happen many times in hospitals when I say the Lord's Prayer, and every time I'm filled with wonder and joy at what it does for people in despair. Most of these folks were older. They knew the Lord's Prayer by heart because they had learned it and prayed it from an early age.

In my experience, at least half of the younger people don't know the Lord's Prayer. In fact, they don't know how to pray at all. But in a crisis, most of them want to ask something of God, and then I can help them to pray.

Commonly, I ask them to repeat after me and we go through the Lord's Prayer phrase by phrase. Occasionally I turn to it in my Prayer book or on a card and we say it together.

With family or friends in a hospital waiting room, the same applies. Whatever the situation, saying the Lord's Prayer acts as a springboard for other prayers, for healing, or courage, or just a simple blessing.

It's helpful to remind people that this is a prayer that Jesus taught his disciples 2000 years ago and that it has brought peace and hope to millions of people since then. What a wonderful gift from God is the 'Jesus Prayer'.

"A poor woman came and put in two small copper coins, which are worth a penny."

Mark 12: 42

Having spent thirty years in business before I was called to the priesthood, I am comfortable talking about money. And we use weekly envelopes to support whichever parish church I'm serving.

But I'm still surprised and hurt when people say, "Every time the church gets in touch with me there's a request for money involved." They even say this about special envelopes included in Easter, Thanksgiving and Christmas greetings.

How does a priest respond to this? There are two approaches in my answer. Both are reasonable and sensible.

First, there's the practical response. Like everything else, having a parish church costs money. Very few have substantial Endowment Funds given by former members.

So the only regular source of income is the voluntary donation by those who participate in worship and other activities. Folks who are regular participants are responsible for most of these donations. Those who come for special occasions need reminders that bills have to be paid.

Second, there's the Stewardship approach, which doesn't focus on bills to be paid, but on sharing the gifts God has given us. Here the message is both theological and inspirational. Everything we have is a gift from God .

As part of God's circle of love in a parish fellowship, we proportionately share our time, talents and treasures so that the mission of the fellowship can be accomplished. The sharing of financial resources will vary according to each member's circumstances. Real stewardship mandates that such offerings should come from the top of your income and not from what's left over after what you have already spent on your personal living.

At the time of Jesus, taxes and tithing were one bundle, with a tithe varying according to what was being tithed. (10% was only one measure) Most people in our world pay over 10% of their income in taxes to provide a basic safety net for everyone. My personal belief and practice is that a minimum modern tithe is 5% of your total income after taxes.

And he cured many who were sick with various diseases, and cast out many demons; and he would not permit the demons to speak, because they knew him.

Mark 1: 34

A healing ministry is wonderful for the persons who are healed, but it is physically and mentally exhausting for the healer. Jesus has spent the whole day and part of the evening with people who don't care for him. They have only come to the house in Capernaum because they want something from him – an affliction cured.

Finally, exhausted, he can do no more. He needs to get away from the crowds, so he goes to a 'lonely place' early the next morning, to pray and to be close to the heart of God, to be refreshed and rejuvenated, because more crowds will be there tomorrow and tomorrow.

We all need a 'lonely place' at various times in our lives; a place where there are no voices demanding our time; a place where peace and quiet will help us rediscover the inner rhythm we need to live abundantly. The word used for lonely place is HERAMOS, and it is not a placid retreat.

Heramos is more like a wilderness, private, but alive with the presence of God, where you can come to grips with what is most urgent about life, what is important about yourself and your relationship with God and others. It is a holy place, where God's will is made clear, and where his challenge to obedience is most demanding.

But Heramos is also a dangerous place, where your own needs and desires are sharply highlighted, and the temptation to do your own thing is most powerful. So obedience and temptation collide, and your mind becomes a battleground.

Obedience is the winner when we really pray, when we are truly connected to God. If necessary, we repeat over and over again whatever words or phrases we have learned will help us focus on God and his will for us. When Jesus went to a 'lonely place' to pray, obedience always triumphed over temptation.

You visit the earth and water it, you greatly enrich it;
the river of God is full of water; you provide the people
with grain, for so you have prepared it.

Psalm 65: 9

We are blessed with living next door to a Conservation Area. Primarily wooded, a substantial number of its mature trees had to be removed recently, partly because of a severe ice storm, and partly because of a bug called the Emerald Ash Borer.

Fortunately, among what is left are a few groups of stately pine trees. They have managed to persevere through changing seasons, regularly harsh weather, pestilence and human encroachment. Every year cones drop from their branches to the ground to begin their participation in the cycle of life.

Some may lie dormant and rot until they fertilize the soil. Some are picked up by people and used for crafting of various kinds. But a few respond to the gifts of rain, sun and wind, the gifts of life itself. They open themselves to share the gifts they have received.

The seeds are released to sink into the earth, and new pine trees ultimately spring forth. They become part of a new generation, part of a built-in chain of blessing which allows them to fulfill their destiny according to God's plan of creation.

As the crown of creation, we too have a destiny to follow. Ours is a two-fold mandate.

The first is essentially practical. God has entrusted us with the responsibility of being the caretakers of all of his creation; taking care to ensure that the 'cones' of every living being are treasured so they can fulfill their destiny from generation to generation. 'Living' includes all plants and creatures, and the environment in which they can flourish.

The second element in our mandate is also practical. As the people of God we are charged with spreading the Good News of Jesus, so that the seeds of God's love and care will germinate into the next generation.

Through us, wherever we are, individually and together as a group, the Kingdom of God will not only be sustained, but grow in quantity and in quality.

And he appointed twelve, whom he also named as apostles, to be with him and to be sent out to proclaim his message.

Mark 3: 14

In my earlier days, I played a lot of sports, Some of them were individual focused – tennis and swimming. Others were team focused – hockey, fastball, soccer, basketball and water polo. In all of these, a place to play and some level of individual skill were needed. But in the latter, the co-operative skills developed through teamwork were of crucial importance.

When I look at the three year ministry of Jesus, I see the group, the team, as his chosen way. It took time, effort and patience. He started with just twelve, and through his continuing gift of the Holy Spirit, there are over three billion today who profess the belief that "Jesus is Lord".

Whether we worship in a church or in some other fellowship form, the real value of our worship is togetherness. For a short period of time, we focus all of our spiritual energy into one concentrated experience of praise, prayer and *learning* with the God whose name is love. As the people of God together, *learning* to live and love each other as followers of Jesus, we demonstrate the presence of a better way of life.

Our common life together can be a powerful witness to God's love and his vision for his creation. It is a witness not only of personal faith but collective love. If I'm not present when our fellowship meets in Jesus' name, I'm missed. God misses me and you miss me. No one can take my place. My absence means that you can't nurture my faith. I can't nurture your faith.

We are a loving fellowship but also a *learning* fellowship. *Learning* to have a more intimate relationship with God; *learning* to accept each other despite differences of age, gender, background, culture, spiritual growth; *learning* how to share our faith experiences; *learning* how to care for the needs of every

person in our fellowship; *learning* to strengthen the faith of each member; *learning* to discover each others' special gifts and how to use them in the life of our fellowship; *learning* to love each other as Jesus loves us.

As God's chosen people, we are called to witness to the joy of living, learning and loving in God's Kingdom, together.

"This is my commandment, that you love one another as I have loved you."

John 15: 12

One of the joyful responsibilities given to a parish priest is to help couples prepare for marriage. Not just to talk about the wedding, but about what it means to be married. A wedding is a few hours – a marriage is a lifetime.

Statistics show that the chance of success in a marriage is increased by 75% if there is proper preparation before the wedding. Proper preparation means much more than talking about love and how they feel about each other with the couple.

We all have a basic human need to belong, to have a close, caring and intimate relationship with a significant other person. This is a need rooted in our very nature – for warmth, understanding, loyalty, affection and trust. To meet that need is the real objective of proper marriage preparation.

Such a relationship is built on more than the sex drive. It demands sharing what makes us who we are, explaining our life experiences openly and honestly. Family background, ethnic and cultural environment, ethical and moral values, critical points of difference, hopes and dreams for the future, health, financial attitudes, all have a bearing on the development of a caring and trusting relationship between two people.

Marriage Preparation helps a couple build a foundation for a long-term togetherness in which each helps the other to become the person God created them to be. It gives two people 'in love' a healthy start to a journey like no other, a lifetime commitment focusing on your mate and not yourself.

The love that Jesus commanded was 'Agape', giving of yourself without thinking of any benefit that might result for you. It's taking a natural liking for someone, and doing something special with it.

'Jesus love' is a *doing* love, being present with your mate no matter what, caring for her needs even at a cost to your own needs or desires.

"Again, the Kingdom of God is like a merchant in search of fine pearls. On finding one of great value, he went and sold all that he had and bought it."

Matthew 13: 45,46

The other day I had to go downtown in Toronto for a meeting. That meant a bus and subway using transit tickets, which I could buy at the local convenience store. A couple ahead of me were buying lottery tickets. Scratch, win another ticket. Scratch, no winner, buy another ticket. Scratch, win another ticket. And so on for ten minutes. Finally, they left. I bought my tickets, missed my bus and had to wait fifteen minutes for the next one.

I don't buy lottery tickets, or a 50/50 draw, but I do play cards for recreation. I play to win because there's a little surge of adrenalin when you see that winning score. For lottery winners there's much more, a vision of getting a treasure that will change your life.

It doesn't surprise me that Jesus told a couple of stories about a treasure. It would help his audience understand his message. One treasure was found by luck, the other the result of a deliberate search. Both men sold everything they had to obtain the treasure they desired, because they recognized its value.

The treasure of Jesus' message was the Kingdom of God, where love of God and love of neighbour rule supreme. We can have it not just in the afterlife when we die, but in the life of today, while we live. It's a world in which we can think, speak and act as God intended us to be, instead of being creatures of our own needs and desires; a world in which self-giving defeats self-taking. This treasure is a gift freely offered, a treasure that cannot be surpassed. You don't have to buy a ticket or wait until a series of numbers is drawn to be a winner.

A lottery can't give a guarantee; the odds are more than a million to one. Just accept God's invitation to become part of his Kingdom, and you'll be an instant winner, a real winner absolutely guaranteed; a payoff which lasts for life eternally; no hoping, no waiting, no disappointment at losing. Instead you'll experience real excitement, real joy, because you've hit the jackpot and it's filled with love.

"For where your treasure is, there your heart will be also."

Luke 12: 34

The disposition of an estate often brings out the worst in people. I've heard the angry statement, "Mother said I was to have her diamond ring" more than once in my ministry.

A man asked Jesus to make his brother share his inheritance with him. Jesus' answer was to tell a story about a wealthy landowner who has enjoyed a very large harvest. He is so self-centred that he talks to himself, and decides to tear down his barns, build bigger ones, and live a pleasure-filled life. He forgets that he has neighbours and workers with whom he could share his good fortune. He forgets that we are remembered by who we are and not by how much wealth we own. He forgets God. Then he dies, and "you can't take it with you."

There are two basic principles here to help us live the Jesus way; how we get our material possessions and what we do with them. The landowner did not create his wealth. He got it from the land, the sun, the rain and the seeds which grew into a bumper crop. All of that came from God.

The tenants or slaves who worked his land were of no consequence to him. He was the successful owner of the whole enterprise, not the caretaker commissioned by God to manage his creation for everyone's benefit. He was self-absorbed, self-seeking and self-fulfilled. At no point did he give thanks to God for his blessings. *Can we hold up our work to God, giving thanks for the joy of being his manager?*

The second principle asks, "What are you doing with the results of your material-producing efforts?" The landowner didn't share, he hoarded. His personal greed ignored other people's needs. Willful, selfish and uncaring, the only thing that crossed his mind was his own pleasure. Unfortunately, as an old Spanish

proverb says, "There are no pockets in a shroud." The only possessions of any real value are those that death cannot take away.

In Colossians 3, St. Paul shares one of his lists with us ... humility, kindness, gentleness, patience, forbearance, forgiveness, harmony, generosity, gratitude, peace, love, acceptance, thankfulness. *At our death, will we have produced riches for self or riches for God?*

So then you are no longer strangers and aliens, but you are citizens with the saints, and are also members of the household of God,

Ephesians 2: 19

When St. Paul talked about the household of God, he was referring to the church; not to the thousands of people who believed in Jesus, but to the faithful in each local community ... like the folks who worship every Sunday in the many parishes I have served. None of those parishes are fewer than 50 years old and a few have been there for over 150 years.

We give thanks for the many thousands of people in the past who worked to build a household of faith in their corner of Canada and the United States. For them, Jesus was not only a cornerstone but also a living presence. They were the 'living stones' who tried to serve the Lord every day, and they gave us an incredible heritage.

As living stones, we are charged with continuing to serve the Lord in our local communities. We can treat the past simply as history, here today and gone tomorrow, which will make the church a household of amnesia.

Or we can treasure our heritage, making it a household of remembrance, using the same foundation of Jesus and his living presence for whatever ministry the Lord directs us to pursue. Such a ministry may be different than what we are presently doing.

Regardless of its form or style, it will continue to provide nurture, support and guidance to each of its worshippers, so that they may live an abundant life within the circle of God's love.

On a Friday two thousand years ago. Jesus gave us his life for us so that we could really be God's people. On the following Sunday, he changed 'could' to 'will'. He guaranteed that, as resurrection people, if we continue to be guided by the Holy Spirit, our household of today and our household of tomorrow will surely be households of God.

But a woman whose little daughter had an unclean
spirit immediately heard about him, and she came and
bowed down at his feet .

Mark 7: 25

Jesus was tired. He needed a rest away from the crowds. So he journeyed outside the Galilee area, hopefully incognito. But it was not to be. His quiet time was interrupted by a woman not of the Jewish faith, who pleaded for help for her grievously ill daughter.

And we have this wonderful dialogue between our Lord and the woman, capped by the healing of her daughter.

What strikes me about this Gospel story is the essential humanity of Jesus. He was exhausted, worn out by the never-ending demands of the crowds – more stories, more healings, more miracles. His energy and his capacity for active living have been overwhelmed by the cries of the needs of so many.

Today we might call it 'drowning in stress', when you desperately must have solitude - no pressure, no deadlines, just a little peace and quiet. For Jesus, that also meant time with God. Yet even prayer seemed impossible.

When someone cried out for help for a child, Jesus couldn't turn away. His initial response was refusal, his ministry was only for the Jews, so "leave me alone". Although the Jews often referred to Gentiles as wild dogs, Jesus put a twist in his comments, by using the word to describe household pet dogs. I can see him speaking with a smile and a sparkle in his eyes.

 Her rebuttal was equally sharp, but not argumentative, saying that even those dogs eat the crumbs under the children's table, the obvious intention being that even a Gentile could hope for an answer to her simple request. Jesus accepted her light humour and told her to go home and be with her daughter, who was now healed.

Clearly we are made to understand that reaching out to someone in need is at the core of Jesus' humanity, and each one of us, as brothers and sisters in Christ, is directed to do the same. Bringing God's love and compassion to others is inclusive, not exclusive.

Arise, shine, for your light has come, and the glory of the Lord has risen upon you.

Isaiah 60: 1

Thus here was a time when I looked forward to the beginning of a new day with excitement and joy. Note that I said the beginning. I still believe that 'this is the day that the Lord has made' and that I should make every effort to serve him as he directs me.

But it's the dread of that first five minutes that prevents me from leaping out of the bed with an exuberant "good morning". Because of my DNA or 90+ years of hard use, or a combination of both, I suffer from lower back sciatica. The lack of movement for seven to eight hours in bed responds with a huge "ouch" when nerves and muscles are made to get moving.

As soon as I go from immobility to mobility, the pain registers 7 to 8 on a scale of 1 to 10. Doctors help me manage the pain (to use their words) through pills and injections, and I'm grateful for their treatment. But those first five minutes!

Fortunately, the Lord who created the new day also created me, and gives me, as part of my creation, the ability to work through the pain of those first five minutes. His treatment is activity – to move, to walk around the house and do a few simple exercises. The pain gradually subsides.

After breakfast and a longer walk, I'm energized to follow whatever God has in mind for me today. Later in the day, I repeat some of the exercises in order to continue managing my sciatica. The really wonderful thing is that I know for a certainty what God has taught me to do, and it works.

So I can live life in all its glorious abundance, each day, one day at a time.

*I will give thanks to the Lord with my whole heart; I
will tell all of your wonderful deeds.*

Psalm 9: 1

Recently I had an appointment with the specialist doctor who is
overseeing my acute pulmonary embolism. After six months of
a combination of rest and exercise, the results of the blood tests,
ultra-sound and CT scan were in.

Alleluia! Praise the Lord! No blood clots! Both the leg and the lungs
are clear! No more blood thinner! No more struggling to put on hip-
length compression stockings! Just be careful when you're flying or on
a long trip.

Some folks will say "Why Praise the Lord? What's that got to do with
God?" My reply is "everything"! The creative endeavors needed to
develop blood tests, make ultra-sound equipment, and manufacture
a huge, complicated CT Scan machine are all gifts of God to certain
individuals. So are the skills required to interpret the results and mold
them into a diagnosis. All are God-given gifts. And my thanks go out
to all of them and their partners in the health professions.

Above all, the Lord who knows my name, and holds me in the palm of
his hands, once again has shown how much he loves and cares for me.
How can I not shout "Praise the Lord "?

Yet, once my exuberance is exhausted, I'm faced with the inevitable
challenge of responding to this special blessing. Giving thanks cannot
be a one-time thing. It surely has to result in God-centred words and
Spirit-directed actions.

I have been given a new lease on life. Now I
have to use it to love and serve God each day
in the world. Not necessarily in the way I've
been doing up to now in limited measure.
Perhaps in a new way. I will leave the continuing path of my ministry up to him

спасибо
GRACIAS 谢谢
THANK YOU
ありがとうございました MERCI
DANKE धन्यवाद
أ شکرا OBRIGADO

*The end of the matter; all has been heard. Fear God
and keep his commandments; for that is the whole duty
of everyone.*

Ecclesiastes 12: 13

Whether this was written by Solomon or is just a collection of his thoughts does`n't really matter. This ending to the book of Ecclesiastes is a very clear direction to the people of Israel.

When I heard this in confirmation class at St. Columba Church in Montreal, I was not only confused but also bothered. Fear God? Why should I be afraid of him? Everything I had learned in Sunday School was about love. Love God, Love your neighbour. Love your family. Do good to those who hate you. Turn the other cheek. I had found it hard to always follow these commands, but they were certainly targets I had to strive for.

Anyway, I didn't really know God, so why should I be afraid of him? I know I could be punished for doing something wrong, but the punishments came from my parents, not from God. When I was afraid of something or someone, my fear was that I would be hurt in some way, physically or mentally. How can God do that? Or so went the mind of a 14-year-old.

Now, 78 years later, I still don't fear God. I now know him a little bit through his man/son Jesus of Nazareth. He was the true example of human love, giving of yourself to others, not asking for anything in return except your love for him.

Yes, I'm in absolute awe of God. He is the one who orchestrated my creation. I'm in wonder at his power. I'm amazed by his patience. I'm astounded by his wisdom. And I'm still trying to get my mind around the fact that He really does love me. Despite all my imperfections and doubts, the Lord of all creation cares about me! What could I possibly be afraid of? His power? His omnipotence?

I understand that the Jews to whom Solomon's pearls of wisdom were directed in Ecclesiastes were 'before Jesus'. They only had the Ten Commandments and the 613 other precepts set down by Moses. To them God was an enforcer, not a lover.

Praise God, it is different now. Jesus is Lord! Hallelujah! Hallelujah for love.

We have gifts that differ according to the grace given
to us: prophecy, in proportion to faith; ministry, in
ministering; the teacher, in teaching;

Romans 12: 6, 7

I visited Annie yesterday, Although her name is Anne, she likes to be called Annie. She lives four blocks from her parish church. Without a car, she walks to church on Sunday. She also walks six blocks to the plaza to do her shopping. People have offered her rides, but she says "I accept them only when I really need them." Not bad for an 88 year old.

She lives in the home she and her husband bought sixty years ago. He went to the Lord eight years ago and she still misses him. Even though they couldn't have children, they had 53 great years together. Annie says her Eddie was the better one of their partnership - gentle, caring and friendly with everyone. I find this hard to accept, because that's a perfect description of Annie herself. Soft spoken, with a welcoming smile for whomever she meets.

Why did I visit Annie? Because she's the historian and archivist for her parish, which recently had its fiftieth anniversary, and I'm their Interim Pastor.

Annie was there from the beginning, and has been active throughout; the gift of land in a new community; the struggle to build a team of interested prospective members; the patience to persuade the Bishop that a church was really needed; the arrival of their first priest-in-charge; Sunday worship in the new community school; getting enough offerings and committed givers to build a church with a big mortgage.

For each year she has at least one or two albums of their parish life …

bulletins, photos, letters, news articles. She took some of the pictures herself, but mostly relied on fellow parishioners.

This is Annie's special ministry. There were times when she wanted someone else to take over, but "God kept telling me He needed me to keep going." Now, with the new technology, her mission is to find someone who will digitalize all her work and then carry on.

Thank God for Annie. Thank God for all the many Annies and Eddies in churches all around the world.

And he appointed twelve, whom he also named apostles, to be with him, and to be sent out to proclaim the message.

Mark 3: 14

The Canadian Women's Senior Basketball team won gold at the 2015 PanAm games, and repeated their victory in the FIBA Americas Olympic qualifying tournament for Rio 2016. Spectators at their games were thrilled at the energy and enthusiasm of the Canadians. Twelve women, ranging in age from 17 to 30, some veterans of international play, some neophytes.

What astounded the pundits was the way they came together as a team; not the usual two or three stars who dominated play, but literally twelve stars working as a well-oiled machine.

No one sat on the bench for the whole game, every player contributed to the final result, no one hogged the limelight, but all supported each other. And they were graced with a coach who built an outstanding team by focusing on the unique talents of each player and binding them together as a whole.

Jesus selected a team, calling twelve men to follow him to disciple-ship in its fullest sense, entering into a common life and fellowship, exchanging their earthly jobs for a higher one, the opportunity to share in Jesus' mission. He coached them through three years of training.

Some say they were slow learners, but with one exception, who was replaced by a worthy substitute, and a last minute addition, their subsequent activities were extremely successful. Their team experience fostered dynamic personal ministries.

A parish church is like a Jesus-selected team, some young, some old, some experienced, some newcomers. All are assured of the same disciple-fellowship that the original twelve had, with the same mission and the same coach, but without his earthly physical presence.

Membership requires faith, and faith demands personal participation, real loyalty, commitment and involvement in the team as an active player of the people of God. The coach is listened to through his Holy Spirit associate.

No one sits on the bench for the whole game. Each one's talents are developed and supported by the rest. There's leadership and it's shared, with no selfish stars. As long as the mission is foremost and each ministry contributes to its goals, a gold medal is a sure thing.

Now there are varieties of gifts but the same Spirit;
and there are varieties of service, but the same Lord,

I Corinthians 12: 4

O ver the past two plus decades since my official retirement, it has been my privilege to serve as an Interim Pastor in twenty-two parishes covering twenty six congregations in the Anglican Diocese of Toronto. To make a list of all the leaders, workers, visitors, teachers, caregivers and helpers would be impossible. Their faith and commitment are the glue that holds a particular Christian fellowship together. But there are some special gifts of personal ministry that I remember:

- Every week she bakes a loaf of bread for the parish Eucharist.

- A major renovation was undertaken using multiple contractors, and he served as the Project Manager, bringing it in on time and on budget.

- She delivers altar flowers to shut-ins with warmth and peace.

- The parking lot was small and the church had unused land which was restricted, being in the flood plain. Patiently she worked through the politics and secured an exception to expand the parking lot.

- The men in a parish woodworking shop converted an unused pulpit into a much used lectern.

- She manages a centuries-old cemetery and chapel-of-ease.

- She researched and settled a land claim against the rectory.

- A small group of women provide a hot meal to the disadvantaged in the community.

  - He keeps the grass cut around the church and rectory.

  - They have a baby shower for the shelter for unwed mothers.

  - He leads an Advent tree of winter clothing for needy families.

- She makes Teddy Bears for an aid charity helping overseas families.

- He makes wooden crosses with leather lanyards for the area prison chaplain.

- For 25 years she has carried on a volunteer caring and chaplaincy ministry in the local nursing home.

- She is a volunteer 'den mother' for the children's area of a local hospital, and the parish regularly provides gifts and toys.

The wonder of these ministries (and dozens more) is that in each case there was a need to which someone in a parish responded without fanfare. They are not only hearers but doers of the word.

"Blessed rather are those who hear the word of God and obey it!"

Luke 11: 28

I participated in the funeral service of a friend, using the Book of Common Prayer. I say 'funeral' because she would never have countenanced the use of some of the modern descriptions, Memorial Service, Celebration of life, etc. In fact, since it included Holy Communion, it could have been called a Requiem Mass.

Her name is Hilda, and she died halfway through her 106th year. To paraphrase Romans 8, Hilda believed and lived that "nothing in all creation could separate her from the love of God through Christ." Without a doubt she is now in the room that her beloved Jesus had prepared for her. (John 14: 2).

Hilda was a worshipping member of St. George's Anglican Church in New Hamburg, Ontario, a town of about 9,000, a parish I was honoured to serve for eight wonderful years. She was a childless widow, comfortably well-off, who had lived in the community for most of her adult life. A devout Christian who actively supported her church and community in every way possible, the image she portrayed was that of a stately, grey-haired lady, a 'grande dame, une femme formidable'

She was strong willed but never overbearing, very proud of her church, community and country but never arrogant, didn't suffer fools gladly but never made them lose face, expressed herself positively but always listened carefully to other opinions. When you got to know her, as I did, she was a warm, approachable, soft-spoken and gentle person, who consciously tried to live her life the Jesus way. Every day.

As her pastor, I shared with her both successes and failures. We grieved together over the death of a close friend, held conflicting loyalties, often had disagreements but never with hostility or anger, and stood side by side against apathy or opposition to Christian faith and practice. No pastor could ever have a more supportive and loving member of our shared church fellowship. Hilda was a good and true friend.

Making your ear attentive to wisdom, and inclining your heart to understanding.

Proverbs 2: 2

T oday I can hear! Really hear! I never realized how much I was missing when people spoke, but both my ears are now recipients of hearing aids. I was told I had had hearing difficulties for many decades, but had compensated by listening more intently.

I was astounded at the patience and skill of my audiologist and his technician. They spent hours determining the exact extent of my hearing loss. They took the test results and a mould of my inner ears and ordered tailor-made aids from a specialty manufacturer.

When the aids were delivered, there was more testing and fine tuning, using computers with special programs, delicate hand-drilling and polishing, followed by training in care and usage. Now they're in my ears and I can hear the world as it really is. Years of straining to listen and missing too much of a conversation, presentation or sermon are over for me. Thank God for the creative invention and human skill and wisdom which has made this possible.

Perhaps the Proverb writer suffered from hearing loss, because he brought ear and heart together, combining wisdom and understanding. It's not hard to hear the voice of God, because you can do it without ears. 'Hearing' is a passive mode. 'Listening' requires opening a channel between the mind and a spirit-filled heart, so that understanding can grow into wisdom.

Experience tells me that this hearing/ listening/ understanding/ wisdom process happens because the time, patience, skill and wisdom of God is transferred with love to the people with whom I have shared life's journey. Hours, months and years of testing and fine-tuning by the Spirit melding with my spirit have gone into helping me trying to live the Jesus way. My

hearing is given aids so that I can learn to listen to the mind of God and so shape my own thoughts, words and actions.

Unfortunately, like my physical hearing, I don't always use those aids, and so I miss out on most of the messages Jesus is sending my way. But when I do use them, my unique hearing and my love-filled listening merge to serve the Lord in the world around me.

And he took them up in his arms, laid his hands on them, and blessed them.

Mark 10: 16

E stablished practice in Ontario is that children are allowed to be absent from school classes on Ash Wednesday and All Saints day, provided they attend a religious program and show authorization when they return to school.

I have planned and carried out a number of programs for these special days. Some have been half-days; some have been full days. Some have been single parish programs; others have involved multi-parishes working together. Most have been Anglican only, but two were co-operative ventures with a local Lutheran parish.

From experience, I favour multi-parish activities, because sharing the cost and equipment means better resources, additional adult leadership, more children, so you can program by age group, more facilities to choose from and greater enthusiasm from parents and parish leaders.

You also have a broader constituency to which promotional materials can be sent, greater commitment and work, because nobody wants to 'let down the side', wider recognition of the program in the local community, more and better ideas for activities from a larger group of leaders and volunteers. Multi-parish programs often involve congregations with different cultural backgrounds, so bringing children together for group activities is an added plus.

Although these programs are intended for parish children, they provide a wonderful opportunity for missionary work when parish children are encouraged to invite friends who have no perceived church connection.

The Lord demands that we serve the world in his name, and expects us to use every opportunity, not only to strengthen the faith of our children, but to spread his love beyond the boundaries of our parishes.

*Then the word of the Lord came to Jonah the second
time saying, "Get up, go to Nineveh, that great city,
and proclaim to it the message that I tell you."*

Jonah 3: 2

Jonah was a prophet who lived in the eighth Century BCE. He
was directed by God to go to Nineveh and publicly denounce
their wickedness. Nineveh was the capital of Assyria, a brutally
militaristic three centuries old nation. He refused to make the trip, and
instead tried to hide from God by taking a ship to Tardish.

A great storm arose, the crew blamed Jonah and threw him overboard,
where he was swallowed by a great fish. In the belly of the fish, he
repented to God and received forgiveness. Three days later, he was
spewed out from the fish. He went to Nineveh, and his cries against
them resulted in a penitent nation.

Biblical commentaries interpret and explain this story in many different ways. For me, it is a clear and positive example of God's loving
concern for each one of us, even when we flagrantly disobey him and/
or turn our backs on him. I call it a 'second chance' story.

Most of us have done things our way instead of God's way, and have
repented and received his forgiveness. In my years in ministry, I have
met a few who could be classed as 'Jonah disobeyers'. Their activities
were blatantly wrong, in fact so severe that the perpetrators were in the
depths of despair, tantamount to being swallowed by a great fish.

They were weighed down by guilt, lives stressed out, feeling isolated in
darkness. God touched them, and from the depths they rose up and
admitted their transgressions. Forgiveness was immediately given.

The lifting of the burden of shame opened new channels to God's love

and care, and joyful opportunities to
serve the Lord. Their second chance
was a gift that could not be, and was
not, ever forgotten.

So also the tongue is a small member; yet it boasts of great exploits.

James 3: 5

I was in the airport in Calgary, waiting to board a flight, the final step in a cross-Canada tour of all-day workshops introducing a new product for my employer. There was an announcement over the PA system about meeting someone at the news stand in the concourse. I thought my name was mentioned. Paying attention when the announcement was repeated, I heard "Would Roy Shepherd please meet me at the news stand in the concourse?" Thinking I had left something in the conference room where the workshop had been held, I hurried over in anticipation.

Standing at the entrance was a smartly dressed man in his early thirties, whom I vaguely recognized. He shook my hand and introduced himself. Fifteen years prior I had been in Halifax, employed as Boys and Girls Director for the YMCA, and he was the president of the Hi-Y club in the local high school.

As a sixteen year old, he was having difficulties at home and in his school studies. On a number of occasions I had one-on-one discussions with him, listening to his woes and trying to bring sensible approaches from my own knowledge and experience.

He was flying to Winnipeg and I was going to Vancouver, We shared a coffee and small talk before our flights were called. Finally he told me that our few private conversations had been a very important influence in his life. When he saw me in the airport, he wanted to meet me and show his appreciation for taking an interest in a muddled-up teen-ager.

I tell the story of this happenstance meeting because it illustrates how our sometimes brief relationships can have a powerful effect on someone else's life without our even knowing it. Sometimes even a simple remark can have far-reaching consequences of which we are unaware. Hopefully for the

better, but we all know that an 'off-the-cuff' comment can also hurt someone's feelings. In the heat of the moment, our tongues can run away from our hearts and our spirits are somehow not in sync with the Holy Spirit.

Let us pray that the Spirit guides us daily in our thoughts, words and actions, because the Spirit knows the difference between delight and despair.

So just as the body without the Spirit is dead, so faith without works is dead.

James 2: 26

I t's September 2015. There's an election underway for Canadians to elect their local Member of Parliament and ultimately their Prime Minister. Does a pastor in a church, synagogue or mosque have a responsibility to participate in moulding the future of the country? Or does the concept of separation of church and state keep them out of it?

No one would deny pastors, rabbis or imams the right to participate in political activities as individual citizens. But their status as leaders in their local religious fellowship puts them in the position of having more influence on the political process than its ordinary members. In many instances, their influence spreads to the whole neighbourhood and even to the broader community.

It would certainly not be appropriate within a community's worship experience to preach a sermon promoting a particular political party. But if there is an issue involving injustice, poverty, corruption, there should be no impediment to speaking out, providing comments have a scriptural base. This can and should be done at any time and it should extend beyond the congregation into the community and the nation. Comments on an issue may seem to favour a certain political party, in which case a simple disclaimer should be noted. When higher church authorities take a public stand on an issue, as many do, they should be locally supported.

Apart from the obvious responsibility to promote member voting in every election, a pastor can, and I believe should, actively participate in political activities, not just during election time, or over a particular issue, but all the time, and should motivate his or her people to do the same. Inevitably this will result in allegiance to a particular political position and sometimes becoming a party member.

Some parishioners may complain, as mine did when I placed a party sign on the Rectory lawn. I held to my conviction and suggested that they take positive steps to promote a different viewpoint. Jesus' teachings were often opposed to the Scribes, Pharisees, Sadducees, Herodians, and Romans, and he did not waiver in pronouncing them.

And he said, "Let anyone with ears to hear, listen."

Mark 4: 9

The parables told by Jesus were 'teachings'. Over a three year period, thousands heard them. Yet, according to scripture, only about a hundred and twenty of his hearers became his followers, and only one whom he healed actually followed him. It's fair to assume that there were others who believed in his message of God's Kingdom and his love, but chose not to actively demonstrate their belief. Today's pundits would say, "all in all, not a very successful ministry".

Over the centuries there have been many speculations as to why he often chose to frame his teachings in parables. Here are a few:

- By telling real-life stories he could better attract a crowd.

- There was safety in story telling – the religious establishment could not accuse him of blasphemy.

- His charisma was best portrayed by his superb story-telling skills.

- They were a challenge to his inner circle of disciples to probe deeply into their spiritual messages.

- He was training his disciples through demonstration how to reach people about God's Kingdom of love.

- He was staying away from the traditional rabbinical style, with its complex system of referrals and minute theological themes.

- People liked to listen to good stories, especially about real life.

Perhaps some of these reasons apply, but I believe there was a deeper understanding of his people and their needs in the mind of Jesus. He knew that the Kingdom of God was a very precious gift, offered with love to every individual. But the Kingdom was not a trivial thing that could be accepted today without commitment, to be replaced with something

else next week. Shallow thought and closed hearts could not move beyond the story told in the parable.

Only a person with an open mind, a yearning heart and a willing spirit could discern and joyfully accept the spiritual message. It was a message so deep, so vital, so wondrous, that faith was essential to its understanding. Since faith itself was a gift from God, Jesus hoped that someone in the crowd could put the two God-given gifts together – faith and a parable.

"*Listen! A sower went out to sow.*"

Mark 4: 3

Most Christians are familiar with Jesus' parable of the sower. Some call it a missionary parable, others a 'marketing' parable. It has been described as a very wasteful method of farming. Agriculturalists today scoff with amazement at a system, which according to the parable, renders three-quarters of the seeds useless. Historians point out that there is considerable exaggeration in the numbers (four kinds of ground?) and that the broadcast method, seeding before plowing, was widely used and considered very effective at the time of Jesus.

Every parable that Jesus told was a capsule of real life in Palestine, often of a farming nature, which is not surprising, since Palestine was primarily an agricultural economy.

But hidden in the story was a spiritual message depicting the Kingdom of God. In the case of the parable of the sower, when you strip away the kind of ground (i.e. people), the ultimate message is the harvest. And the harvest is enormous – ten times present day yields. It evokes astonishment at the power of God.

Take this scenario. A local parish church wants to increase its membership. They focus on a particular Sunday event – Harvest, Christmas, Easter. Posters are placed in strategic locations, flyers dropped off in area homes. Lighted signboards proclaim the attraction.

Present members are encouraged to invite someone they know – family, friends, neighbours. Considerable time, talent and money are invested in making this missionary effort successful.

On the appointed day four new people attend worship. Two months later, one of the four has become a regular practicing member. Parish decision makers say it was a failure, a waste of time and energy that could have been put to better use.

They focused on the sowing, not on the harvest. And what a harvest! One stranger brought into God's circle of love and introduced to Jesus. Hallelujah!

To whom then will you liken God, or what likeness compare with him?

Isaiah 40: 18

On the Jewish people's journey to freedom in the promised land, escaping slavery in Egypt, travel conditions were far from ideal. Trekking in the desert with little food and water was tiring and painful. Many died along the way. Not only did they grumble to the God who delivered them, but they built a golden calf to which they offered obeisance. Instead of worshipping God, they began to worship an idol.

Each one of us is on a journey, a journey of life. Travel conditions are often less than ideal; sometimes tiring, sometimes stressful, sometimes painful. Disappointments, failures, shattered dreams, sickness, broken relationships, problems of many kind are potholes and detours in what is supposed to be a journey of happiness and personal achievement.

Rather than walking with the Lord, who is a constant source of hope and peace, we set our sights on something or someone else. In effect, we worship, (make worth of) an idol of our own creation. Not a golden calf, but an idol nevertheless.

We can make a list of our own idols - money, power, popularity, ambition, heroes, material possessions, intoxicating substances. They become the driving force in our own self-awareness vision. The tragedy is that we rarely recognize that an idol has become the focus of our journey.

A true life journey is one without idols, but a journey with God. Only the Lord can release us from the prison of idols and give us the freedom to become the fully alive persons we were created to be.

The journey will not be without doubts, problems and disappointments, but God will always be making the journey with us, guiding, protecting and sustaining us.

*"And I have other sheep that do not belong to this fold,
and they will heed my voice. So there shall be one flock,
one shepherd."*

John 10: 16

Every five years, the Government of Canada conducts a census, an instant picture on a particular day of every person in the country, noting basic details of age, gender, marital status, children and so on. A comparison of the results since World War II in almost every area of the country, particularly in the urban centres, reveals some widespread changes in the local demographics.

In the fifties and sixties, most of the mainline Christian churches planted dozens of neighbourhood churches in the burgeoning cities. But primarily through immigration, increasing numbers of local residents are now members of cultural churches or non-Christian religions. Local parishioners have neighbours who worship in synagogues, mosques or non-mainline churches. One Anglican church which sixty years ago had a Sunday School of over 500 children recently had to close its doors.

A case in point illustrates the situation and the challenge. I was the Interim Pastor of a seventy year old neighbourhood church, which at one time was a thriving community hub, but had experienced yearly decreases in membership and participation for the past 20 years. Membership now stood at 130 households. Sunday worship attendance at two services averaged about 80 persons – usually with no children or just one or two. What's more, only 16% of the people lived in the community, the majority driving from outside the parish to attend Sunday worship.

Census data records that 27.6% of the 6,700 persons living within a two kilometre radius of that church had no religious affiliation. That's a staggering 2,000 individuals who needed to hear the story of Jesus and be invited into God's circle of love.

The real challenge is not to 'sheep steal' among those who already have a faith foundation, but to reach out into the community, be an active participant in its common life, and share our faith with those who have not yet met Jesus. The form and content of that sharing will vary from person to person, but the result must always be **demonstration** and **proclamation**, show and tell of each member's own life with Jesus.

Make a joyful noise to God, all the earth; sing the glory of his name, give to him glorious praise.

Psalm 66: 1,2

I seldom meet anyone who doesn't like or appreciate some form of music, and that's especially true of children. They love to sing songs that are easy to learn and easy to remember. God has gifted me with not only a real love of music, particularly music with a beautiful melody, but also an ear for it. Growing up, I played the ukulele and the mouth organ (sometimes together), and thanks to my parents, I learned to play the piano.

I spent many happy years with children on Sunday morning, leading them in singing Christian hymns and songs, usually strumming on a guitar. When I became a priest I was introduced to 'Children's Time' during Sunday worship, in which I was expected to tell the children a story and lead them in a prayer. From my former Church School experience, I added the singing of a short song, still strumming on a guitar.

But none of the simple stories I told, had songs attached to them; and although there were many books of children's songs, I had difficulty matching the songs to the stories. As usual, the Holy Spirit took over and directed me to use the gifts God had given me to compose appropriate songs every Sunday. Thirty years later, I'm still doing it, with three changes:

- I strum a banjo, a gift from my wonderful wife.

- I sit on a chair, instead of on the chancel step .

- I print the words for the congregation, so they can sing along.

Here's a sample of one song (using Phonetic Do-Ray-Me).

Give your love to God
Do Do Do Me Ray
Give your love to God
Ray Ray Ray Fah Me
Give your love to God
Me Me Me So Fah
Jesus says to you.
Ray Fah Me Ray Do

Vs.2 Love your neighbour too
Love your neighbour too
Love your neighbour too
What you say and do.

Vs.3 Jesus' rules are two
Jesus' rules are two
Give your love to God
Love your neighbour too.

This is easily sung as a round, coming in after the second line.

***Then Jesus ordered them to tell no one, but the more he
ordered them, the more zealously they proclaimed it.***

Mark 7: 36

A man who was deaf and had a speech impediment was brought
to Jesus, who put his fingers in his ears, and touched his mouth
with spit and said "be opened". Immediately the man could
hear well and speak plainly. The Aramaic word 'ephphatha', which
is translated 'be opened', was more than a directive to the ears and
mouth. It was a command to the man himself. Through the healing
acts of Jesus, the whole man was healed. What a wonderful experience
that must have been! The chains of deafness and being tongue-tied had
been lifted, and a new freedom shone forth.

Then Jesus demanded that no one was to be told of this healing. Why the
secrecy? The healed man wanted to shout out loud, to joyfully share his
'new creation', not only with his family and friends, but with the whole
community. For him to be silent would be unnatural and ungrateful.

But note from the story that Jesus took the man aside and healed him
in private. The healing was a personal encounter between Jesus and the
sick man. It was not an experience to be sensationalized, or for applause
wherever he went. It was simply the result of God's love and grace for one
of the crown of his creation.

Unfortunately, as we say today, the medium is the message. The
medium of an incredible miracle obscures the message of love that
Jesus was bringing to the people. His deeds were sensational and no
requests for silence could prevent them from being excitedly proclaimed by all who experienced or witnessed them. The sick man was
healed, transformed into a new person.

An encounter with Jesus, whenever and wherever it happens, doesn't

have to be a miraculous change in a
physical or mental condition. Nor
does to be 'opened' by Jesus mean no
more problems, no more struggles,
no more pain.

It does mean that when we accept Jesus as Lord in our lives, we will be given an inner strength and peace from the Holy Spirit so that the vicissitudes of life do not push us into hopeless despair. An encounter with Jesus can transform us into the person God created us to be. I call that 'healing'. I call that a miracle.

But their delight is in the law of the Lord, and on his law they meditate day and night.

Psalm 1: 2

What a heart-stirring way to begin a book of 150 spiritual songs, written and compiled thousands of years ago! Shining like a powerful beacon to me is the word 'delight'. Its usage is part of our common language, but seldom found in common conversation. We find it most in storytelling, poetry, and dramatic literature, like a Roman candle bursting in the sky.

Sometimes delight evokes a burst of laughter, sometimes just a soft smile. Angels are delightful. So is the purr of a cat or the wagging of a dog's tail. We walk into a room filled with familiar faces and have an inner sense of belonging - that's delight. In the sorrow of a funeral, we recall moments of joy with our departed friend - that's delight. Our toes tingle as they move to the beat of a stirring melody – that's delight. We smile at achieving something we've never reached before – that's delight.

We're working on a difficult project and all of sudden the solution comes to us. A granddaughter takes her first step and there are smiles all around. We meet someone new, and instinctively our inner self jumps at the gift of a new relationship. Even though we have seen it performed in many places by different performers, over and over again a particular musical lifts up our spirits. What a wonderful gift of creation it is to be able to experience delight so often in God's world!

There's a downside to delight. Some folks are delighted at the pain or misfortune of others. Some take delight at lording it over someone they have bested. The chests of some swell out in pride at securing more power. With 'manly' delight some boast over the killing of a deer.

Many millions are never able to feel delight, because they live under oppression and poverty. For some, delight faces a barrier because of the bitterness in their soul.

There are many shades of joy and many degrees of delight. We find all of them in the Book of Psalms, for they are about life. We pray that, as God's Kingdom continues to come into our world, more and more people can experience the true delight of creation – living in the circle of God's love.

For by grace you have been saved through faith, and this is not your own doing, it is the gift of God.

Ephesians 2: 8

In the 2015 Pan Am Games, a men's 4 by 100 relay team won the race by a wide margin, but they were not awarded the gold medal. One of the judges determined that, in passing the baton from one runner to the next, the receiver had placed his foot on the line designating his lane. There was no intrusion on another runner, but a rule is a rule. It was a bitter disappointment to a team that had spent months in training. I recall in my high school gym class that we were taught to pass the baton running, and this emphasized the importance of sharing and good hand-eye co-ordination.

In his letter to the new Christians at Ephesus, Paul made it abundantly clear that we are not in charge of our own salvation. It is simply a gift from God. We can't earn it, or deserve it, or claim that we have it.

Yet we do play an important part in it. Grace is offered by God. Faith is also the result of God's action. In both cases, however, what is offered must be accepted in a conscious and affirmative way. It is our choice to accept or reject them.

People without faith, God's accepted gift, cannot be saved by God's grace, because they are unable to recognize that a gift is being offered. Some theologians may declare that God can do anything, but we are not puppets, since he gave us the gift of free will.

Both faith and grace are like passing the baton in a race – the race of life. God is the runner with the batons –  the baton of faith and the baton of grace. He runs up to us and puts the baton of faith in our hands. It is now our choice to reject it, or grasp it and run with it. Now we are running with faith, and he offers us the baton of grace. We run with the two batons and our lives are changed forever. It can happen at any time and in any place.

There are no special lanes to run in, and no judge to disqualify us because we stepped on a line. Incredibly, if we drop a baton, God picks it up, chases after us, and puts it in our hand again. What a race to be in!

Then the Lord called "Samuel! Samuel!" and he said
"Here I am."

I Samuel 3: 4

My study Bible places I Samuel 3:2-10 under the heading 'The Call of God to Samuel'. We treat this event as something special. There's even a beautiful modern hymn by Daniel Schutte entitled 'Here I am, Lord'. Whether the call was out loud or just in the mind of Samuel is really of no consequence – a call was heard and an action reply ultimately resulted.

Most Christians today see this event as an example of God selecting someone to a special ministry, such as ordination as a Pastor/Priest, or Youth Leader, or overseas missionary.

Unfortunately, this has tended to push into the background what we read in 1 Peter 2:9 … "You are a chosen race, a royal priesthood, a holy nation, God's own people." This is inclusive, not exclusive, and makes it clear that every believer is from time to time the recipient of a call from God.

Let me suggest the following:

- *you visit a friend in the hospital*

- *you send a birthday card to a friend living far away*

- *you pray for your uncle who has just lost his job*

- *you drive an elderly lady to the poll to vote*

- *you bake 5 dozen chocolate chip cookies for a church bake sale*

  - *you help wash the dishes after a parish luncheon*

  - *you take on the task of Warden in your parish church*

  - *you deliver altar flowers to a homebound parish member*

  - *you make a substantial donation to a children's charity*

- *you invest a day a week as a hospital volunteer*

Each one is a response to a call from God. The result is a special ministry, whether it be short term or long term. We can never evaluate the importance of each call, because its true value depends, not on the responder, but on its meaning to the recipient.

God makes millions of calls each day for people to serve others. A visit to a friend in hospital is a short term response, when compared to ordination. But to God, the value is not the nature of the response, but the fact that his call resulted in action. Each response, in its own way, builds up God's Kingdom of love.

The steadfast love of the Lord never ceases, his mercy never comes to an end.

Lamentations 3: 22

Mandy had a caring husband, three great sons and a wonderful family. Because of lower back pain, she took pills; not just those prescribed by her doctor, but anything she could purchase from the drug store. Many days found her physically and mentally lethargic, unable to do household tasks.

Her best friend sat with her, challenged her, prayed with her and brought God back into her life. With the help of counselling and a pain management program from health professionals, Mandy is on the way to being the wife and mother she is capable of being. Where is God's mercy?

Will loved to gamble; poker, professional sports, lotteries, but especially the horses. His job as a salesman left him free of being chained to a desk, but most afternoons, instead of talking to customers, he was at the track. His credit cards were maxed out. He owed money to loan companies. He even took grocery money from his wife's purse.

She went to her parish priest, who consulted a retired police captain in the church. He recruited a former gambler. Over many months they met with Will, prayed with him, arranged to gradually pay off his debts, and helped him deal with his obsession. The family is no longer facing financial ruin. Where is God's mercy?

Sam had a successful career as an insurance underwriter. However, he mismanaged family finances, and to cover the shortfall, he falsified some documents and took money from customer accounts. He was caught, convicted and sent to jail.

Parish members helped his wife and children stay afloat in new quarters after a mortgage default. The parish priest visited him often – formal confession/ absolution/ forgiveness. A model prisoner, he could be released after serving 1/3 of his sentence. But he didn't have a job to go to. The priest found a parish member who owned a business and offered Sam full-time work on probation. He's now out of prison, working and back with his family. Where is God's mercy?

- God is patient with those who are afflicted.

- God suffers when one of his people suffers.

- God finds someone with faith to intervene as a helper.

- God listens to the prayers of the afflicted and the helpers.

The Lord is my strength and my might, and he has become my salvation; this is my God, and I will praise him, my father's God, and I will exalt him.

Exodus 15: 2

She had a name, but I can't remember it. She was 12 feet tall. She had an 8 foot tail and a large belly that rested on the ground. Her head was small, with a large snout. She had serrated edges on her back from her head to her tail. No one was afraid of her, because she was made of green fiberglass. She was a big, beautiful, imposing dragon, the mascot of St. George's Anglican Church in Grafton, Ontario. When an event took place at St. George's, the dragon stood tall in front of the church hall.

Grafton is a small town about two hours east of Toronto. St. George's is a small church, seating fewer than 100. When I was the Interim Pastor there in 1995, it was brimming with vitality, despite its small membership. Sharing an organist with another church, its six voice choir led the congregational singing. The parish also shared its priest with another church down the road, so they had learned years before the importance of lay leadership.

Bible Study programs – yes. The children had an activity every Sunday morning. There was an annual memorial service for their cemetery. Weekly community social events were well-attended. When anyone was sick or in the hospital there was always a caring, practical and helpful response.

In co-operation with other local churches, the people of St. George's started and continued to support a retirement residence in the community.  Inter-church co-operation was an important option for many community activities.

One of the features of Grafton's Canada Day parade the summer I was there was St. George's big green dragon, high on a float with a warden dressed in armour to represent St. George. Not particularly scriptural, but who cares on a beautiful sunny July day? Parish members distributed flags, candies and prayer cards to the cheering spectators along the route.

And who would expect 42 adults and young people to fill a school bus, driven by one of the wardens, to travel to the west end of Toronto for an exciting performance of the light opera Godspell? But it happened. At St. George's in Grafton.

Small is not only beautiful, but powerful. That's what the Holy Spirit can do with a committed and hard-working group of believing worshippers.

That you may be filled with the knowledge of God's will, in all spiritual wisdom and understanding.

Colossians 1: 9

S hortly after I arrived at one parish, I discovered that three young people from 14 to 16 years of age were interested in Confirmation. After negotiating a date with the Bishop, I began a weekly program of home study and group teaching with two boys and a girl. The second week, the girl's mother asked if she could have a chance for a study like the young people.

The Church recognizes that adult members may participate in what is called a 'Re-affirmation of Vows' – that is, the promises made in their confirmation, through a study program. I happened to have such a program, and within a week the word got around and five more members asked if they could also take part. The result was six adult members in a ten week course of home study and weekly group discussion.

Both courses worked well. All nine parish members were confirmed or re-affirmed in an inspiring service with the Bishop. Since then, in almost every parish of my many interims, when a Re-Affirmation program is suggested, it is enthusiastically received.

Here are some impressions I have learned:

- most Anglicans are confirmed in their very early teens and have little formal faith training after that, and many of them feel a real need for a deeper understanding of their faith;

- the program must be planned and organized to result in a formal Re-Affirmation service with the Bishop;

- the program works best combining home study and group teaching;

- participants should meet weekly to share home study assignments and to be moved forward by the leader;

- there must be an active leader, usually but not necessarily the priest, to co-ordinate efforts and to be sensitive to members' concerns;

- weekly meetings should involve group prayer. The best plan is to have a schedule of members leading this prayer;

- the program cannot be shortened with irregular meetings and a shorter time frame – a minimum of ten weeks is recommended, but more than 12 weeks results in scattered weekly attendance;

- the support of parish leaders and the Bishop is essential.

"Truly I tell you; whoever does not receive the
Kingdom of God as a little child will never enter it."

Luke 18: 17

It was a small town in rural Ontario. The Anglican church there had seen better times. Now it was a little congregation with only a handful of children. Because there were few children's' activities in the area during the summer, the wardens thought we should have a Vacation Bible School. For three or four children ages 3 to 12, impossible. But the Holy Spirit said "Talk to the other pastors in town." The Presbyterian and Roman Catholic churches were 20 miles away; they would encourage their children to attend if it happened, but that's all. That left the United and Pentecostal Pastors in town. One was lukewarm, the other enthusiastic. Finally the decision was a 'go'. Each church recruited two leaders. We chose a curriculum from a Pentecostal resource for a one week program.

At this point, it was the last week of school. The principal gave us a plug in their final assembly. Posters were placed in stores and buildings, flyers were sent home with the children from the school. The Roman Catholics and Presbyterians sent flyers to their children, as did we three. Finances? We agreed to share the cost of the course materials, craft supplies and snacks.

On opening day we were greeted by 30 children and two parent volunteers. Day two saw our numbers increased to over 50 children – children are the best recruiters of other children. By day three everyone was feeling part of a happy and successful adventure.

Each day there was an assembly with storytelling, singing and prayers. Then the children were split into three age groups for crafts and learn-ing, using two church halls across the street from each other. Lots of fun! Lots of excited children! The week ended with a campfire - stunts. skits, games, songs, prayers, hot dogs, drinks and prizes … nearly 100 children and parents.

The talk at the post office the next Monday morning was all about the wonderful program run jointly by the churches. To the Anglican wardens - mission impossible. To the Holy Spirit, a little wisdom, a lot of love and commitment by a small group of Christians working and praying together. Not Mission Impossible, but Mission Accomplished.

If your enemies are hungry, give them bread to eat,
and if they are thirsty, give them water to drink.

Proverbs 25: 21

L ast week I saw a young boy help an older woman whose shopping
cart had tipped going off the curb, spilling some of her groceries
on the ground. They were both smiling.

We have a neighbour whose wife is in a wheelchair and in constant
pain. He takes care of her day and night and has been doing so for
many years. He has a soft voice, a gentle smile and a warm heart.

A small group of women were concerned about the abuse of women in
their homes. For months they actively engaged the police, social agen-
cies, hospitals, doctors, all levels of government and the general public
in becoming aware of the magnitude of the problem. Their commitment, hard work and fund-raising activities resulted in the purchase
of a house, the hiring of staff, and the opening of a shelter for abused
women and their children. It was called 'Nova Vita' – new life.

Some liberal modernists decry this proverb. Don't give a man food,
give him an economic system where there's food for everyone. I can't
disagree with this principle, but it doesn't have to be an either/or.
Surely you can feed a starving man, while advocating for a fairer economic system.

That's what Jesus did. Wine for the wedding guests, food for a hungry
crowd, sight to a blind beggar – those were Jesus' actions and that's
what God expects of us. To help someone in need is to make a difference in somebody's life. That's what the boy did; that's what my
neighbour is doing; that's what those women did;
that's what Jesus did. Sometimes it's short-lived,
sometimes it lasts a lifetime, sometimes it changes
a community. But in each case it makes a difference in someone's life.

Making a difference involves two things – recognizing a need and doing something about it.
Recognition means being constantly aware of life

and the people around us, Sometimes in simple ways, like the helpful young boy. Sometimes like our neighbor, personally and willingly meeting a long-term need. Sometimes like the women, alert to a community issue. In every case, recognition was followed by action. That's making a difference. Hallelujah!

Let them praise the name of the Lord, for he com-
manded, and they were created.

Psalm 148: 5

I n Psalm 148, the word 'praise' is repeated 13 times. Both the
opening and closing stanzas are 'Praise the Lord'. A modern hymn
translation of the psalm gives it the title "Let All Creation Praise
The Lord"; praise from the angels, the sun and moon, the stars, sea
monsters, fruit trees, creeping things, to kings, princes, rulers, men,
women and children.

Two questions arise. Why is the Lord praised and how is he to be praised?
The 'why' is answered in the psalm "for he commanded and they were
created, and he established them forever and ever." Whether or not a sea
monster can reason and understand, the simple fact is that at some time,
through evolution or otherwise, the species was created and became living
creatures. In our case, through reason, imagination and understanding, we
can be conscious of the 'why' of praising God, because our very existence
is the result of God's same creative activity.

When we praise the Lord, we are expressing our gratitude for something good that has happened to a friend, a family member or ourselves. Gratitude is a 'me' emotion – a reflection attributable to self-
satisfaction for what has happened. It is also giving thanks to someone
– recognizing that God is not only responsible for the reason for praise,
but also for our ability to express our appreciation. We say 'praise' in
prayers, sing it in our songs, and it often comes out as a spontaneous
response to what we see as a God-given situation.

Surely the Lord who loves and cares for us should receive more than
gratitude for what he does and gives to us.
In its truest sense, our praise should be a
commitment to a God-created universe.
That means having a relationship with him
on a conscious level, and understanding our
responsibility as co-managers of our fragile
earth home.

Are the spring blossoms of the apple tree its expression of gratitude for its existence? Are our 'Praise the Lord' responses our apple blossoms of gratitude?

*Now during those days he went out to the mountain to
pray; and he spent the night in prayer to God.*

Luke 6: 12

T hirty-four years ago I went on a three day retreat. I had completed
some studies and training, and the purpose of the retreat was to
determine whether the church was satisfied that God was truly
calling me to ordination as a priest in the Anglican Church of Canada.
And also for me to be sure that I really wanted to accept God's invitation to a different role in my church. For an always focused, always
busy person, the many hours of 'nothing' was both a challenge and
a revelation.

To blot out the world with its complexities was not easy for me. The
techniques I'd read about were only mildly helpful, since I soon discovered the truth of the research that says "the mind is always busy".
Being completely open with the Lord in body, heart, mind and spirit
is like talking on the phone while the radio is blasting in the same
room. It was a learning experience which deepened my relationship
with my creator.

Many years later I have had the privilege of being a leader for two
men's weekend retreats. The theme of the first was 'Living my faith in
the world'. There was plenty of sharing, small group discussion, fellowship, as well as some quiet personal time. We sang and did some
praying together. There was structure and a final personal goal. It was
quite unlike my three day retreat, but it helped a dozen men from a
parish to focus on faith in their worlds.

The second retreat was different. It focused on scripture and faith understanding. There was a lot of personal time for meditation, prayer and

reflection; with less time for sharing, fellowship and group prayer. Many of the men had
participated in the first retreat, and it was at
their request that there was less structure and
more personal freedom to explore the dimensions of their own faith.

Both were retreats, in that they removed the participants from their normal environment and distractions.

Both resulted in some meaningful spiritual experiences. And because of the prayerful preparation and being there, my own faith was deepened and strengthened.

*Therefore we must pay greater attention to what we
have heard, so we do not drift away from it.*

Hebrews 2: 1

Jimmy and his wife are active members of a local church. The new pastor is doing things they believe are wrong. So they stay away from Sunday worship for a couple of weeks … which become a few months.

Evelyn, a young teen-ager, is confirmed and says "I've graduated. I don't have to go to church anymore."

The Jones family moves from one city to another. In the hustle and bustle of getting settled and the kids into a new school, church is forgotten.

Leslie says grace before meals at home, but not in a restaurant because "it would embarrass people."

Mary tells her pastor she won't be in church for a few weeks, because she's got company visiting from out of town.

It's so easy to stray away from our faith, to stop praying, to forego worshipping on Sunday, to give a pass on reading the Bible. We don't realize we've drifted away from God until one day something happens to make us consciously aware of it. Many ignore that recognition and let the drift continue. Others are really using the church as their social milieu, a form of country club, so drifting away means moving on to something else.

Although it's easy to drift away from God, it's often not so easy to drift back. Most people discover that, for each Sunday you miss going to church, it's more difficult to go back. Not because of the warm welcome

 when you walk through the door, but because of your own embarrassment at going back with no real reason for your absence. That's too bad, because every Sunday you're away, you are missed. And no one can take your place. A fellowship is like that.

Praise the Lord, the Holy Spirit is working throughout the drifting process, pressing the drifter to stop, turn around, and come back into God's circle of love. Sometimes the Spirit intervenes through a member of the fellowship, sometimes through a friend who understands the emptiness of absence. Sometimes an event occurs in which the drifter really needs and seeks out the wisdom, power and love of God. However it happens, the Spirit is always there.

Rejoice always,

1 Thessalonians 5: 16

It's August 1945 and the war's over! The Blue Jays won the World Series! My nephew got the news that he was free of cancer! The party I supported was elected with a majority! My grandson and his fiancée bought a house! My heart was full of joy at each one of these events. We experience great happiness when good things happen. Everyday happenings don't usually evoke joy.

St. Paul sends a letter to his fellow Christians at Thessalonica to bolster their spirits. Some of their members have died, and the promise of the second coming of Jesus has not happened, so they will miss it. Hope is being undermined by doubt. In one short paragraph he shows his tremendous love for them, with an explosion of caring admonitions designed to support and build up their faith.

Here's a small sample. "Be at peace … encourage the faint-hearted … help the weak … be patient with them." And the ones above. "Be joyful … pray … give thanks." I favour the translation of 'rejoice" over 'be joyful'. It has more 'zing' and helps me open my mind, heart, spirit and emotions about our common faith,

We feel happy in the spirit of Christmas, but Easter is different; When we say "The Lord is risen!" there's a punch in our joy. We really feel like rejoicing. Our spirits are buoyed by a sense of great joy. We have hope without doubt.

Every Sunday morning is a resurrection day, a time for joyful celebration as we join together in praise, prayer and thanksgiving for the wonderful gift of Jesus. When our worship is over and we leave, rejoicing in the power of the Spirit, we have been nurtured, built up in the faith, so our joy can spread the love of Jesus to the world in which we live.

"*Then they shall be my people, and I will be their God.*"

Ezekiel 37: 23

The people of the parish of Christ Church, in the town of Ayr, were preparing to celebrate their Seventy-fifth Anniversary. One evening, Shirley, a member of the Chancel Guild, phoned me, distraught. Two of the stained-glass windows had been broken. I called Steve, one of the wardens, and we met at the church to examine the damage. Some of the panels of the windows were smashed. There were five stones lying on the floor, surrounded by pieces of coloured glass. Someone had thrown them from outside.

I still vividly remember my sense of sadness and anger looking down at those pieces of glass, most of them quite small. Why the stones had been tossed we would never know. Together these pieces had formed a beautiful picture; a picture which for some had delivered a particular spiritual message; and for others the remembrance of someone special for whom a memorial had been dedicated.

A few thought it was a wonderful piece of art. It was also a picture which declared to the community that people who believed in God gathered together; a picture which, as Henri Nouwen said of other such windows, 'revealed the face of God to the world.' But now, as we looked on it with dismay, it was just two broken windows.

Many years later I see each of those pieces of broken glass as members of that relatively small church fellowship. Individually, they tried to serve God in ways that he demanded. Together, they portrayed a dynamic picture of God at work in the world. But the real face of God was not found in those beautiful stained-glass windows; it was found in the lives of the people who gathered there.

Does your parish church play an important part in the life of its community?

Postscript: Thanks to proper insurance coverage and the skill of professional artisans, the windows were repaired and shone their message for
our big celebrations.

"You search the scriptures because you think that in them you have eternal life, and it is they that testify on my behalf. Yet you refuse to come to me to have life."

John 5: 39,40

Due to the Montreal educational system at the time, and not to my academic brilliance, I entered McGill University at the age of 16. My chosen degree path was science, with honours in physics and chemistry. Although I managed to struggle through advanced calculus and trigonometry, my downfall came in second year electricity. I studied and could ream off fact after fact, but I failed every test miserably.

Finally my professor, the famous Dr. David Keyes. called me in and said, "Mr. Shepherd, if you wish to pass this course, I advise you to throw away everything in the textbook about electricity and study the remaining 70% of the material. Your mind seems to be unable to live in the world of amps and ohms." That's what I did. And I scraped through. When I returned to McGill after the war, I switched courses to honours sociology.

Studying the Bible is like that experience. I can read all about Noah, Abraham, Joseph, Moses, Joshua, David, Jesus, Peter, Paul, and have a mind full of knowledge, even some insights into ancient Jewish history and culture. I can read the Gospels, acquiring a mountain of facts about Jesus' preaching, parables and miracles.

But I'll never be a real Christian until I meet Jesus, until I open my heart and spirit to the voice of the Lord, calling me into fellowship with him. I must change from the pursuit of knowledge to the experience of a person ... from a 'knowledge degree' to a 'faith degree'. The words I read then will be Jesus speaking to me, as I live with him at my side, living with joy in the world of faith.

Incredibly, when I read with faith, I can share the building of a boat with Noah, travel the desert with Moses, erect a Temple with Solomon, join

Jonah inside the big fish, catch some fish with Peter, be shipwrecked with Paul. and eat some chunks of bread and small fish with thousands, having spent the day listening to Jesus.

***But Martha was distracted by her many tasks, so she
came to him and asked, "Lord, do you not care that my
sister has left me to do all the work by myself? Tell her
then to help me."***

Luke 10: 40

I t was a bright Sunday morning. I sat in church with my wonderful mate, and my mind wandered. Our pastor was preaching, but I couldn't understand what she was saying. In the last minute rush to get ready for church, I had forgotten to put my hearing aids in. My sloppy tardiness prevented me from hearing what Audrey later told me was a gem of a spiritual message. It was my loss.

At the confession, I didn't say the words in the Prayer Book with my fellow worshippers, but silently asked God to forgive my failure to prepare for worship. Hopefully repentant, I promised to correct my bad habits.

Will it happen again? I hope not. But the mind is very susceptible to creating distractions.

- A line in a hymn strikes a special chord in my memory and the rest of the verse is forgotten.

- The leader of the Prayers of the People petitions God's help for the residents of Fort McMurray from a devastating fire, and I immediately remind myself to make a donation and I don't hear the next petition.

- A story in the sermon triggers a similar personal experience, and the next two minutes are lost.

I'm sure you can add many such personal distractions.

We usually apologize when such flights of the mind turn us away from the subject at hand. But they are nothing to be ashamed of. My own experience tells me that often they are specific messages from God to remind us of something or direct us into some future thought or action.

I believe that my momentary distraction from the community at worship somehow nurtures my own participation.

It doesn't excuse my forgetting my hearing aids!

But would you not rather say to him, "Prepare supper for me, put on your apron and serve me while I eat and drink; later you may eat and drink."

Luke 17: 8

J esus told a story of a servant who had worked all day in the fields. When he came home he could do nothing for himself until he had served his master. At that time, if you were a servant, you were a slave. Your labour, talents and time all belonged to the master. Constant obedience or exceptional work didn't merit special favours or even a thank you.

The intent of the story was not to condemn slavery, but to send a strong message about our relationship with God. It was a stern warning about having a bookkeeping attitude to God - that he has a ledger for each one of us in which he enters our personal balance sheet, the credits or debits for each day based on whether we had been a faithful servant. Not so, was Jesus' message. If we believe in God, we voluntarily agree to be his servant, to do what he wants us to do without any thought of reward. No merit, no thanks, no credit balance - we just do our duty.

But what is my duty in my relationship with God? I may be a servant, but I'm not a slave. My creation gives me free will to make choices, something a slave cannot do. God's master/servant relationship with me is based on love. The breadth of his love for me is beyond imagination, and any command to me is a request for obedience based on that love. My response to that command is determined by the depth of my love for him.

My love is based on trust - trust that God will never do anything to harm me, but will always want the best for me. Obedience - based on love and trust, my love and my trust in God. That's being a faithful servant of God. It can be a full-time job or a part-time job, depending on the strength of my commitment to him.

> **OBEDIENCE**
> IS EASY IF WE
> **LOVE**
> AND
> **TRUST**
> **GOD**

Incredibly, at the end of each day, if I have made some wrong choices, and I admit my mistakes and ask for God's forgiveness, he will keep no record, but will wipe the slate clean. Tomorrow I can start fresh, living in faith and obeying God with love and trust, because I know he still loves me.

For your name's sake, O Lord, pardon my guilt, for it is great.

Psalm 25: 11

M y friend Jerry is tall and somewhat slender for his age. He eats like a horse and never puts on weight. I'm shorter and a little flabby, and my life has been a constant battle to keep off the pounds through diet and exercise. The battle is not usually stressful, and I can step on the scales without having a conniption fit. However, I can very easily fall off my weight regime. When I do, I can add ten pounds almost within the blink of an eye.

Then frustration begins, because taking the excess pounds off is not only hard, but requires considerable disciplined effort. A personal trainer once told me that when I felt the urge to splurge, I should put a ten pound weight in a backpack and wear it for a few days. That should be sufficient motivation for me to resist the urge. I've never tried it, but use the excuse of low metabolism instead.

Feelings of guilt and shame are like pounds on the flesh. When you say or do something that hurts someone, even if you're in the right, your inner self has feelings of guilt. You can try to remove your guilt by asking forgiveness of the injured party. An extra pound on the scale doesn't seem like much, but it can easily become ten pounds if you don't act to prevent it. So it is with guilt. It can weigh on your mind and spirit and become heavier and heavier if you don't deal with it.

The trouble with feelings of guilt is that, even after you've asked and received forgiveness from the victim, you are still ashamed that your behaviour made the whole thing happen.

That's where God comes in. With a repentant heart, take your shame to God and ask forgiveness. The result is wonderful! The weight of your shame is immediately lifted. You are free from it. As a bonus, the forgiveness of the Lord overflows and blesses all your future relationships with others.

Then Peter came and said to him, "Lord, if another member of the church sins against me, how often should I forgive? As many as seven times?" Jesus said to him, "Not seven times, but I tell you seventy-seven times."

Matthew 18: 21,22

My immediate reaction to this teaching of Jesus is 'Who's counting?' If someone has done me wrong, I have not forgiven him and harbour a grudge against him. Our relationship has been severely blemished.

I can refrain from further relationship, in which case there will be no further opportunity for wrongdoing. On the other hand, I can accept further slights as just the way things are between us. Numbers don't matter. Resentment and revenge are the opposite of forgiveness and compassion

It was Jewish teaching at the time that if a wrongdoer repents, apologizes and makes restitution, *it is the duty* of the injured party to forgive, and if necessary, to forgive three times, *but not a fourth time.* When Peter answered his own question, he went beyond accepted teaching. Seven times to him signified an excess of mercy.

Jesus' reply shattered even Peter's generosity. By using seventy-seven times (or seventy times seven, depending on your interpretation of the Greek) he clearly reversed the concept of unlimited hatred described in the Song of Lamech (Genesis 4: 24).

In the old days there was no limit to resentment or revenge, but now, if you are a follower of the Lord, you can never refuse to forgive a wrongdoer. Forgiveness is unlimited. Hatred is not tolerated.

For most of us, there is an obvious tension between unlimited forgiveness and our ego-driven humanity. A wrong against me hurts my self-esteem, and I resent it. There are always two people in a disagreement.

One carries the revenge-burden of the victim. The other carries the guilt-burden of the perpetrator. With repentance and forgiveness, both burdens are lifted.

"So my heavenly Father will do to every one of you, if you do not forgive your brothers and sisters from your heart."

Matthew 18: 35

These are Jesus' final words on his teachings about life. Peter had asked him how many times he should forgive someone for a wrong committed against him. The reply from Jesus was "Unlimited."

But there are two sides to every coin, and Jesus followed this dialogue with the parable of the Unforgiving Servant, a man who was forgiven an enormous debt, then refused to forgive a small debt that was owed to him. When the 'original forgiver' found out, he threw the man in jail.

The message of the parable is clear. When we are repentant of a wrong doing and apologize to the injured party, God is always ready to forgive us. But if in our lives we request forgiveness and refuse to give it to others, we will pay the penalty at the Final Day Of Judgment. Each time we say the Lord's Prayer ..."forgive us our trespasses, as we forgive those who trespass against us ..." we accept the fact that if we do not forgive others, there will be dire consequences.

If God is the 'original forgiver' in the parable, it's reasonable to ask how we can believe that forgiveness is unlimited, since he first forgave the man, then took back his forgiveness and punished him?

God's forgiveness is a gracious gift, freely given. When it is misused, it  is of no value. It is lost. We cannot receive any of God's blessings, in this case forgiveness, unless they are then reflected in the manner in which we treat our relationships with others.

A life without forgiveness to others is a life in which forgiveness does not exist, and that includes the unlimited forgiveness of God.

"There is a boy here with five small barley loaves and two small fish. But what are they among so many people?"

John 6: 9

The story of the 'feeding of the five thousand appears in all four Gospels. All of them refer to five loaves and two fishes, but John tells us that they were the offering of his lunch by a boy.

Rather than having one person read the whole passage at Sunday worship, it is ideally suited to be presented in dramatic form, because it's a great story with four characters – Jesus, Phillip, Andrew and the boy. In one parish, we gave the boy a name, Nathan, and made it his story of what had happened.

Many churches use a dramatic reading of the crucifixion narratives on Palm Sunday and Good Friday. There are many other Gospel readings that will have far greater impact if they are converted to multiple-part readings. (I once heard the Parable Of The Sower in which the seeds were given personalities and told the story dialoguing among themselves; it was a wow!) Here are some tips I've learned about dramatic presentations:

- Make sure the message from scripture doesn't get lost.

- Don't hand out the parts to people as they arrive for worship. A rehearsal is best, but at least give them out a few days ahead.

- Always have extra copies of the script. Someone will forget.

- Props are not necessary if you have good readers. If you use them, either have a full-fledged stage presentation or one simple garment to identify the character, which readers put on as they move from their seats to the chancel.

- Position the characters in the chancel or nave as best fits the story. Don't have readers standing side by side on the chancel steps.

- Encourage the congregation to picture what's happening and make themselves part of the picture For instance, they might try being Hebrew soldiers as David confronts Goliath.

- Experienced directors/producers of plays could say much more. For most parishes, keep it simple.

I sink into deep mire, where there is no foothold; I have come into the deep waters, and the floods sweep over me.

Psalm 69: 2

A few years ago a parish member buttonholed me during the after worship coffee hour. Everything in her life was going wrong. Her son and daughter-in-law were almost at blows over the choice of a new living room set. They gave her a new job at work and her employees were fighting among themselves. To top it off, her hot water tank was leaking and had to be replaced. Where was God in all her woes? She believes in him, but he seems to have deserted her.

I listened to her. She was looking for an opportunity to vent her emotions, but she also needed words of comfort and wisdom. I think the Holy Spirit was at work, because I said, "Sylvia, when you get home, take out your Bible and read Psalm 69."

A couple of days later she phoned me. "Wow! That person in the Psalm was in dire straits. Things couldn't be worse. Not only was he in pain, but all those around scorned him. Yet he could talk about it with God. (quoting the Psalm) '… rescue me from the mire; do not let me sink; deliver me from those who hate me, from the deep waters …'

"Can you believe it?" Sylvia went on. "In the depths of despair, he cried out to God, *knowing that God was listening!* And he was confident that God would do something about it. Then he said (she quoted) 'I will put God's name in song and glorify him with thanksgiving!' He's giving thanks even before finding out what God will do to help him in his suffering"

Well, Sylvia laid it all out for God, described all her problems and feelings, asked forgiveness for being angry at him, and prayed that he would guide her thoughts, words and actions in the coming days. She gave thanks to God for listening to her, because in listening, he lifted the burden of depression from her.

*And hope does not disappoint us, because God's love
has poured into our hearts through the Holy Spirit that
has been given to us.*

Romans 5: 5

Before Jesus, it was almost impossible for people to get close to God. Even in the Psalms, a compendium of all human relationships with God and each other, in which individuals, groups and nations gave voice to those relationships, God was still a stranger. He was an untouchable entity, a mighty power who could do wondrous things but would also allow horrible things to happen. He was unreachable. He could not be a friend, just a 'supreme being', and you lived in awe and fear of him.

Then Jesus came and made God visible. In three short years of ministry, he brought us into the haven of God's grace, his eternal blessings and love. In a wonderfully human way, he introduced us to God. He opened the door to enter into God's presence, where we can build a relationship with him.

Unfortunately, even that is difficult, because we live in a world which denies God most of the time. Living the Jesus way, trying to be the people God created us to be, ends up in a battle against Satan and the wicked powers in the world.

Praise the Lord, we are given God's Holy Spirit, who wraps around our spirit, giving us wisdom, power and courage to live in God's Kingdom and serve him as members of his circle of love.

This Holy Spirit is the channel of God's love and, through Jesus, the visible witness to it. Through this Spirit we are infused with the life and teachings of Jesus, increasing day by day, one day at a time, our understanding and our ability to follow and obey God's desired direction to our lives.

All this amounts to my simple understanding of that complex doctrine developed by the early Christians called the Holy Trinity; three aspects of God's personality, three revelations of his being. God made me. Jesus saved me. The Holy Spirit guides me.

As a deer longs for flowing streams, so my soul longs for you, O God.

Psalm 42: 1

For many years now I've been saying to people, "I've got great DNA. I'm going to live to at least a hundred." That's a rather idiotic and arrogant comment. It may happen that way, but I shouldn't brag about it.

I don't believe that the Lord looks in a special book and determines that in three years, five months, eleven days and thirty-four minutes, I will die, or for that matter, that I will die tomorrow. Whatever, it's a done deal. My time will have come.

The God who created me, the Jesus who showed me what a real human being could be, the Holy Spirit whose attempts to guide me have often fallen on deaf ears, would not plan my demise that way. I live in the world of his creation. He made it good, and generation after generation of his so-called 'caretakers' have messed it up.

But some day there will be 'a new heaven and a new earth'. I don't know when that will be. Meanwhile, my DNA, my parents' upbringing, my lifestyle, my feeble attempts to do God's will and my advancing years will finally force my body to succumb to gravity and lack of restoration. Whenever that happens, God will say he's glad I arrived safely.

Jesus promised us eternal life, meaning living in God's Kingdom, within his circle of love. I can do that now. I don't have to wait until I die. Eternal life, living in God's Kingdom, is mine today. I have to let the Holy Spirit really guide me so that each day, one day at a time, I can walk hand in hand with Jesus. My death will just mean moving from a beautiful world here, to an even more beautiful world in another of God's spaces.

Of course, I still want to make it to a hundred.

Glory to God, whose power, working in us, can do infinitely more than we can ask or imagine. Glory to God from generation to generation in the church and in Christ Jesus, forever and ever. Amen.

Book of Alternative Services, Page 214

This is not a Bible quotation, but a Doxology that most Canadian Anglicans stand and declare at the conclusion of the service of Holy Eucharist. It is a short paraphrase of Ephesians 3: 21, the key words being glory, power, work, more, imagine, church, Christ Jesus.

I have in my possession a children's toy called an 'Energy Stick', given to me by my friend Gerry. It's an eight inch long, one inch in diameter, transparent plastic tube, with ¾ inch metal coverings at both ends. Inside are some thin metal wires connected to each end, and some loose capped ends. When you grasp both ends with your hands, the small caps at the end of the wires light up and there is a great singing noise.

At coffee hour at Christ Church, Scarborough Village and at St. Theodore of Canterbury, North York, I asked everyone to join hands in a circle, making sure they were in one long unbroken line. I then joined the circle, grasped one end of the Energy Stick and had the person beside me grasp the other end. The stick lit up singing. There were close to one hundred hands in the circle. One person held up a hand and the light and the singing stopped. It didn't take any coaxing for everyone to repeat the Doxology.

Every parish is like an Energy Stick. Every parish, focusing on Jesus, empowered by the Holy Spirit, can do infinitely more they can ask or imagine. They'll not only become the 'light of the world' but they will make a joyful noise doing it.

"As you go, proclaim the good news, saying 'The Kingdom of God has come near."

Matthew 10: 7

Jesus said these words to his twelve disciples as he sent them out on their first mission. In addition to preaching, they were also charged to heal the sick, raise the dead, cleanse lepers, and cast out demons. Then he admonished them, "I send you out as sheep in the midst of wolves, so be wise as serpents and innocent as doves."

I'm sure he gave them some training, but time was limited, so there were no Masters of Divinity in evidence. We don't know how long their mission was supposed to last, but from the rest of his instructions, it wasn't just a weekend to test the waters.

What I read sounds scary – more like a baptism of fire. Healing, raising the dead, cleansing and casting out demons all depend on the power of the Holy Spirit, and if these actions happen (as they did), then most people would be inclined to listen when you tell them about the Kingdom of God.

As a preacher, I would love to have heard what they said when they talked about the Kingdom. Assuming I don't regurgitate an old sermon, I know from personal experience that to write and rehearse a clear message requires at least eight to ten hours of my time.

You may say that if I paid attention to the Holy Spirit, it shouldn't take that long. I do listen to the Holy Spirit, who tells me to reflect on the three Scripture readings for the day plus the Psalm, and I will find the message which the Lord wants me to deliver for that time and that congregation. This reflection takes time. Then I have to put words together and deliver them with faith and conviction.

Perhaps the disciples' audience was different than today's, but I don't think so. The people all wanted, and still want, to hear about the saving grace of

God. I can only conclude that they were preachers with a simple direct message that didn't involve a lot of reading.

Meanwhile, I'll do what I think the Lord wants me to do – prepare his message so that it means something to my friends in the local congregation, proclaiming the Kingdom.

Then he said to his disciples, "The harvest is plentiful but the labourers are few; therefore, ask the Lord of the harvest to send out labourers into the harvest."

Matthew 9: 37,38

During my early teen years I was fortunate to be able to spend every summer at the Montreal Boy Scout Camp Tamaracouta in the Laurentians. Shy and pudgy, I worked hard at Scout achievements. I earned the Bushmen's Thong, and was one short of Gold Cords, but there was still a lot of spare time.

The Waterfront Director, Bill, (all I can remember of his name) noticed that I was good at swimming and got me into life-saving programs. But what do you do when camp is over and you have a lot of Royal Life Saving Society awards?

I was a long time 'Y' member, and they had recently built a beautiful new facility on Royal Avenue. One day, as I was coming out of the pool, the Program Director, Roby Kydd, asked me if I would like to help in the swimming program.

By springtime, under Roby's gentle guidance, I had moved up from lifeguard to teacher and organizer of the Parents' night. While this was happening, George Paige, the Physical Director, noticing my extra flab and lack of confidence, mentored me in an exercise, gym and event planning program.

Three men took an interest in a shy, overweight teenager. They changed my self-esteem and my life. The 'Y' is a Christian Association, and most of the Scout troops were church sponsored, so I'm sure the Lord played an important part in my maturing process. I didn't recognize it until many years later. But I'll never forget Bill, Roby and George.

Who has touched your life in a special way?

*__Then the Lord put out his hand, and touched my
mouth, and the Lord said to me, "Now I have put my
words in your mouth."__*

Jeremiah 1: 9

I t's over 2500 years ago. You're a young man, of the Hebrew priestly class, but not wealthy, and certainly not experienced in the world of inter-nation politics. God elects you to be his spokesperson to the leaders of your country. Because you don't know when and how to be God's mouthpiece, God tells you not to be afraid. He will give you the words and he will be able to speak to them through you.

Your name is Jeremiah, and for forty-one years, covering five differ-ent Kings of your country, you will constantly warn them about the dangers of becoming involved in the struggles for supremacy among the three big powers of Assyria, Egypt and Babylonia.

Involvement meant breaking the country's covenant with God, chang-ing many traditions, defying prescribed religious practices, even to the point of worshipping pagan idols. Time and again Jeremiah prophesied against this. But to no avail. Over just a few years, Jewish armies were defeated, the Temple and Jerusalem were razed to the ground, and all but the poorest of their citizens shipped into captivity in Babylon, 1500 kilometers away.

Today, every Christian is elected to be a Jeremiah, a spokesperson for God. In Matthew 28:19, we are charged to "make disciples of all nations", and in Acts 1:8, "you shall be my witnesses ... to the ends of the earth."

Our instructions could not be more explicit. We have the authority of God, the directions of Jesus, and the power of the Holy Spirit. And we have the teachings of Jesus which will "put God's words in my mouth."

There's no risk. We don't have to be afraid. Just remember God's promises in Psalm 91. "I will protect you – I will deliver you – I will answer you – I will be with you – I will rescue you – I will honour you – I will satisfy you – I will save you."

I will – eight times. That's enough for me.

"A new heart I will give you, and a new spirit I will put in you and I will remove from your body the heat of stone and give you a heart of flesh."

Ezekiel 36: 26

Ezekiel prophesied during the captivity of the people of Israel. As a member of the priestly class, he was one of the captives.

The faith of the Hebrews was anchored in three things:

- God had made them an independent nation through the exodus and the promised land

- The Temple in Jerusalem was where God was present to his people

- They had a covenant with God, who had made them his chosen people, who would show the world what God was like.

They broke the covenant over many years of disobedient behaviour, resulting in the destruction of Jerusalem and the Temple and the loss of their land. In strong language and images, Ezekiel spoke out against their disobedience and declared doom on the surrounding nations. When decades of captivity fostered loss of hope for a forlorn people, he then prophesied that God would restore them as his chosen people. But they would be a transformed people, replacing their old hearts of stone and spirits of disobedience with new hearts that would listen and new spirits that would act according to God's will. The prophesy was realized many years later.

A 'biblical heart' is the centre of my personality, the core of my being. A 'biblical spirit' is the force that determines my behaviour. Both were transformed when I was baptized. That's true of everyone who is baptized. But just as a transformer in electricity must be well maintained for the power to pass through and be changed, so it is with a transformed heart and a transformed spirit. Rust (selfish lack of commitment) and dirt (evil powers and temptation) can easily alter and misdirect the flow of God's covenant love through the Holy Spirit.

You and I are called in our own local church to be God's people today – to be a beacon to the community of the true nature and character of God. The more we are able to rid ourselves of the rust and dirt that our worldly environment throws us, the closer we will become a fully transformed fellowship of love. When people see us, they will see God's Kingdom at work

Then Jesus asked, "Were not ten made clean? But the other nine, where are they?

Luke 17: 17

I don't remember where I heard this story, but I will never forget it.

Jeremy had a severe case of leprosy. He lived in a cave, isolated from the rest of the town. An angel appeared to him and Jeremy pleaded to be healed of his affliction. "I will heal you," said the angel, "and in seven years I will return to see what you have done with your new life." Jeremy was healed.

Samuel lived in the same town. With crooked legs and a distorted body, he spent his days and nights as a beggar. He implored the angel to heal him of his physical deformity, so he could work and stop begging. The angel told him, "I will heal you, but in seven years I will return to see what you have done with your new body." Samuel was healed.

Timothy was blinded in an accident when he was very young. Now in his early twenties, he lived with his widowed mother. Hearing about the angel, he prayed, "Please help me so that I will no longer be a burden on my mother." The angel appeared and declared, "I will heal you, and in seven years I will return to see what you have done with your new eyes." Timothy was restored to full sight.

Seven years passed, and the angel returned. Before he knocked on the door of Jeremy's new house, he changed into a leper. Jeremy opened a window and yelled "Go away! I don't want to catch your horrible disease." Immediately Jeremy became a leper again.

As a crippled beggar with tattered clothes, the angel knocked on Samuel's door. Waving a heavy stick, Samuel screamed, "Get off my property or I'll beat you." Immediately his legs and body were contorted into a crippling deformity.

Finally the angel visited Timothy, changing into a blind man with a white cane. When Timothy opened the door and saw him he said, with a smile on his face, "Welcome! Welcome!

Come in and sit down. This is your lucky day. Seven years ago an angel gave me my sight. He'll be here in a few minutes and I'm sure he'll do the same for you."

"He removes every branch in me that bears no fruit.
Every branch that bears fruit he prunes, to make it
bear more fruit."

John 15: 2

P eople are wonderful! Some people are especially wonderful! Every time I put A Word from Father Roy to paper, which I hope and believe is a message God wants me to write, that same Lord tells me to submit the words to my Editor. I do so not only to correct my typing mistakes, which occur despite Spell Check, but to be sure that what I have written clearly conveys God's message in an easily understood manner.

Following God's instructions is sometimes difficult, and just because he says "my words shall be your words" doesn't mean I play no part in the exercise. I love the Lord, but I am not a puppet with him pulling the strings.

Our connection is more like an IPhone where God speaks to me and tells me what he wants me to write and relies on me to listen and follow through. Unfortunately, my mind is the go-between God's message and the words that end up on the paper. Often this results in the true meaning of God's message being muddled up by the combogulation *(not a word! Ed.)* of words coming off my pen. It's not intentional on my part. Somehow the idea or theme is confused and unclear.

That's where my Editor comes in. She is a skilled and experienced writer and publisher. But she is also tuned in to the Lord, so she can

tell whether the message is clear or muddled. She asks me what I mean by a particular passage, and then gently shows me where a few changes could make all the difference in the impact of the message. There's never any suggestion to change the message itself, just to improve the manner in which it is expressed.

To further enhance the presentation, she also finds and adds an appropriate graphic illustration, sometimes re-arranging the paragraphs to fit it in. Everything she does makes it easier for you to read.

Her name is Audrey and she's been my adorable wife since 1947. In her honour and with immeasurable appreciation, the last page of this book of spiritual messages features her description of the meaning of The Eucharist.

THE EUCHARIST

The candles shed their light upon the altar.
The incense sends its clouds of prayer to heaven.
The organ swells with grand, triumphant music.
The priest and those surrounding kneel, adoring.
"This is my Body" - and the bread is offered.
"This is my Blood" - and sacred drink is given.
And Jesus stands among us - Alleluia !

A family gathers in the dim-lit sickroom.
A table holds the paten and the chalice.
A priest puts on his stole, and in the quiet
A house becomes a chapel for consoling.
"This is my Body" - and the bread is offered.
"This is my Blood" - and sacred drink is given.
And Jesus stands among us - Alleluia !

The conference is over. Priests and people
All gather for a picnic in the sunshine.
And someone says, "Let's celebrate Communion.
As holy things, we'll use these rolls, this fruit juice."
"This is my Body" - and the bread is offered.
"This is my Blood" - and sacred drink is given.
And Jesus stands among us - Alleluia !

The sacred is around us as we journey.
We see God in the eyes of friend and stranger.
We hear God in the silence and the clamour.
We know God in the Eucharist he gave us.
"This is my Body" - and the bread is offered.
"This is my Blood" - and sacred drink is given.
And Jesus stands among us - Alleluia !

©AOS2016

Printed in Canada